Pascal and Theology

Je vous demande pardon, Monsieur,
dit M. Pascal à M. de Saci, de
m'emporter ainsi devant vous dans
la théologie . . . ; il est difficile
de n'y pas entrer, quelque vérité
qu'on traite, parce qu'elle est
le centre de toutes les vérités.

Pascal
and
Theology

JAN MIEL

The Johns Hopkins Press
BALTIMORE AND LONDON

*The portrait of Pascal reproduced on the title
page is attributed to Philippe de Champaigne
and dated 1656 or 1657. Photo Giraudon. A
detail of a view of Port-Royal engraved by
N. Bocquet is reproduced on the front and
back covers.*

For my wife

Elizabeth

*theologian
in spite of herself*

Contents

Preface

The study of Pascal's "image" through the last three hundred years is a subject of some interest quite apart from the study of Pascal himself. Prior to the renewal of Pascal studies in the twentieth century, two characteristic pictures of Pascal may be said to dominate: first, that of the great scientist, mathematician, and (potential) philosopher who unfortunately turned to religion and wasted his last years in mysticism and arid controversy; we tend to associate this view with the eighteenth century. The other, the romantic image, attempts to retain the mystic as valuable but can understand the supernatural only in terms of tension, paradox, anguish. Common to both these views is the notion of a great gap dividing his rational, scientific, mundane thinking from his religious and theological thinking—a gap crossed only by a dramatic conversion, understood in terms of a mystical or pathological experience. Twentieth-century scholarship and criticism have greatly altered these views. With regard to the subject of this book, we now recognize that Pascal's theological concern preceded the *nuit de feu* of 1654 by many years, and influenced even his approach to science as well as his whole understanding of human nature. We also know that his scientific activity did not cease abruptly with the so-called second conversion. Yet the myth of the mundane scientist who "got religion," a myth started in the seventeenth century and perhaps even encouraged by Pascal himself, is still to some extent with us, and at least part of the aim of this book will be to dispel that myth by showing to what extent Pascal's thinking is most centrally theological during all his adult life.

The study of Pascal's religious thought has been further complicated, at least for Catholic scholars, by his Jansenism, that problematic heresy of which it seems almost impossible to take an unbiased view. The history of the Jansenist movement is even now being rewritten by such scholars as Jean Orcibal and Louis Cognet, and their works once assimilated are certain to clear the air for future discussion of Pascal's Jansenism. In the meantime, two attitudes prevail: there are those for whom Jansenism is still more or less anathema and who tend therefore to see it as foreign to Pascal—grafted onto his thought but never really embraced by him (e.g., Baudin, Steinmann, Réguron); and there are those who admire the richness and solidity of the Port-Royal theologians and who try to show how much Pascal got from them and to interpret him in terms of their theology (e.g., Laporte, Russier). Both attitudes seem to me unsatisfactory; the first because it is simply false; the second because, although it may clarify certain points in Pascal's works, it tends finally to obscure what is most interesting, namely, what is not borrowed—and could not be: Pascal's own theological thinking, that is, his way of approaching theological questions, including his own particular use of traditional terms, even his understanding of earlier theologians.

Besides those who regard Jansenism sympathetically, and those who regard it as a kind of fanatical cult which unfortunately drew Pascal under its spell, there are among readers of Pascal a third group—undoubtedly the largest—who regard the whole Jansenist controversy with indifference, who see it as arid, academic, and irrelevant; they wonder, as Jean Cocteau put it, "qu'un esprit comme Pascal . . . ait pu consentir à examiner de telles balivernes."[1] It seems to me, however, quite impossible to understand the thought of someone as theologically oriented as Pascal without taking his theology seriously. Pascal's theological thought represents the efforts of a great mind to come to grips with the relation between God and man, a relation that was for him the absolutely central question of human existence. Theology may aim at saying something about God: it inevitably says something about man;

1. Jean Cocteau, *La Difficulté d'être* (Monaco, 1953), p. 33.

those who find Pascal unconvincing on God must still understand his theology if they are to understand what he says about man.

In fact, the question that occupied Pascal is just as actual today as it was then, namely, the question of freedom. Few questions have been so debated in recent years by both analytic and existentialist philosophers, though the philosophical question is only parallel to, not identical with, the theological one. But in contemporary theology also,[2] the relation between grace and freedom is an important issue still dividing Protestants from Catholics, and often seeming to underlie other disagreements; a Jaspers and a Bultmann, for example, may seem to differ mainly on questions of method, but underlying, and perhaps determining their choice of method is the fact that Bultmann is an Augustinian on the question of freedom and grace, while Jaspers is a neo-semi-Pelagian.

But can we really expect Pascal's Jansenism to be relevant to modern discussions? I believe so. Pascal is a peculiarly modern figure. Two of his major scientific achievements—the invention of the "machine arithmétique" and the discovery of the "règle des partis"—had relatively little immediate influence; Descartes had far more impact on the history of science and philosophy in the eighteenth and nineteenth centuries. Yet these two discoveries make Pascal the grandfather of computer science and probability theory, both of which have only come into their own in the twentieth century. Likewise, Pascal's rigorously empirical approach in science is far closer to present-day scientific method than is Descartes' rationalistic mechanism. So in theology, many thinkers consider that we are now in a distinctly post-Cartesian age, one in which notions of subject and object, mind and body must be radically redefined. Pascal offers us a concept of God that is not rational or moralistic, but personal, which means that His relations with man are historical and dialectical and ultimately mysterious; and Pascal's theology is correspondingly positive and

2. It is surely no accident that the first important book to take a truly "existential" view of theology was Hans Jonas' *Augustin und das paulinische Freiheitsproblem* (Göttingen, 1930).

analytic and much concerned with the precise limits of human discourse in the realm of the supernatural.

This book, then, attempts to explore Pascal's theological thinking, especially his theology of grace. As this necessarily involves the question of his Jansenism, and as I cannot pretend to take an unbiased view of that movement, I have at least tried to show some justification for my bias in an historical introduction to the problem of grace and free will in the Christian tradition. Then I turn to Pascal's *Ecrits sur la grâce*, writings which, owing perhaps to their unfinished and repetitious character, have been much neglected by Pascal scholars. From these writings I try not only to extrapolate Pascal's fundamental theological positions but also to draw something like a theological method. In the remaining chapters, I analyze the theology of his other writings, not just to show a simple influence of Jansenist theology, but to see the development of his theological thinking in the context of other problems and purposes. Such an approach to Pascal will undoubtedly seem to some to be narrow and one-sided; even in the sphere of religion, I concentrate mainly on theology, giving little attention to the rich tradition of Jansenist spirituality. This narrowness is the inevitable, if regrettable, result of focusing one's lights on a particular area; it is necessitated by sheer practical limitations, and justified, if successfully carried out, by the amount of light the one area, when sufficiently illuminated, may reflect upon others.

Writing about a figure as much studied as Pascal necessarily involves a good deal of scholarly documentation and discussion. I have tried, however, to relegate all material of a specialized nature to the notes in order to leave the text accessible to any general reader interested in Pascal or theology or both, but not especially interested in scholarly controversies. Those familiar with the scholarly literature will find most of my positions defended in the notes; with what success, they will have to judge.

I have chosen to refer primarily to the "Bibliothèque de la Pléïade" edition of Pascal's works[3] because at the time I began

3. *Oeuvres complètes*, ed. Jacques Chevalier (Paris, 1954).

this book it was the only one readily available that contained all the known texts.[4] In referring to the *Pensées,* I give the page number in the Pléiade edition and also, as is the custom, the number of the fragment in the Brunschvicg edition.

Readers who may not be entirely at ease with Pascal's French are referred, for the *Lettres provinciales* and the *Pensées,* to the excellent translations by A. J. Krailsheimer in the Penguin Classics series. *The Essential Pascal,* edited by Robert W. Gleason, S.J. (New York: Mentor-Omega, 1966), includes several of the shorter works, notably the important *De l'Esprit géométrique.* As the *Ecrits sur la grâce* are not available in English, I have provided, in an Appendix, translations of the most important passages discussed in Chapter II.

I wish here to acknowledge my debt to many people and institutions. To the libraries of Princeton, Harvard, and Yale Universities, and of their respective divinity schools; to the libraries of The Johns Hopkins University and of Woodstock College; and to the manuscript division of the Bibliothèque Nationale—I am grateful for their generosity and many courtesies. I wish to thank Wesleyan University for a series of summer grants, which enabled me to continue my research, and to thank especially The Johns Hopkins Humanities Center, and its director, Professor Charles S. Singleton, for giving me a year as a Fels Foundation Fellow there in which I was able to complete the actual writing of this book. Finally, although many people have aided me with discussion and criticism, I must mention two in particular to whom I owe most: the late Professor E. B. O. Borgerhoff, whose humane and insightful teaching first interested me in Pascal, and who was thus for me an *adiutorium sine quo non*; and Professor Ira O. Wade, who directed an earlier version of this book as a dissertation, and who by his aid and encouragement, always promptly and generously given, was my *adiutorium quo.*

J. M.

Middletown, Connecticut

4. The edition called "L'Intégrale," ed. Louis Lafuma (Paris, 1963), is now also available.

Abbreviations

AN   Alexander Roberts et al. (eds.), *The Ante-Nicene Fathers of the Church,* 10 vols., American edition (Grand Rapids, 1951).

BA   *Bibliothèque augustinienne: Oeuvres de saint Augustin,* 85 vols. (projected), (Paris: Desclée de Brouwer, 1945–).

Br.   Followed by a number, refers to the number of a "Pensée" in the various Brunschvicg editions.

Denz.   Denzinger-Bannwart, *Enchiridion Symbolorum* (23d ed., rev.; Freiburg, 1937).

DTC   E. Amann, E. Mangenot, A. Vacant (eds.), *Dictionnaire de théologie catholique,* 15 vols. (Paris, 1930–50).

GE   L. Brunschvicg, P. Boutroux, F. Gazier (eds.), Pascal, *Oeuvres complètes,* 14 vols. (Paris: Collection des Grands Ecrivains de la France, Hachette, 1908–25).

OC   J. Chevalier (ed.), Pascal, *Oeuvres complètes* (Paris: Bibliothèque de la Pléiade, 1954).

PG   Migne, *Patrologia Graeca,* 162 vols. (Paris, 1857–66).

PL   Migne, *Patrologia Latina,* 221 vols. (Paris, 1844–64).

Biblical quotations in English are from the Revised Standard Version; quotations in French or Latin are as they appear in the author under discussion, and in the case of Pascal are usually his own translations from the Vulgate.

Pascal and Theology

Chapter I Grace and Free Will:
An Historical Introduction

It is surprising how many scholars have written on Pascal's Jansenism or his lack of it, his orthodoxy or his heretical tendencies, and on the departure of both Jansenius and the Molinists from the true doctrine of the Church—all as if Jansenism really were a doctrinal heresy, and as though it were obvious in what way this heresy deviated from a supposed orthodox Catholic tradition. Yet attempts to say precisely in what this heresy consists, if they try to do more than echo the polemics of the period, meet with a great many difficulties. For one thing, the Church itself did not, during the time of the Jansenist disputes, pronounce any official doctrine on the important questions involved: all that it proclaimed was a truce; the condemnations of various theologians were primarily political in their implications, and none of them is in any sense a definition of doctrine. And then, the nearest thing that one can find to an official Catholic position on grace and free will (usually taken to be the central issue involved) is the declarations of the Councils, especially those of Carthage (418), Ephesus (431), and Orange (529), which followed and recommended the position of St. Augustine. But this source is complicated by the fact that the majority of subsequent theologians have not found the Augustinian doctrine acceptable in its totality and have introduced deviations that considerably alter the import of the doctrine; and also by the fact that not a single one of the Early Church Fathers holds the same view as St. Augustine and most hold views quite incompatible with his.

The purpose of this rapid survey of the problem, then, will

not be to extract the "official Catholic position" from available texts, in order to show how Pascal did or did not deviate from it, but will be to show some of the major shifts of position within the tradition of the Church, and what difficulties and influences produced these shifts, in order to evaluate Pascal's place within this tradition. Pascal's orthodoxy is not a serious question: he was a Catholic thinker who dealt with a problem variously treated by other Catholic thinkers; if it could be shown his position coincided exactly with that of St. Augustine or St. Thomas, it would then be equally true that it differed in important ways from that of St. John Chrysostom or St. Robert Bellarmine.

It must be admitted, however, that the question of orthodoxy plays a large role in Pascal's own writings, and one of the major pieces in his polemic is that there is an orthodox tradition which the Jesuits either ignore by citing only quite recent books, or deliberately do violence to, and that if one turns back to the Fathers of the Church, one finds the Jansenist doctrine fully vindicated. In a passage in the second of the *Lettres provinciales*, however, the tradition on which the Jansenists depend is cited more accurately:

> *Cette grâce victorieuse, qui a été attendue par les patriarches, prédite par les prophètes, apportée par Jésus-Christ, prêchée par saint Paul, expliquée par saint Augustin, le plus grand des Pères, embrassée par ceux qui l'ont suivi, confirmée par saint Bernard, le dernier des Pères, soutenue par saint Thomas. . . .*[1]

Missing from this genealogy are three centuries of Christian writings from St. Paul to St. Augustine; and the truth is the writings of the Early Fathers, before Augustine, are virtually unanimous in their consistent affirmation of the freedom of man's will, and in their lack of a doctrine of sin that would mitigate that freedom. We must leave aside discussion of real or implied doctrines concerning grace and freedom in the writings of Saints Paul and John: not only because biblical

1. *Lettres provinciales, OC*, p. 683; cf. *OC*, p. 687 and *passim*.

scholarship is a highly specialized discipline—quite beyond this author's competence—but also because Scripture is not part of the tradition we are studying but the source or point of departure for it. Let us begin, then, with one of the first important apologists, Justin Martyr. After using the apologetical argument that Christ fulfills the sayings of the prophets, Justin sees that these arguments might lead some to think that all men's actions are foreordained;[2] he argues then that "unless the human race have the power of avoiding evil and choosing good by free choice, they are not accountable for their actions," and since the prophets also teach "that punishments, and chastisements, and good rewards are rendered according to the merit of each man's actions, he must have freedom of choice."[3] In support of this refutation of fatalism, he cites a text abridged from Deuteronomy 30:15-19: "See, I have set before you good and evil; choose good";[4] and a similar passage from Isaiah 1:16. In the *Second Apology*[5] he specifically mentions the Stoic doctrine of fate, which he refutes

2. *First Apology,* chaps. 43-44; *PG,* VI, Cols. 391-95; trans., *AN,* I, 177-79; hereafter cited as *I Apology.*

3. *I Apology,* chap. 43.

4. The text in its entirety reads: "See I have set before you this day life and good, death and evil. If you obey the commandments of the Lord your God, by walking in His ways, and by keeping His commandments and His statutes and ordinances, then you shall live and multiply, and the Lord your God will bless you in the land which you are entering to take possession of it. But if your heart turns away, and you will not hear, but are drawn away to worship other gods and serve them, I declare to you this day, that you shall perish; you shall not live long in the land which you are going over the Jordan to enter and possess. I call heaven and earth to witness against you this day, that I have set before you life and death, blessing and curse; therefore choose life, that you and your descendants may live." The context, both historical and religious—the "life" and "good" to be chosen are simply prosperity in a specific place in the near future; and the obedience demanded is to the Mosaic "statutes and ordinances"—render the passage virtually irrelevant to this theological use of it. Also, Justin has confused this text with the words of the Lord to Adam, for he says that Moses spoke them to the first man.

5. *Second Apology,* chap. 7; *PG,* VI, cols. 455-58; *AN,* I, 190-91.

3

by showing that there would be no such thing as morality if everything were determined by fate, and yet the Stoics themselves continue their moral teaching.

Before going on to the other early Christian writers, let us examine Justin's arguments. The most central is a philosophical argument from morality: (1) if man and his actions are moral (i.e., worthy of praise or blame), he must be free to choose between good actions and evil ones; (2) man is moral; (3) therefore, he is free in his choice. In support of (2), he will cite not only the "legislators and philosophers" (including the Stoics themselves) who command some actions and forbid others,[6] but also the authority of Scripture; it is this that makes his argument theological. But his citations of Scripture are all taken from the Old Testament: the morality is still the Judaic morality; there is no recognition of a new, specifically Christian relation of man to God. Furthermore, we should note that, although he has been led by a discussion of God's foreknowledge to refute fatalism, he makes no attempt to reconcile man's freedom with this foreknowledge,[7] merely affirming, somewhat redundantly, that God in his foreknowledge of man's actions has foreordained rewards for good actions and punishment for his evil ones.[8]

Certain features of Justin's position are not difficult to explain. The whole discussion is inspired, as he himself tells us, by the Stoic doctrine of fate (*heimarmene*), which was generally linked with an astrological fatality common to most of the popular religions of his time. Justin's argument from mor-

6. *Ibid.* In *I Apology,* chap. 44, he attempts to draw support from Plato by citing the famous *Aitia 'elomenou; theos anaitios,* "Blame goes to him who chooses; God is blameless," from the Myth of Er (*Republic,* X, 617E). However, in this myth, the choice referred to is made by the soul before birth and the whole course of our worldly life is fatally determined by it. Justin's use of the quotation is hardly enhanced by his assertion that Plato learned that man is free by reading Moses and the prophets.

7. Cf. A. W. F. Blunt, *The Apologies of Justin Martyr* (Cambridge, 1911), p. 64, note.

8. *I Apology,* chap. 44. For an exposition and some discussion of Justin's position, see also L. W. Barnard, *Justin Martyr: His Life and Thought* (Cambridge, 1967), pp. 114–17.

ality was part of the traditional refutation of astral fatalism, an argument probably almost as old as astrology itself and certainly common coin since Carneades in the second century B.C.[9] The one difference between Justin's argument and the philosophical one is his use of Scripture to prove that man is moral and has choice. However, as his use of Scripture is not specifically Christian but rather Judaic, it is not surprising that his argument is virtually identical with that of Philo of Alexandria, even including the same quotation from Deuteronomy.[10] In fact Philo, with his more profound knowledge of Scripture and a more meditative cast of mind, arrives at a position more "Christian" than that of Justin, for he sees man's free will as a grace of God—a special gift which, like all of God's gifts, it is a grave injustice to attribute to ourselves.[11] The influence of Philo on all of early Christian theology is well known and needs no special discussion; the closeness of Philonic doctrine to that of Justin leads us to remark two important ways in which this doctrine will differ from later positions: first, Justin's affirmation of free will is not directed either against God's omnipotence nor against a doctrine of grace, but against a pagan idea of fate; and second, his doctrine of freedom is not in any way related to the coming of Christ or the Christian revelation.

Justin's pupil, Tatian, writing in the middle of the second century, is more acutely aware of the problem of evil, and his account of the origin of evil and free will is more picturesque (and closer to Manicheism) than that of his master. According to Tatian,[12] the first-born of the angels resisted God and became a demon; others imitated his transgression and gave up their free will to follow their infatuations. But men form the material of their apostasy, for, "having shown them a plan

9. See D. Amand, *Fatalisme et liberté dans l'antiquité grecque* (Louvain, 1945), pp. 195–207 and *passim*.

10. Philo, *Quod Deus sit immutabilis,* 10, 50; cited in Amand, *Fatalisme,* pp. 86–87. Cf. Harry A. Wolfson, *Philo* (Cambridge, Mass., 1947), I, 432–38.

11. Cf. Wolfson, *Philo,* I, chap. 8, and Jean Daniélou, *Philon d'Alexandrie* (Paris, 1958), pp. 175–81.

12. *Address to the Greeks, PG,* VI, cols. 803–88; *AN,* II, 65–83.

of the position of the stars, like dice-players, they introduced Fate, a flagrant injustice." [13] Not only is Fate an illusion of the demons, but Death also: "Why are you fated . . . to die?" he asks. "Die to the world, repudiating the madness that is in it. . . . We were not created to die but we die by our own fault. Our free-will has destroyed us; we who were free have become slaves; we have been sold through sin. Nothing evil has been created by God; we ourselves have manifested wickedness; but we who have manifested it, are able to reject it." [14] So Tatian too rejects the Greek notion of Fate, sees it as the invention of the demons, and strongly affirms man's free will. However, his vision of evil seems to have overpowered his vision of man's freedom; he saw demons everywhere—in everything Greek, or sensual, or even material; he turned toward encratism and died an apostate.[15]

Tatian's difficulties, however, bring us to another important argument for free will: the argument from evil. The idea of this argument is to show that without free will one cannot explain the origin of evil, either moral or cosmological. For God, the creator of everything, is good, and would not produce anything evil; yet there is evil in the world; so man, although not evil in himself (for God created him) must be capable of evil, i.e., free to do evil, and the evils that are not the direct result of man's actions (e.g., misfortunes, ill health, floods, etc.) are sent by God as punishments for men, and so are really a good in disguise. This was a traditional Judaic view. But whatever the schematic advantages of this view, it seemed to many to offer certain empirical disadvantages. Moral evil may seem to originate in our decisions, but the evils that befall us seem more often than not to be unrelated to any sins of our own. The righteous man is seen to suffer and the vicious man to prosper; and floods, wars, etc., destroy whole populations without regard to the individuals' virtues. Judaism found several replies to these objections: (1) the sins for which one

13. *Ibid.*, chap. 8, *PG*, VI, col. 821; *AN*, II, 68.
14. *Ibid.*, chap. 11, *PG*, VI, col. 829; *AN*, II, 69–70.
15. F. Cayré, *Patrologie et histoire de la théologie*, 3 vols. (Paris, 1927–44), I, 124–25.

is punished may not be obvious ones; (2) the evils that befall the righteous man are not real evils but rather adversities sent to cure, or try, or improve him; and (3) a man may suffer for the sins of his ancestors.[16] The philosophers, who had no doctrine of personal providence, were not troubled by these problems: they had only to give a cosmological account of evil without justifying the ways of God to man. However, there was another religious system rivaling the developing "orthodox" Christian doctrine in the second century, which accounted for evil and also personal salvation: some discussion of Gnosticism, and especially of Christian Gnosticism, is absolutely essential for an understanding of the course of Christian theology in the second and third centuries.[17]

The origins of Gnosticism are still obscure and likely to remain so;[18] one can say in general that some sort of Gnostic religion or movement antedates Christianity, and that it was probably of oriental inspiration.[19] It is also often held that there was a Judaic Gnostic movement out of which arose the Christian Gnostic sects. However, one of the characteristics of Christian Gnosticism most important for our subject is its rejection of the Judaic tradition: the Old Testament was regarded as the work of a "dieu maudit" who in an imperfect act created a world full of evil of which he remains the master, enforcing his laws with cruelty and running the world according to a relentless (astral) necessity.[20] Salvation came not from obedience to the law, but consisted in being freed from all law and necessity, and St. Paul's remarks to this effect have

16. See Wolfson, *Philo,* II, 280–83.

17. Cf. F. M. M. Sagnard, "Intérêt théologique d'une étude de la gnose chrétienne," *Revue des sciences philosophiques et théologiques,* XXXIII (1949), nos. 2–3, 162–69.

18. H.-C. Puech, "Où en est le problème du gnosticisme?," *Revue de l'Université de Bruxelles,* XXXIX (1934–35), 137–58, 295–314. For a more recent discussion, see Hans Jonas, *The Gnostic Religion* (Boston, 1958), esp. pp. 33–34.

19. Puech, "Où en est le problème du gnosticisme?," pp. 152–56; cf. Jean Doresse, *Les Livres secrets des gnostiques d'Egypte,* 2 vols. (Paris, 1958–59).

20. Puech, "Où en est le problème du gnosticisme?," pp. 146–47.

been cited by some as an expression of this doctrine; indeed, some historians (e.g., Harnack) have seen in Christian Gnosticism the first truly Christian theology, freed at last from Judaic legalism and giving the proper emphasis to the radical novelty of Christ's teaching. However, a Christ come to free us from the cruel God of the Old Testament can hardly be understood as the Son of that God, but must be sent by a truly good God who has existed from all eternity above and beyond the created universe, and who made an appearance as the Christ to show the way to the elect few capable of understanding his doctrine. As H.-C. Puech puts it, "Le drame de la chute et du salut est, pour ainsi dire, joué de toute éternité . . . le Jésus historique n'était pour la Gnose qu'un fantôme: l'essentiel était le Sauveur préexistant." [21] All important, then, was the *knowledge* (*gnosis*) of salvation, attained through a "mythologizing" interpretation of Scripture, that is, an understanding of scriptural events in terms of cosmological mythologies, as well as through mysterious rites and initiations; on the moral level, whether one obeyed the law or sinned greatly was ultimately of no importance for true salvation—both asceticism and libertinism were taken as logical consequences of Gnostic doctrine;[22] morality concerned only the soul (psyche), while true salvation was spiritual (pneumatic) and transcended the world of good and evil.

Now, whatever may be the origins and characteristics of oriental Gnosticism, the rise of Christian Gnosticism has still to be understood in a Christian context. One important element of the new doctrine is what has been called the Hellenization of Christianity. The true God of the Gnostics is not the personal God of the Jews, but the pure Being of the philosophers, an object of contemplation and knowledge, not of worship or obedience. Another feature has been called the "mythologizing" of Christianity, undoubtedly connected with the increasing disillusionment among Christians of this period

21. *Ibid.*, p. 306. An excellent discussion of Gnosticism and Christianity is: L. Cerfaux, art. "Gnose préchrétienne et Biblique," in *Dictionnaire de la Bible: Supplément,* III (1938), cols. 659–701.
22. Jonas, *The Gnostic Religion*, pp. 46–47, 270–77.

with the failure of Christ to reappear. We know that the Second Coming was taken by the first-century Christians to be imminent, a belief largely responsible for the living, evangelical faith of the early Christians. When, however, no such real historical Coming materialized, the real historical Christ began to lose ground and new allegorical interpretations of the Gospels came into favor. This new interpretation made faith no longer a fidelity to the historical Christ, a waiting for his return "as the bride awaits the bridegroom," but a belief in the new doctrine of salvation, and then, for the Gnostics, a knowledge of the secret truth which was salvation, known only to the elect and passed on by those who possessed this perfect knowledge.

Given the nature of Gnostic systems, it is not surprising that none of them develops a theory concerning grace and free will. Yet in the system of Marcion (second century) at least, the gratuity of the Gnostic revelation is stressed, and parallels have been drawn with statements by St. Paul about Christ's "grace freely given," while others would see Augustine's notion of gratuitous predestination as Manichean, and ultimately Gnostic in origin.[23] Leaving aside the question of historical influences, we may note, with Jonas, that while the grace of which St. Paul speaks is a free gift of the Creator to creatures with whom he has a complex historical relationship (involving disobedience, guilt, repentance, mercy), the Gnostic grace is rather the spontaneous gesture of a God entirely outside creation who has no relation to creatures other than that paradoxical gift.

It is also worth noting that the whole Gnostic cosmology is an attempt to solve the problem of evil. There is no longer a personal God whose will must be shown to be just, as in the Judaeo-Christian tradition, but the world, including men's souls and bodies, is the creation of a demiurge, an emanation from the true God and hostile to him, and whose world is full of evil and ruled by necessity. This demiurge came to be equated with the God of the Old Testament, and Christians who did not rise above that conception could save their souls

23. See *ibid.*, pp. 143–44; Cerfaux, "Gnose préchrétienne," col. 694.

by good works, but could never see that their little drama of salvation was merely part of an immense pattern the true nature of which was known only to the "spirituals," or Gnostics. This spiritual knowledge, which was the only true salvation, did not depend on a choice or act of the will, but was a recognition that choosing and willing are illusory or, at the very best, futile. Nor was this recognition an act of knowledge of which one could question whether it originated in man or in God; it was the discovery of a secret knowledge, revealed by the good God through enigmatic parables, rites, and myths, the meaning of which was passed on by the adepts who were capable of explaining these things allegorically. This meaning, once revealed, freed one from all illusion, including the laws and commandments. There is no need to emphasize the difference between this point of the doctrine and the teaching of Saints John and Paul: although the full value is given here to the force of "revelation" in the New Testament, the truth that will "make you free" is never conceived by either St. John or St. Paul as sufficient in itself, but as freeing one from evil in order to practice virtue, liberating from the Law only to practice the new law of charity. Gnosticism, insofar as it includes a fusion of Hellenistic philosophy and Judaic personal religion, is thus parallel to, but very different from the synthesis of John and Paul. For these latter, salvation was not in the hands of man but of a God who had made himself known once in the person of Christ and would come once again; it did not depend exclusively either on morality or on rational knowledge, but on a personal, historical relationship. Gnosticism likewise was not moralistic—we have already noted that moral acts were considered irrelevant to true salvation— nor was it rationalistic—the knowledge of the Gnostics could not be attained by the right use of reason: it was mythical. The movement was a kind of intellectual pharisaism in which the key to salvation was not an elaborate set of laws but an elaborate set of beliefs; like moral pharisaism, it was present at the birth of Christianity and would remain a permanent temptation throughout its history. The possibility of confusing the knowledge we have of our salvation, or of our freedom, with salvation and freedom themselves seems, as the Reformation showed, to be always with us.

But, to return to the Early Fathers, Origen, in his *De Principiis* (written in the first quarter of the third century), points out that certain heretics "practically destroy free will by bringing in lost natures, which cannot receive salvation, and on the other hand saved natures, which are incapable of being lost." [24] These heretics are identified [25] as the followers of Marcion, Valentinus, and Basilides, Christian Gnostics who cite Scripture to their purpose, and whom Origen wishes to refute, having proved the free will by the same scriptural passages used by Philo, Justin, et al.; and also by the freedom implied by the Old and New Testament commandments considered together with God's righteous judgment. He argues as a true theologian, carefully reflecting on all the passages from Scripture that seem contradictory or opposed to what he considers basic doctrine. The several passages where God has hardened someone's heart or, in his mercy, softened it[26] are examined at length, and it is shown, first, that when God is said to have hardened a heart, He has not actually hardened it but allowed man to harden his own heart by his perverse tendencies: the evil all originates in man, God merely permits it by withholding his grace, that is, the punishments which would have shown him the evil of his ways.[27] But he must still explain why some men are thus abandoned to their evil ways, while others are saved. This he does by comparing God to a physician who sees that some diseases may be cured quickly while other cases require that the disease run its full course, for a quick cure might lead to an early relapse.[28] Origen is especially careful to remind us that it is not only this life that is involved, but an immortal soul, and he points out that even Pharaoh, whose heart remained hardened until his death, may

24. G. W. Butterworth, *Origen on First Principles, Being Koetshau's Text of the 'De Principiis' Translated into English* (London, 1936), p. 169 (III, i, 8).

25. *De Principiis*, II, ix, 5; *ibid.*, p. 133.

26. Exod. 4:21, 7:3; Ezek. 11:19–20; Rom. 9:18; Is. 63:17–18.

27. *De Principiis*, III, i, 8–12.

28. *Ibid.*, III, i, 13.

have received God's mercy after his death on account of his usefulness in the fulfillment of God's plan.[29]

So evil in the world is of two kinds: the evil that men do, out of their own perverseness, when left by God to their own devices; and the evil that God visits on men as a punishment and that, as in the traditional Judaic view, is therefore a form of God's mercy. This explanation of the origin of evil would have stood as an adequate one, and a sufficient refutation of Gnostic theories at least on scriptural grounds, if it weren't for certain other passages of which the most important (the very one that led St. Augustine to change his own earlier views) is Romans 9:6–24. In this passage St. Paul points out that God said, "Jacob I loved, but Esau I hated . . . though they were not yet born and had done nothing either good or bad." Thus the evil that befell Esau was no just punishment for anything he had done but was decided before his birth, as it was also decided before his birth that he should not be granted God's mercy but was to be abandoned to his own wicked ways. "So then he has mercy upon whomever he wills, and he hardens the heart of whomever he wills," and his will does not seem to depend in any way on man's actions.

Origen is one of the few early writers to face this problem squarely. However, the radical nature of his solution has been obscured by the fact that most of the pertinent writings are preserved only in Rufinus' Latin translations, which are often apologies for, or dilutions of, the originals, rather than straight translations. It seems clear now, both from some of the Greek fragments and from quotations of Origen by his attackers,[30] that his solution to this difficulty depends on a belief in the transmigration of souls. At one point, he says, "As . . . it will happen in the day of judgment that the good will be separated from the evil and the righteous from the unrighteous and every individual soul will by the judgment of God be allotted to that place of which his merits have rendered him worthy . . . so also in the past some such process, I think, has taken

29. *Ibid.*, III, i, 14.
30. *Ibid.*, II, ix, 7–8; III, i, 21–24. Cf. Butterworth, *Origen,* pp. xv ff., and p. 72, n. 8.

place." And again, "Even before the present life there were rational vessels, either wholly purged or less so, that is, vessels which had purged themselves or had not, and . . . each vessel received according to the measure of its purity or impurity, its place or region or condition in which to be born or to fulfill some duty in this world." [31] If the soul has not actually been born into other bodies, it has still had an existence prior to this one during which it was capable of somehow acquiring merit and purifying itself, or the reverse. The dependence on Platonic doctrine is obvious here, and in fact there is a very close resemblance to the picture of the preexistent soul found in the Myth of Er. [32] Such a mythical resolution was not, of course, acceptable to more orthodox Christians, most of whom had already abandoned the transmigration of souls as a possibility; yet it is important that Origen looked hard at the real difficulties presented by the passages in St. Paul, and that his reconciliation of human responsibility and determinism (though it was a very limited determinism as compared with the Greek fatalism) depended, as in Plato, on putting the responsible choice into the past, even if that past was highly mythical.

St. Irenaeus[33] was another great opponent of the Gnostics who was concerned to assert the identity of God the creator and God the father; but he refuted also the transmigration of souls, even to the point of almost admitting the materiality of the individual soul, which took the shape of the one body it inhabited.[34] Yet he asserted the freedom of the will and the case for our meriting reward or damnation so strongly that some writers have accused him of Pelagianism.[35] His argu-

31. *De Principiis*, II, ix, 8.

32. *Republic*, X, 613E ff.

33. An excellent summary of Irenaeus' doctrine of redemption can be found in J. N. D. Kelly, *Early Christian Doctrines* (2d ed.; New York, 1960), pp. 170–74.

34. See Etienne Gilson, *History of Christian Philosophy in the Middle Ages* (New York, 1955), p. 23 and note.

35. E.g., F. Vernet, art. "Saint Irénée," in *DTC*, VII, col. 2460; and P. Beuzart, *Essai sur la théologie d'Irénée* (Paris, 1908), p. 64. Denied by Gilson, *History,* and by John Lawson, *The Biblical Theology of Saint Irenaeus* (London, 1948), pp. 223 ff.

ments reduce for the most part to the two basic ones we have already seen: from morality and from evil.[36] His citations from Scripture, though, are at least taken largely from the New Testament, but are the same sort as those used by Philo and others, that is, they are not passages affirming that man is free, but commands, and occasions where men are rewarded for faith or goodness. He does not consider the passages that seem to imply a lack of freedom, but, as one author puts it, "c'est contre le fatalisme et le dualisme gnostique qu'Irénée a été amené à souligner ainsi la libre responsabilité de l'homme," [37] and also to deemphasize man's present need for grace. However, he fully recognizes that Adam's Fall was an important event for all mankind and he is one of the first to develop the parallelism between Adam and Christ, the Fall and the Redemption, in his theory of "recapitulation." [38] Even more important, however, are his notions of the childhood and growth of man;[39] seeing Adam as man in his infancy, he ascribes to him only a relative perfection which still needed spiritual growth. Even in his present state, man is neither radically evil nor yet perfect, but is able to grow spiritually and must live in the expectancy of a future perfection that is greater even than that of Adam before the Fall; this expectancy was based on the conception of the Millennium, which has since been discredited, but as developed by Irenaeus it is part of an historical and eschatological vision now considered essential to Christianity;[40] and it opened the way for certain features of the Augustinian doctrine of Redemption.

Irenaeus' disciple, Cyprian, was not so much a theologian as a practical man, a good pastor, but with a mystical spiritual-

36. See *Adversus haereses*, IV, 37; *PG*, VII, cols. 1099–1104; *AN*, I, 518–21.

37. Th. Camelot, review of Lawson, *Biblical Theology*, in *Revue des sciences philosophiques et théologiques*, XXXV (1951), 312. See also F. Sagnard (ed.), *Contre les hérésies* by Irénée de Lyon (Paris: coll. "Sources Chrétiennes," 1952), Introduction.

38. See Lawson, *Biblical Theology*, chap. 11.

39. *Ibid.*, chap. 12.

40. See Jean Daniélou, "S. Irénée et les origines de la théologie de l'histoire," *Recherches de science religieuse*, XXXIV (1947), 227–31.

ity which in its own way also prepared the way for St. Augustine; the latter will not hesitate to quote St. Cyprian against the Pelagians, and certain passages seem well suited to his purpose: "For who resists God, that he may not do what he wills? . . . We pray and ask that God's will may be done in us; and that it may be done in us we have need of God's good will, that is, of His help and protection, since no one is strong in his own strength but he is safe by the grace and mercy of God."[41] Or again: "Moreover the Lord of necessity admonishes us to say in prayer, 'And suffer us not to be led into temptation.' In which words it is shown that the adversary can do nothing against us except God shall have previously permitted it."[42] However, in these remarks he is speaking of the struggle between flesh and spirit, familiar from St. Paul, in which "we cannot do those very things that we would,"[43] and implies the need of an auxiliary grace to help us against temptation, but also seems to imply that we are free to ask for that grace, which is clearly somewhat short of the position St. Augustine will maintain, and in any case has nothing to do with the difficult questions posed by predestination and the passages that suggest it. Cyprian's spirituality is nevertheless one of great dependence on the Lord and certainly emphasizes our need to pray continually if we are to have the strength to perform good and meritorious works.

Meanwhile another argument for the freedom of the will has made its appearance, though it is not one that we need linger over. It was perhaps first introduced by Irenaeus, is mentioned in Tertullian, and developed at some length by Gregory of Nyssa. Very simply it is that, since Scripture says we are created in God's image, this implies that we are, like God, free. Now since it is nowhere explained in Scripture in what way we are like God—and it is clear that we are also in many ways quite different from Him—this argument is primarily an invention of philosophical theology, an interesting speculation but without any value as dogma, and Tertullian

41. *De Oratione Dominica, PL,* IV, col. 528; *AN,* V, 451.
42. *Ibid., PL,* IV, col. 536; *AN,* V, 454.
43. *Ibid., PL,* IV, col. 537; *AN,* V, 451.

puts it forth as such, using the usual Philonic arguments and citations from Scripture to support it.[44] But Tertullian's view deserves further discussion on other grounds. He is probably the first Christian writer to use the term "liberum arbitrium." [45] He is also, however, the first to elaborate and emphasize a doctrine of original sin and use the term "vitium originis." [46] To see more clearly his position on these questions, we must first outline his doctrine on the origin and nature of the soul. Partly under the influence of the Stoics and certain medical theories,[47] Tertullian believed in a material soul, created at the time of birth out of the souls of the parents; so our souls, like our bodies, are all quite literally descended from Adam. Now Tertullian, anxious to refute the Platonic and Gnostic dualism,[48] which led so many other early Christian writers (especially among the Greeks) to think of sin as being solely of the flesh, maintained that sin had its origin in the soul— men often sin in thought without involving the flesh at all. So when Adam sinned, he corrupted his soul but also the souls of all men born after him, and this corruption became as a second nature to men.[49] However, the guilt of this sin was not transmitted—each man is born innocent—nor was the inherited corruption such as to destroy the freedom and complete responsibility of each individual.[50]

44. Cf. H. A. Wolfson, "Philosophical Implications of the Pelagian Controversy," *Proceedings of the American Philosophical Society,* CIII, no. 4 (August, 1959), 556.

45. J. Morgan, *The Importance of Tertullian in the Development of Christian Dogma* (London, 1928), p. 53.

46. *Ibid.,* p. 172.

47. Cf. G. Verbeke, *L'Evolution de la doctrine du pneuma du stoïcisme à s. Augustin* (Louvain, 1945), pp. 518–28.

48. A. J. Festugière, "La Composition et l'esprit du *De Anima* de Tertullian," *Revue des sciences philosophiques et théologiques,* XXXIII, nos. 2–3 (1949), 143–46; Festugière maintains that Tertullian went much further in the direction of a corporeal soul than he need have gone to refute his opponent.

49. "Naturae corruptio alia natura est." *De Anima,* 41, 1, ed. J. Waszink (Amsterdam, 1947), p. 57.

50. For Tertullian's doctrine of the soul as outlined, see Festugière, "Composition," and G. Bardy, art. "Tertullian," in *DTC,* XV, cols. 152–54.

This general doctrine of the origin of the individual soul must in turn be understood in the context of the other doctrines current at the time. Tertullian's system of the transmission of souls, often called "traducianism," is in direct opposition to the Platonic doctrine of the preexistence of souls, such as was adopted by Origen. Traducianism in one form or another, though usually purged of the notion of the materiality of the soul, was widely accepted in the West, and seems to be the doctrine accepted by St. Augustine himself, although he vacillates on this question. The Eastern Fathers tended to favor a different view, a sort of compromise between Platonism and traducianism usually called "creationism"; for them each soul is an individual creation *ex nihilo* by God as in the Platonic theories, but is joined to just one body at the time of its birth, as in the traducian theories. This theory is essentially that of Philo, though each writer has certain nuances of his own. Tertullian, a confused and highly unphilosophical thinker, never saw the possible predestinarian implications of his theories of traducianism and original corruption; and although Philo was too Platonic for him in these matters, he out-Philoed Philo in his emphasis on man's freedom and merit, being perhaps the first Latin writer to give the question that peculiar twist which seems characteristic of the Roman legal mind. As Tixeront puts it:

Cette théorie du mérite et de la satisfaction, mise en relief surtout par Tertullien, est peut-être, dans toute son oeuvre, celle où se trahit le plus son esprit de juriste. Il a créé pour elle une terminologie qui a subsisté et qui reste caractéristique de la théologie latine. . . . Si nous agissons bien, nous méritons auprès de Dieu, nous méritons Dieu. . . . Dieu devient notre débiteur. . . . Au contraire, par le péché nous offensons Dieu et nous devenons ses debiteurs, mais nous devons et nous pouvons lui satisfaire. . . . Inutile d'insister sur le caractère propre de ces expressions: elles sont bien représentatives du génie positif latin.[51]

51. J. Tixeront, *La Théologie anténicéenne*, cited in *DTC*, XV, col. 154.

So, while he laid the basis for the doctrine of Original Sin, Tertullian at the same time invented the "liberum arbitrium" and gave it that context of debt and merit, tinged with the sense of profit and loss, which will become characteristic of a whole current of thought in the West.

The Eastern Fathers did not follow this lead. On the whole loyal to Philo, they were largely unaware that a controversy was building up. St. John Chrysostom in particular was soon picked up and cited by the Pelagians themselves in defense of their position. His doctrine has indeed much in common with at least the semi-Pelagian views: he believed that God calls all men to salvation, that those only are saved who answer the call by their good will, that God then helps them in acts of virtue; God's grace is important and necessary, but it is not prevenient—it is consequent upon a necessary act of the will. He defends the free will at all costs and fears that a denial of it will result in despair or negligence of salvation. On predestination, he is afraid of making God the author of sin, and because of his inability to distinguish between a doctrine of election and a doctrine of reprobation, Chrysostom, in his embarrassed commentary on the passage in St. Paul's Epistle to the Romans—the one which would lead St. Augustine to develop his doctrine—reduces predestination merely to a foreknowledge on God's part.[52]

Gregory of Nyssa was one of those who tried to demonstrate the existence of our free will on the basis of our likeness to God.[53] He distinguishes two different freedoms: a structural freedom (the Greek *eleutheria*) which was ours at creation, in which we were the true image of God and free to communicate with Him and all His creation; and a functional freedom, or freedom of choice (*proairesis*). The first was lost by Adam's sin, but men not only retained the freedom of

52. See A. Kenny, "Was St. John Chrysostom a Semi-Pelagian?," *The Irish Theological Quarterly*, XXVII, no. 1 (Jan. 1960), esp. pp. 27–29; and G. Bardy, art. "Saint Jean Chrysostome," in *DTC*, VIII, cols. 660–90.

53. This exposition is based mainly on J. Gaïth, *La Conception de la liberté chez Grégoire de Nysse* (Paris, 1953).

choice: by the proper use of that freedom they can aspire to the earlier freedom of communion.[54] Further, Gregory virtually equates freedom of choice with reason and seems to consider that the very fact that to deny the one also destroys the other is a sufficient argument for the freedom of the will. Finally, for him as for so many of the pre-Augustinian Fathers, any theory of predestination would have smacked of an astrological fatalism and was to be violently rejected.[55]

So at the end of the fourth century the Greek Fathers, steeped in Platonism, influenced by Philo, and shunning an oriental fatalism, believed man to be absolutely free in his choice of good and evil and were on the whole untroubled by the theological difficulties implied by certain biblical texts; when questions were raised, the texts were ignored or explained away. The Latin Fathers were meanwhile developing a sense of original sin and corruption, and of the need to "pay off" this sin in some way, but as yet the doctrine of free will had not been seriously affected. Virtually all the pre-Augustinian Fathers held to what Professor Wolfson calls "the conception of absolute freedom of the will." [56] Yet, as we have seen, various troubling questions had been raised, especially in the West, and bits of doctrine had been formulated which were to become parts of a whole new theory of grace and predestination; and underlying it all, as a foundation waiting for its superstructure, was the Greek "conception of relative freedom": the will as free only in the sense of being free from external compulsion. In fact this is the doctrine of both Plato and Aristotle, to whom a cyclical theory of creation meant not only that the laws of nature were fated, but that man's actions also were mere repetitions of previous existences and certainly fated also, even if "relatively" free. Philo and the Jewish thinkers had modified these doctrines to fit in with a conception of linear rather than cyclical time and of a free, miracle-working God. St. Augustine will take the same basis and, modifying it in a different way, change the whole future of Christian thought on grace

54. Gaïth, *Conception,* pp. 79–81 and *passim.*
55. Amand, *Fatalisme et liberté,* pp. 418–31.
56. "Philosophical Implications," pp. 554–55.

and freedom; it is a radical change and will meet with much resistance, but the way had been prepared,[57] and when Augustine formulated his views they were accepted and recognized as the true Christian doctrine. Let us now turn to that doctrine.

Besides producing an important shift in the Christian tradition, Augustine's doctrine of grace caused a revolution in his own thought. This change can even be fairly accurately dated: it occurred between the writing of the *De Libero arbitrio*, finished in 395, and of the *De Diversis quaestionibus ad Simplicianum*, begun in 396. As was pointed out by Augustine himself,[58] this latter text represents his arrival at his basic doctrine on the subject, and so this doctrine was formulated well in advance of the Pelagian controversy;[59] in fact, it was St. Augustine's doctrine, as expressed implicitly in the *Confessions* in the year 400, which led the Pelagians to formulate their objections.[60] This is important to note for the reason that those in the Middle Ages and later who have wished to temper the Augustinian doctrine have sometimes claimed that the Doctor of Grace in his need to combat the Pelagian heresy went beyond his own true doctrine; the letter to Simplician can serve as a guide to settle any such claims.

We have tried to show that this sudden break with the doctrine of three centuries of Christian thought was prepared by various notions and spiritual undercurrents which preceded it; that such influences were at work is amply attested by the simple fact of the relatively quick and widespread acceptance of the Augustinian doctrine. Another puzzle remains, however: what led St. Augustine himself to such a sudden change of heart? In his writings prior to 396, and especially in the *De Libero arbitrio*, man's freedom is stoutly upheld along the

57. In the fourth century, the Latin writers Hilary, Ambrose, and the Ambrosiaster were especially important; cf. Kelly, *Early Christian Doctrines*, pp. 353–57.

58. *Retractationes*, II, i, 1; *BA*, XII, 450–53.

59. This was insisted upon in the authoritative article of E. Portalié, "Saint Augustin," in *DTC*, I, cols. 2268–2472, and by many subsequent writers on the subject.

60. See Wolfson, "Philosophical Implications," p. 555.

traditional lines. In particular, in the early writings against the Manicheans, the freedom of the will is a cornerstone of his argument concerning the origin of evil. This is most clearly put forward in the famous dispute with Fortunatus in August of 392,[61] and is one of those books on which the Pelagians will draw to cite Augustine against himself. So, for instance, in one passage we find:

but Evil comes from a voluntary sin of the soul to which God has given free will. If God had not given this free will, there could have been no just reason for [our] punishment, nor any merit in our doing right, nor a divine commandment to repent our sins, nor that forgiveness of our sins which God has given us through Jesus Christ. For whoever sins involuntarily does not sin at all.[62]

It is most interesting to note the context of this passage: the free will is defended here not in its capacity to choose salvation, but as the source of evil in the world. Pascal and his age assumed from Augustine's writings that the Manicheans denied free will and it is one of his points that the Early Fathers' remarks in defense of the freedom of the will are directed against the Manicheans, who are for him Lutherans before the fact.[63] It is only in the present century that we have gained any really solid knowledge of the Manicheans,[64] and although they are certainly tainted with the oriental fatalism against which the Early Fathers did so often inveigh—thus vindicating Pascal's argument, if not his historical accuracy—their denial of free will is in the sense in which Augustine here affirms it, namely, as the source of evil in the world. As regards salvation, the Manicheans required

61. *Acta seu disputatio contra Fortunatum Manichaeum, BA,* XVII, 118–93.

62. *Contra Fortunatum,* 20; *BA,* XVII, 164.

63. *OC,* pp. 1016, 1022–23.

64. See H.-C. Puech, *Le Manichéisme: son fondateur, sa doctrine* (Paris: Musée Guimet, Bibliothèque de la Diffusion, 56, 1949); and S. Augustin, *Six Traités Anti-Manichéens,* ed. R. Jolivet, M. Jourjon; *BA,* XVII, Introduction and notes.

a vigorous and active struggle against the "evil nature" and believed anyone educated in the True Religion could engage in this struggle. The effect of the Manichean cosmology is to place evil outside the enlightened soul and to release that soul from its power—St. Augustine is called on thus to explain how evil got into man's free soul in the first place (unless God put it there) and in reply he gives, already in 392, an exposition of the consequences of Adam's Fall which is fairly pessimistic.[65] Particularly important is his theory of the habit (*consuetudo*) of sin, which is our punishment for Original Sin, and which is not a necessary nature (as is the sinful nature according to the Manicheans), but a habit of the flesh which can be changed to a habit of virtue; man since the Fall is sinful as surely as snow is cold, but just as snow can be melted and become hot, so man can change that sinful nature (which is really only an attribute) and become virtuous.[66] But the weight of the habit of sin is depicted in detail and is considered an empirical fact, the vision of evil is strongly there, and the ground has been laid for his speculations on that most basic habit of sin, concupiscence; in the *Retractationes,* St. Augustine himself underlined the importance of this passage for his future views.[67]

The *De Libero arbitrio* is St. Augustine's major work on the will before his change of position, and it too is stuffed with affirmations of man's freedom which the Pelagians will take up to support their cause.[68] And rightly so: there is no denying the optimism of the work, especially of the first book. But once again, one must bear in mind that it is a work concerned with the origin of evil and with proving the existence of a good God who has nevertheless permitted evil—all this, of course, still as an attack on Manichean dualism. The question of the necessity of grace simply is not raised. Augustine, during this period, was simply not preoccupied with such questions, but if he had been it seems obvious that although he had ac-

65. *Contra Fortunatum,* 22; *BA,* XVII, 175–77.
66. *Ibid.,* pp. 177–81.
67. *Retractationes,* I, 16; *BA,* XII, 376–79.
68. A list of such passages can be found in *BA,* VI, 500.

cepted many elements of his later doctrine—the importance of Original Sin, the notion of the *massa peccati*, the need for God's help to perform virtuous actions, etc.—he still thought of the *initium salutis* as being entirely dependent on man's free choice.[69] The vocation came from God but man's assent came only from man. And from there it is a short step to the semi-Pelagian view: that believing and willing are ours and merit the graces which we receive to aid us in good works. So although St. Augustine did not change his thinking on anything but the question of the *initium salutis*, nevertheless that change was a radical one.

Our question of why this change occurred still remains unanswered. Some scholars would see in St. Augustine's own spiritual life the source of his new attitude: as a new convert, advancing daily in Christian virtue, triumphantly denouncing Manichean heresies, he experienced an optimism and enthusiasm for his new religion, which slowly and naturally subsided, giving rise, by 395 or so, to a more realistic view of man's sinful nature even after baptism, and of his need for help to lead a virtuous life.[70] Professor Wolfson thinks that he arrived at his doctrine of man's concupiscence after the Fall through his own experience of the difficulties of living in continence and from a mistranslation of a passage from the Wisdom of Solomon (8:21).[71] However, the theory of concupiscence has even better scriptural authority in a passage from St. Paul (I Timothy 6:10): "Radix omnium malorum est cupiditas," which Augustine had quoted earlier against Fortunatus;[72] also, the passage to which Wolfson refers is in the *Confessions* (VI, 11, 20), written after he had formulated his new doctrine and in which he plainly states that earlier, when he had trouble remaining continent, he believed in the power of the free will.

In fact, a careful reading of the letter to Simplician in which his new doctrine of the necessity of grace and predestination

---

69. Cf. Portalié, "Saint Augustin," in *DTC,* I, cols. 2378–79.
70. See, for example, Bardy in *BA,* VI, 501–504.
71. Wolfson, "Philosophical Implications," p. 558.
72. *Contra Fortunatum,* 22, 21; *BA,* XVII, 168.

are first put forward makes quite clear that the passage from Romans (9:10–29) was the decisive factor; that, in spite of his own reluctance to admit it, Scripture forced him to a belief in God's predestination of souls before any occasion or even prevision of merits; as he stated himself: "In the solution of this question, I labored all for the freedom of man's will; but the grace of God was triumphant, and I could not but understand the most limpid truth of what the Apostle has said, 'Who then discerns you? For what have you that you have not received? And if you have received it, why glorify yourself as though you had not?'"[73] It is clearly a humility before the words of Scripture that led St. Augustine to a position earlier Christian thinkers had found incompatible with the philosophical implications of other scriptural passages. Without denying the importance of his spiritual life in this change, we may remember that a very similar spiritual experience had already found expression in other Christian writers without their having formulated a new doctrine of grace. What is new in St. Augustine is his refusal to ignore or explain away the biblical passages that indicate man's total dependence on God's will, as had been done previously with the aid of Greek philosophy, Philo, and allegorical interpretation. The best guess as to what brought about this change is that of Professor Buonaiuti[74] that it was a reading of the commentaries on St. Paul of the Ambrosiaster.[75] These commentaries, which also, incidentally, in-

73. *Retractationes,* II, 1, 1; *BA,* XII, 453.

74. E. Bonaiuti [*sic*], "The Genesis of St. Augustine's idea of Original Sin," *Harvard Theological Review,* X (1917), no. 2, 159–75. Additional force is given this view by the fact that Augustine follows the Ambrosiaster's misreading of Rom. 5:12 to the effect that death passed to all men because all sinned *in Adam*. See Kelly, *Early Christian Doctrines,* pp. 354, 363.

75. *Commentaria in tredecim epistolas B. Pauli, PL,* XVII, cols. 45–508. These commentaries, written by an unknown author between 374 and 379, were long incorrectly attributed to St. Ambrose; it was Erasmus who saw the mistake and gave the author the name Ambrosiaster. In spite of their anonymous origin, they are considered by some to be the most important commentaries on St. Paul in all of Latin Christendom. See G. Bardy, art. "Ambrosiaster," in *Dictionnaire de la Bible: Supplément,* I, cols. 225–41.

spired Pelagius,[76] gave to Augustine, if not a new doctrine of grace, at least a new respect for the literal and obvious meaning of Scripture; and so, asked by Simplician to tackle one of the many passages in which a notion of predestination seems implied, he followed the text rather than the philosophers. The resulting synthesis of Pauline spirituality with the Greek-inspired writings of the earlier Fathers amounted to a new doctrine binding together already accepted notions of Original Sin, grace, divine prescience, and Sacred History in a way that would serve as a point of departure for virtually all future Christian thought.

Let us try to state as succinctly as possible just what this doctrine is;[77] then we shall see to what further precisions (and perhaps also exaggerations) St. Augustine was led by the Pelagian controversy. The central question involved for St. Augustine was, as we have already seen, the *initium salutis*, that is, whether the very first step or movement of the individual toward salvation came from man or God. Philo and the Early Fathers all allowed that God came to man's aid with various gifts or helps when asked, but all—including Augustine himself before 396—maintained that the first step, or at least the answer to God's call, must come from man. And the argument, as we have seen, ran mostly along moral lines: such a step was necessary if man was to be held responsible for his sins and to merit salvation. Now it was this last requirement

76. See G. de Plinval, *Pélage, ses écrits, sa vie et sa réforme* (Lausanne, 1943), pp. 86–92.

77. For this outline of Augustine's doctrine of grace, I depend primarily on two works: the article "Saint Augustin" of Portalié in the *DTC* cited above (n. 59), and the more recent work of J. Chéné, *La Théologie de saint Augustin: grâce et prédestination* (Le Puy-Lyon, 1962). All the essential texts are cited in the first, quoted at length in the second. E. Gilson, *Introduction à l'étude de saint Augustin* (2d ed.; Paris, 1943), pp. 185–216, is helpful but is too synthetic in its attempt to reconcile all phases of Augustine's thought. Cf. B. Romeyer, "Trois problèmes de philosophie augustinienne: à propos d'un livre récent" (review of Gilson), in *Archives de philosophie,* VII (1930), no. 2, 200–43. G. Bonner, *St. Augustine of Hippo* (Philadelphia, 1964), chaps. 8–9, gives a good account of the development of the Pelagian controversies.

that suddenly seemed superfluous to Augustine and even in contradiction to many statements of St. Paul. "What have you that you have not received?" he kept asking himself, and if all good things are gifts from God, surely the greatest good of all, our salvation, is also a gift freely given, and therefore not merited. There is a difference though: *all* good and virtuous acts are the result of God's grace—they are prepared by a grace that is totally unmerited, though they may in turn merit further rewards; such gifts are granted to pagans as well as Christians, enabling them to lead "naturally" virtuous lives. But salvation demands a special grace, and the acts of faith and prayer are the result of these special graces. These two cases will, in the Scholastic period, be developed into the theory of the two orders: natural and supernatural. St. Augustine does not establish any such thorough separation of orders, even in his theory of the two cities. Nevertheless, he clearly distinguishes, in discussing God's graces, between those required for meritorious acts unrelated to salvation, and those which lead to salvation itself. This latter "sanctifying" grace is defined as absolutely necessary for salvation, as totally gratuitous, and as efficacious, i.e., infallible in its results.

Now our sinful acts, on the other hand, are by no means gifts from God nor are they in any way attributable to him; man is responsible for his sins, and that for the reason given by all the Early Fathers and by Augustine himself when he argued against the Manicheans: because he is free. His will is free always to choose between good and evil, even though, since the Fall of Adam, this choice is not "indifferent" but heavily weighted on the side of evil. Nevertheless, St. Augustine consistently affirms this essential freedom of the will.[78] How then are these two concepts of an efficacious or infallible

78. Those passages in his later writings where he states that, through Adam's Fall, the "libre arbitre" was lost, are shown by Portalié to need correction on the basis of semantics ("Saint Augustin," in *DTC,* I, cols. 2404–2405), or are rhetorical exaggeration: "Si, comme le montre l'histoire de son influence, de graves contresens ont été, si souvent, commis sur sa véritable pensée, Augustin en est lui-même, pour une large part, le premier responsable." H.-I. Marrou, *Saint Augustin et l'augustinisme* (Paris, 1957), p. 55.

grace and of the essential freedom of the will to be reconciled? The answer lies in an understanding of the nature of the human will. Our will is free to choose, but it is also determined in two ways: it acts according to motives, choosing always a greater good over a lesser; and it does not choose—but must choose among—the objects presented to it. Man has no control over either the external objects presented to his choice, nor the internal images or motives which will govern that choice: these are sent by God. Now the way in which God supplies the objects and motives of our will so that, if he wishes it, we infallibly choose the good—yet retain our freedom to choose evil—depends on his prescience, or rather simply his science, for, although this knowledge was present to him even at creation, it is always and eternally present and not prior to our acts. Nothing is easier, then, than for God to give us exactly the circumstances and motivations necessary for us freely to choose our salvation, knowing as he does the minutest details of our lives both internal and external. To the external "calls to faith"—the Gospels, the example of Christ, the teaching of the Church—correspond also internal aids, which both enlighten our ignorance and attract our wills, making us see and want our salvation. Our wills being what they are, they will respond to such solicitations both freely and infallibly; their freedom is not merely a lack of constraint but also a genuine power to choose, even though in fact we will choose what God has foreseen we shall. Professor Wolfson has shown[79] that this theory of St. Augustine depends on a distinction made by Aristotle between what is necessary by the internal nature of a thing, and what is compelled by an external force. When we say, "God is immutable," it does not mean that anything compels God to remain always the same, but rather it is his nature to be so: he is immutable by definition. So the human will is concupiscent by definition and although it sins freely and without being compelled, yet it could not do otherwise and still be the same human will. When, however, it is transformed by grace, its very nature is changed and it turns necessarily—again without any compul-

79. "Philosophical Implications," pp. 559-61.

sion—toward the good. This distinction can be seen as roughly equivalent to that between logical necessity and physical causation, and it is clear that this is exactly what St. Augustine has in mind when he says, for example, that he would accept the concept of Fate (*fatum*) in his system provided it were taken in its etymological meaning of that which is spoken, rather than seeming to depend on the movements of the stars.[80] This then is St. Augustine's way of reconciling the peculiar infallibility of grace and the freedom of the will.

As for the necessity of grace, the problem raised was that of God's desire for universal salvation: if God wishes the salvation of all men, but only gives these totally effective graces to some, doesn't he give to the rest of mankind a grace at least sufficient for salvation, provided they choose to accept it? Such a notion of a grace sufficient for salvation but not leading to it infallibly—not to be confused with the "natural" gifts of virtue mentioned above, which are freely given to many men but are outside the realm of salvation—would be contrary to the very notions of the nature of the will and of God's omniscience invoked above. An infallible grace is absolutely necessary for salvation: its reconciliation with God's desire for the salvation of all is a mystery, but there is no injustice involved, as we shall see. For the gratuity of grace, on which Augustine insists most strongly,[81] means to him, not only that this grace is given prior to any consideration of individual merit, but also that it is unmerited by humanity in general. It is an act of pure mercy on the part of God, given that primitive curse under which we all are born. To understand this we must look at the Augustinian conception of Original Sin.

This doctrine was already widely accepted at the time, but not with all the implications which St. Augustine will find in it. Most earlier theologians had supposed that, with the first sin, Adam lost (for himself and his posterity) his immortality and several other attributes such as an enlightened mind, a freedom from passion (*apatheia*), etc. Augustine makes it clear however that these attributes were not part of our human

80. *De Civitate Dei*, V, 9; *BA*, XXXIII, 676–79.
81. See J. Chéné, Introduction to *BA*, XXIV, 10–15.

nature (to which we might consider ourselves entitled), but special divine gifts; it is with perfect justice that God withdrew them and left us in a state in which we are drawn about by our senses and passions, and will end our limited existence sooner or later in death. Salvation is a matter of returning us to something like that earlier state, by sanctification, which is our adoption through Christ; it requires a grace which is above that required for mere natural virtues, and doubly gratuitous as it returns us to a state which we had no claim to even before Adam's Fall. This double gratuity can best be seen in regard to perseverance: Adam had the grace of the power to persevere in obedience to God (the *adiutorium sine quo non*) which was sufficient to enable him effectively to do so; if we, in our fallen state, were given only this *power* of perseverance, our weakness would still make us fall away. We are in effect given the grace of perseverance itself (the *adiutorium quo*), and because of it, even though we retain the freedom to turn away from God, we do not do so. That Adam's freedom was greater than ours, is due to our concupiscence. This controversial term was already mentioned in connection with the change in Augustine's position around 396; we must add here that much of the confusion concerning it comes from the tendency of Augustine's own disciples to identify it with Original Sin itself. The temptation was great, for Augustine was fond of pointing out the close connection of concupiscence with reproduction and thus (if we accept a traducianist point of view) with the transmission of Original Sin. In fact, Augustine never finally accepted traducianism nor did he actually identify concupiscence and Original Sin; concupiscence is rather a consequence of that Sin, as is clear in his views on Baptism. For Original Sin is destroyed by Baptism, but concupiscence remains. What is destroyed is the imputation to us of Adam's concupiscence (sometimes called "original guilt"), as also of his ignorance, pride, etc. We are released from the curse, but not from the effects of it.

One final feature of his doctrine, which St. Augustine had arrived at before the Pelagian controversy, was his acceptance of predestination. This was at the heart of the very text of St.

Paul (Romans 9:10–29) which he had agreed to explain to Simplician and was perhaps the hardest pill to swallow. But Augustine could see no other explanation of St. Paul's meaning than that God chooses out of this mass of sinners some who are to be saved: their number is fixed and their election assured from all eternity; the rest, of course, are damned. But at the same time he will maintain that all men have the possibility of being among the elect if they wish to, and that it is God's will that they be saved, though only the elect will want to be saved. Although apparently paradoxical, if we think once again of the distinction of Aristotle outlined above, the position loses some of its contradictoriness. As Augustine had argued against the Manichean, Fortunatus, it is snow's nature to be cold, but this only means that snow is cold by definition —it can still be melted and heated. So if man is by definition sinful, yet, with God's grace, that nature can be changed and the same man become saved. And nothing actually prevents us from willing our salvation, even though God knows that not all of us will do so. But His knowledge of these things is absolutely inscrutable, and as Augustine says, especially in his preaching, "since you don't know whether you are among the elect, strive as though you were." This is the last word on the subject: beyond that is only the mysterious will of God.

The polarity of St. Augustine's system is obvious and is made even more explicit in the notion of the two cities, the one celestial, the result of God's mercy, the other infernal, but in accord with God's justice;[82] many have seen a latent Manicheism still present in his later thought. Be that as it may, in the question of grace, St. Augustine always maintains the two poles in equilibrium—an equilibrium, however, which will be frequently upset in the subsequent history of doctrine. The Medieval and modern writers on grace can readily be classified by the extent to which they are attracted to one pole or the other—they will tend either to exaggerate predestination to the point where free will becomes impossible, or to insist so on free will that predestination seems excluded.

82. Cayré, *Patrologie*, I, 672.

But even in those who manage to maintain both extremes of Augustine's doctrine, there is a further temptation open. Augustine's synthesis depends not only on the notion of the two cities, celestial and otherwise, but also on the dogma of the Fall of man from a semi-celestial state.[83] Both to him are real historical facts; they are revealed by faith and cannot be demonstrated by reason. So our sinful nature and our vocation to salvation are the results of real events in time; they are not different orders of the physical world, nor different aspects of human nature. Likewise their reconciliation can only be historical. The importance of this early development of a theology of history has been insisted upon in many recent works.[84] We need only keep in mind the points essential to the doctrine of grace, namely: that the free state of man existed in Adam in a period now ended; that the post-lapsarian age may in turn be subdivided into *ante lege, sub lege,* and *sub gratia;* that we live in the latter, that is, under the new dispensation of Christ; and that his dispensation is also an historical one which will not reach its fulfillment until all those predestined to salvation are gathered into the kingdom, and those who remain under the curse of Adam are justly punished. Any attempts to reduce this historical dimension will tend to make of Christianity either a philosophy, which for Augustine it was not, or a merely Gnostic religion, which it was not either.

In his own lifetime, Augustine's great opponents were, of course, the Pelagians. Although few of his writings are known directly, most historians agree that Pelagius himself went pretty far in the direction of a purely naturalistic and Stoic-

83. *Ibid.*, II, 172.
84. E.g., Oscar Cullman, *Temps et histoire dans le Christianisme primitif* (thesis, Neuchâtel-Paris, 1947), and also his *Christ et le temps* (Neuchâtel-Paris, 1947); H.-C. Puech, "Temps, histoire et mythe dans le christianisme des premiers siècles," *Proceedings of the 7th Congress for the History of Religions* (Amsterdam, 1951); Jean Daniélou, "S. Irénée et les origines de la théologie de l'histoire," pp. 227-31; H.-I. Marrou, *L'Ambivalence du temps de l'histoire chez saint Augustin* (Montreal-Paris, 1950); J. Chaix-Ruy, *Saint Augustin, temps et histoire* (Paris, 1956).

inspired religion.[85] He began as a moral reformer, urging men to obedience to the Law. As he ran up against the notion, in St. Augustine and others, that man could not obey the Law without a special grace from God, he became more confirmed in his opinion of man's natural goodness, praised natural virtues and the moral conscience, eventually finding all "natural instincts" good in themselves. He rejected Original Sin, or at least any corruption resulting from it, and consequently found Baptism unnecessary except as a means of erasing our individual sins. The grace of Christ was a purely external affair and consisted primarily of his teaching and example. He claimed man could both will and do anything he wished, and needless to say he excluded any form of predestination. Finally, he emphasized merit in a way that was legalistic, or even commercial, and it is not hard to make the jump from the notion of dealing with God in merit to dealing with the Church in indulgences: Pelagius, the reformer, fell into a doctrine that led in exactly the opposite direction from that which he intended. Even if he had been responsible only for this doctrine of merit, his error would still have been obvious: such a notion, in fact, puts God in our debt, makes Him subject to our freedom.[86] In any case, the Church of the early fifth century was not ripe for such a movement, for even though many of these questions had remained open to differing interpretations up to this time, St. Augustine managed to get Pelagius to admit and retract his errors; and his disciples, Celestius and Julian of Eclanum—more dedicated theologians who refused to retract —were persecuted and exiled. Cassian, who had also fought against Pelagius' errors, did so not so much in the name of the Augustinian doctrine as from the point of view he had learned from the earlier Fathers, especially the Greeks. What Professor Wolfson would have us believe of Pelagius himself [87] is entirely true of Cassian: he merely followed the Philonic doctrine of

85. See Cayré, *Patrologie,* I, 381–83; Plinval, *Pélage*; Chéné, *La Théologie de saint Augustin,* pp. 21–23.

86. See F. Earle Fox, "Biblical Theology and Pelagianism," *Journal of Religion,* XLI (1961), no. 3, 169–81.

87. "Philosophical Implications," p. 562.

absolute freedom which had been the tradition of the Church up until St. Augustine, yet this very doctrine was also condemned and later labeled "semi-Pelagian." There is no need to outline that doctrine here as it is essentially that of Philo or St. John Chrysostom, admitting the need for God's call and for his grace to help us to virtuous actions, but insisting that our answer to the call, our faith, merits the aids to action which God subsequently gives us. St. Augustine himself having instigated the condemnation of Pelagius' views at the Council of Carthage in 417–418,[88] his doctrine on grace and free will was made official by the Council of Ephesus in 431, and again by papal decree in 520,[89] and the second Council of Orange in 530–32, condemned semi-Pelagianism by citing St. Augustine, often textually.[90] In this same period, however, Augustine's friend, Prosper of Aquitaine, somewhat softened the rigor of his doctrines by insisting that predestination was neither a cause nor an impulse toward evil, and that God wished to save all men and gave to all the opportunity for salvation. It is still disputed whether Prosper was strictly faithful to Augustine, or whether he, like Cassian, should not be labeled semi-Pelagian, but he seemed to most to be within the bounds of Augustine's doctrine, if not of his intentions, and his more moderate view gained general acceptance. In 475, the Council of Arles saw fit to condemn an exaggerated predestinarianism.[91]

Because of the weight of all this official ratification of the Augustinian doctrine, the whole question of grace and free will was, in the Medieval period, to some extent forced underground. This is not to say it was not discussed: on the contrary, numerous are the sentences, commentaries, treatises *De Gratia et libero arbitrio* throughout the Scholastic period; for although the essential doctrines had to be maintained—the necessity and gratuity of God's grace had to be affirmed along with the

88. Denz., Nos. 101–108, 109a.
89. Denz., No. 173a.
90. Denz., Nos. 174–200.
91. Denz., Nos. 160a–b.

freedom of man's will—yet the way in which these doctrines were understood and reconciled was left open. The only major eruption of the problem that actually threatened the solidity of doctrine took place in the ninth century: the exaggerated predestinarianism of Gottschalk produced a battle which raged through most of the century and involved Scotus Erigena and several Councils—Gottschalk was condemned by the Council of Quiercy-sur-Oise (853).[92] Out of these disputes there emerged not only a general acceptance of at least an anterior will of God to save all men,[93] but also a condemnation of what was known as "double predestination"; that is, it was maintained that only the elect are actually predestined: the damned are condemned on the basis of the prevision of their sins.[94] But this dispute, on the eve of the Scholastic period, is the last before the sixteenth century to involve basic doctrine. So it would perhaps be most accurate to say that during the Middle Ages the surface of the problem was frozen, but that if we are to understand why, with the thaw of the Renaissance, it burst forth again, not only considerably muddied but ready to overflow its Augustinian confines, then we must see what underground springs, what subaqueous obstacles, what freshets of thought were at work beneath the surface rigidity.

I shall attempt to distinguish only three major steps in the Medieval treatment of grace and free will which seem to me the fundamental influences on its subsequent development: first, the "rationalization" of the problem; then, its "naturalization"; and finally the effect of Duns Scotus' "voluntarism" on the whole affair.

Boethius was, in some respects, the first Scholastic philosopher. He was largely responsible for the transmission of Aristotle to later Medieval thinkers,[95] and we might say for the introduction of Aristotelian method into our problem.

92. See E. Portalié, art. "Développement historique de l'augustinisme," in *DTC*, I, cols. 2527–30; and Denz., Nos. 316–19.

93. Denz., Nos. 317–18.

94. Denz., No. 316; see H. Rondet, *Gratia Christi* (Paris, 1948), pp. 177–79.

95. See F. Copleston, *A History of Philosophy*, Vol. II, *Medieval Philosophy: Augustine to Scotus* (London, 1950), pp. 101–3.

Working from the philosophical puzzle of the "future contingents," Boethius manages to divorce God's prescience from any necessity operating on us by saying that since God's knowledge is eternal and always present, consequently He does not cause events in advance, but knows them as they happen whether past, present, or future.[96] The same idea is repeated by St. Anselm in the eleventh century and will be repeated throughout the Scholastic period.[97] Now this may be ingenious, and it is certainly free of doctrinal error, but it has also, in its endeavor to found its conclusions on rational or speculative theology alone, excluded that vital element of man's present relation to God: historical time, in which our relation to God is known only through revelation. This omission is characteristic of virtually all Scholastic theology, which is architectonic rather than existential. The result, during the Middle Ages, is not so much error as confusion, and the Medieval systems of grace become progressively more subtle and elaborate in their attempts to invent the right formula while leaving out an essential ingredient. It is this that I call the "rationalization" of the problem: the abstracting of the element of historical time—essential to Augustine's doctrine, based as it is on biblical revelation—in the attempt to understand it by means of a rational or speculative theology. An excellent example of this process is afforded by the now familiar distinction between the natural and supernatural order. This distinction, which is not to be found in St. Augustine,[98] was considered to be implied in his account of Adam's condition before and after the Fall: our human nature was not destroyed by the Fall, but rather we lost the supernatural (or preternatural) gifts that God had given to Adam. Now to miss this point in St. Augustine leads directly to the misinterpretations of Luther and Calvin; but to erect what in Augustine's doc-

96. Boethius, *Consolationes philosophiae* (London: Loeb Classical Library, 1918), V, prosae 2–6, pp. 370–411; cf. Gilson, *History of Christian Philosophy*, p. 103.

97. Anselm, *De Concordia praescientiae, praedestinationis et gratiae cum libero arbitrio*, II, 2; *PL*, CLVIII, col. 520 B, cited in Rondet, *Gratia Christi*, p. 182, note.

98. See Portalié, art. "Augustinisme," in *DTC*, I, col. 2530.

trine are merely states or conditions of man into two orders existing side by side leads to other temptations, namely an exaggerated emphasis on "human nature" as virtually independent of God and the supernatural order, or in other words to a philosophical humanism that no longer needs God. So the rationalization of the problem leads directly to what I call its "naturalization." The "discovery of nature," which can be said to take place in the twelfth century and which received added impetus and sustenance from the increasing acquaintance with and assimilation of Aristotle, not only reinforced this emphasis on the question of human nature, but involved also the attempt to explain that nature and the grace which transforms it in terms of Aristotelian causality.[99]

These tendencies are developed through a whole series of treatises *De Libero arbitrio* in the twelfth and thirteenth centuries in which it is discussed whether the *libre arbitre* is a faculty or a *habitus,* whether it is dependent on *ratio* and *voluntas* or independent of them, and so forth. St. Anselm, Peter Lombard, and St. Bernard are all entirely faithful to Augustine in their balance of freedom and election, and St. Bernard in particular was a great favorite of the Jansenists and is often quoted by Pascal as a defender of the true Augustinian doctrine and the last of the great Fathers;[100] he was instrumental in the condemnation of Abelard's Pelagian tendencies.[101] St. Bonaventure gives us a particularly interesting attempt to reconcile Augustinism and Aristotelianism.[102] But let us confine ourselves to looking at only one representative of this develop-

99. See M.-D. Chenu, *La Théologie au douzième siècle* (Paris, 1957), chaps. 1–3; also O. Lottin, *Psychologie et morale aux XIIe et XIIIe siècles,* Vol. I, *Problèmes de psychologie* (Louvain, 1942), pp. 11–207.

100. See the quotation at the beginning of this chapter; also, E. Jovy, "D'où vient l'*Ad tuum, Domine Jesu, tribunal appello* de Pascal? Pascal et s. Bernard," in his *Etudes Pascaliennes,* III (Paris, 1928), 54–87; and B. Jacqueline, "Les Milieux jansénistes français au 17e siècle et saint Bernard," *Citeaux in de Nederlanden,* VI (1955), 28–30. For Bernard's doctrine, see E. Gilson, *The Mystical Theology of Saint Bernard* (London, 1940), pp. 47–48.

101. See Rondet, *Gratia Christi,* pp. 183–86.

102. See E. Gilson, *La Philosophie de saint Bonaventure* (Paris, 1924), pp. 271–73, 325–78.

ment: the system of St. Thomas Aquinas, and that, not because he was the most extreme in his views, but because he was the most influential. We shall attempt first to grasp some of the Scholastic vocabulary, and then to see the implications of the Aristotelianizing of the Augustinian doctrine.

When St. Thomas Aquinas speaks of grace,[103] he most often means not the actual grace of which St. Augustine speaks almost exclusively, but an habitual grace.[104] He distinguishes first, using St. Bonaventure's terms, between *gratia gratum faciens*—an infused, sanctifying grace (the source of, though not identical with the infused virtues)—and *gratia gratis data,* or "free grace," a grace that enables us to act and work for the salvation of others though not necessarily conferring or producing the sanctification of the individual who receives it. This distinction does not correspond precisely to that between actual and habitual grace, but it seems to be St. Thomas' view that sanctifying grace is most often of the habitual sort; this is the way in which God transforms a natural creature into a supernatural one and prepares him for his supernatural end, which is the beatific vision. On the other hand, actual grace is usually a free grace (also called *motio* or *auxilium speciale,* a term that becomes the source of controversy at the Council of Trent), freely given at a certain moment for a certain purpose but not sanctifying.

Both of these kinds of grace can be subdivided into *operans* and *cooperans:* grace is operative when it is the direct action of God's will moving ours; it is cooperative when our will responds and cooperates with it to produce acts of virtue. In much the same manner, that first action of God on the will

103. My account of St. Thomas' doctrine is based primarily on the following: F. C. Copleston, *Aquinas* (London, 1955), esp. pp. 178–91; E. Gilson, *Le Thomisme* (5th ed.; Paris, 1948); Cayré, *Patrologie,* II, 604–608; R. Garrigou-Lagrange, *The One God* (London, 1946), pp. 487–717; idem, art. "Prédestination," in *DTC,* XII, cols. 2940–56. The essential texts are assembled and translated in A. M. Fairweather, *Nature and Grace: Selections from the "Summa theologiae" of Thomas Aquinas,* Library of Christian Classics, Vol. XI (Philadelphia, 1954).

104. See Portalié, art. "Augustinisme," in *DTC,* I, col. 2531.

may be termed "prevenient" and the later action of a grace aiding our actions as "subsequent." He further recognizes an exterior grace (*ad specificationem actus*) as opposed to an interior grace (*ad exercitium actus*) according as to whether an act is considered with regard to its final or efficient cause.

As to the distinction between sufficient and efficacious grace, which will play such an important role later, this distinction is not an integral part of the system of St. Thomas himself, though he does use the terms, for instance to refer to Christ's act of redemption as being "efficacious for some, but sufficient for all." It is a distinction arising out of the larger question of predestination, and the need to reconcile God's desire to save us all with his actual damnation of some. As the doctrine of God's will to universal salvation had by then been accepted, it must be explained how, being all-powerful, God can fail to carry out this will. St. Thomas distinguishes an antecedent and consequent will (the distinction is not new with him, of course), but only the consequent will is efficacious for the reason that in the actual carrying out of a plan, often some things must be sacrificed to achieve a greater good, as when a man may wish to save both his family and his furniture from a fire, but leaves the furniture in order to get his wife and children out safely. So God wishes to save us all, and Christ dies for us all in a way that is "sufficient" in the sense of compatible with his plan; nevertheless he does not in fact save us all through Christ and his grace, just as he does not bring all fruits to perfect ripeness. Thus God's antecedent and consequent will are the basis for the later Thomists' distinction between sufficient and efficacious grace. It is clear that in this context the sufficient grace of Christ is not in fact sufficient in the way the Molinists will later wish to make it seem.

Now through all this proliferation of kinds of graces, St. Thomas never deviates from the essentials of Augustinian doctrine; this variety of distinctions arises out of his subtle analyses of the problems and controversies that had obscured that doctrine: the distinctions always serve the purpose of preserving even the most rigorous features of Augustine's view. But if St. Thomas' version turns out to be so much more elaborate, it is surely because of the difficulties presented by his attempt to explain that doctrine in Aristotelian terms. Professor Gilson has shown[105] how Thomas Aquinas was led—perhaps through his rejection of the views of the Platonizing Arabic and Jewish theologians—to abandon Platonic philosophy in favor of the Aristotelian philosophy, taught by his master Albert the Great, as a basis for Christian theology. This decision was basically on epistemological grounds, but a whole mode of perceiving the world was involved. For Augustine, the will of God rules the world, and it is his Logos that speaks through the world; our destinies are spoken in eternity and our only proof of God's existence is in the internal awareness of his Logos—as may be expressed in the ontological proof. For St. Thomas, however, God is the cause of the world and we can see His effects and reason back to the creator (all St. Thomas' proofs of God's existence are cosmological); and the creatures of this world, including man, are not directly dependent on the Word or will of God, but on the tendencies and capacities of their natures, although these natures, to be sure, were created and are sustained by God.

One can see, then, that there are two important ways in which St. Thomas' use of Aristotle will affect the problem of grace and free will. The first is the application of the Aristotelian theory of causality to the problem of grace. Now St. Thomas handles the whole question with great finesse; he insists at one point, for instance, that "as an accidental quality of the soul, grace acts on the soul not efficiently, but formally, in the way in which whiteness makes things white," [106] which seems to correspond to Augustine's view that grace determines us logically rather than physically. But there is no doubt that this posing of the problem in terms of physical causality led to the controversial "physical predeterminations" and "physical premotions" of the sixteenth-century Dominicans, an orientation that is quite incompatible with St. Augustine's system.

105. E. Gilson, "Pourquoi saint Thomas a critiqué saint Augustin," *Archives d'histoire doctrinale et littéraire du Moyen Age,* I (1926–27), 5–127.
106. Ia, IIae, q. 111, art. 2; see Fairweather, *Nature and Grace,* p. 168.

The second way in which Aristotle's influence will subtly modify the question of grace and free will concerns the question of human nature. We have already mentioned the tendency to reduce St. Augustine's historically defined "states" of man (before the Fall, after the Fall, etc.) to possible states or natures; but St. Thomas will speak of "man in the state of pure nature," [107] and even though he does so only hypothetically, it is a short step from there to the consideration of "natural man," an abstraction that has no place in the Augustinian system. These tendencies do not, of course, seem particularly subversive within the context of Scholasticism, where the concern was with architecturally sound but static systems; with the new dynamism of the Renaissance, however, such concepts will take on different meanings, as we shall see.

The third major event of the Scholastic period that produced serious alterations in the problem of grace and free will is Duns Scotus' theory of the will, and what is often called his "voluntarism." [108] It would, of course, be a mistake to suppose that Scotistic "voluntarism" implies libertarianism as it is understood in connection with our problem, or to assume that this doctrine of the primacy of the will over the intellect led directly to a more action-oriented, militant point of view such as one might associate with the Jesuit order or the new Humanism. The forces at work here are more complex than that: the moral concern of the Protestant Reformers and of the Jansenists shows as much of Scotus' influence as do the Counter-Reformation and the humanistic emphasis on the power of natural man.

Duns Scotus does indeed assert the primacy of the will over the intellect and so sets his doctrine into contrast with the "intellectualists," notably St. Thomas Aquinas. One reason for

107. E.g., Ia, IIae, q. 109, art. 8; Fairweather, *Nature and Grace,* p. 151.

108. For Duns Scotus' doctrine I rely principally on the account in E. Gilson, *Jean Duns Scot: Introduction à ses positions fondamentales* (Paris, 1952), esp. chap. IX, pp. 574-624; and on B. M. Bonansea, "Duns Scotus' Voluntarism," in *John Duns Scotus, 1265-1965,* ed. Bonansea and J. K. Ryan, *Studies in Philosophy and the History of Philosophy,* III (Washington, D.C., 1965), 83-121.

this primacy is the primacy of love (a function of the will) over wisdom. Another reason—and this is more important for our question—is that knowledge is dependent upon and bound to its object, but for Scotus the will is not. He distinguishes between the will as simple *appetitus naturalis,* passively and necessarily directed toward happiness, and the *voluntas libera,* or the will in its essential freedom. This essentially free will has freedom of contrariety (to choose one of two opposing acts), and freedom of specification (to choose between possible acts or objects). Duns Scotus therefore rejects St. Thomas' position that the will, like the intellect, is determined by its object; he must allow, of course, that the object of the will has some bearing on the act of volition, that it is a *causa sine qua non* or partial cause of the act of volition, but he maintains that this does not prevent the act of the will in volition from being completely free and self-determining, as that is its essential nature. He does not allow that this free act can be caused either by an object of the intellect (as St. Thomas maintained) nor by a phantasm (as was maintained by Godfrey of Fontaines); nothing extrinsic to the will is the cause of volition— "nihil aliud a voluntate est causa totalis volitionis in voluntate."

Now the consequences of this position as it is applied to the Augustinian doctrine of grace are very serious indeed. For St. Augustine, as for virtually all theologians from the Early Fathers to St. Thomas Aquinas, the will was conceived in terms of freedom from constraint, a freedom to follow its natural objects (whether the general good or a particular good, or even an evil conceived as a good); and whether the object of the will was conceived of as primarily exterior or interior, as an object of perception and intellect or a phantasm of the mind, it was still the object that attracted or moved the will. This is absolutely essential to the Augustinian doctrine of grace and predestination because, for Augustine, God has only to control the attractiveness of the object (the *delectatio*) in order for the will to be moved as He foresees that it will, without His interfering in the will's essential (but relative) freedom. In the Scotistic system, however, the will is divorced from its objects and becomes a subjective, arbitrary faculty, not only absolutely free but something approaching a pure but empty power. To conceive such a will in relation to the Divine Will becomes immediately more problematic; the Divine Will, if it is to be triumphant, must impose itself as one power overruling another; predestination must inevitably take on an overwhelming and sinister character, as of a tyrant imposing his will from above, or at least pushing us from behind, rather than calling or inviting as a desirable object. There are two possible reactions to this view of predestination: the total repression and subjection of the human will in favor of the Divine Will (the way of Luther and Calvin); or the rejection of the traditional formulas of predestination, and the attempt to modify traditional doctrines so as to safeguard man's essential freedom (the way of Lessius and Molina). Both ways depend on a new conception of the will which is not that of St. Augustine and fits ill with his doctrine. And this new conception of the will no doubt had other sources than Duns Scotus (e.g., his teacher Henry of Ghent); just as the naturalization of theology was prepared by more than a century of speculation before St. Thomas Aquinas, so the new voluntarism was in the air before Duns Scotus was being widely read, as is evident from the rapid acceptance of his views on the primacy of the will. A kind of anti-intellectualism was in the air in the late Middle Ages, which Occam's nominalism, the new Humanism, the development of positive theology, and even Boehme's mysticism can be seen to represent in different ways; but for our problem, Duns Scotus represents it most decisively and influentially.

If we turn to the Reformation with this in mind, we shall not, then, find it so difficult to account for such things as radically divergent views both claiming to be Augustinian. What is perhaps for us the most familiar debate on grace and free will—that between Luther and Erasmus[109]—does not

109. The texts are: M. Luther, *Tractatus de libertate christiana* (1520) in *D. Martin Luthers Werke* (Weimar, 1863–), VII, 49–73; *idem, De Servo arbitrio* (1525), Weimar edition, XVIII, 600–787; Erasmus, *Diatribe seu collatio de libero arbitrio* (1524) in *Opera omnia*

seem nearly so radical as it might otherwise. The scriptural, textual approach of Erasmus of course had its influence at Louvain;[110] but his main effect was rather a kind of mood or spirit than a doctrine. It is safe to say (and also a kind of tribute in these matters) that he contributed nothing new to the doctrine of grace and free will. He advocated peace and moderation in all disputes on these questions, and this was the prevailing policy of the Church during the next two embattled centuries. And he argued that the effect of a theology like Luther's on the life and morals of common men must be taken into account: the denial of free will would lead ignorant men to continue in perversity, rather than to try to observe the Law; to despair rather than to reform. His primary non-scriptural argument for free will is that without it man is inconceivable, a useless and senseless creation—and if man were convinced this were his case, he should certainly be demoralized; an argument that may be modern in tone, but in substance is the same as that of the Early Fathers.

Luther's reply is scornful and vitriolic: such considerations are opposed to the Truth, the Word of God, and to faith in Jesus Christ. He points out that the everlasting hair-splitting of the Scholastics in their efforts to save the free will had led more men to despair than its open denial. Doctrinally, he flatly denies free will as freedom of choice; he turns to ridicule the attempts to reconcile God's foreknowledge with such a freedom —clearly if God knows we are going to do one thing, we are not free to do something else; and he proclaims that God wills and works all in all, including evil and damnation as well as salvation. A notable weakness in this doctrine is a tendency to equate will and works, and so to ignore the role of will in the act of faith itself. The resulting notion of faith as an

(Leyden, 1703–6), IX, cols. 1215–48; *idem, Hyperaspistae Diatribes libri duo contra servum arbitrium Martini Lutheri,* Leyden edition, X, cols. 1249–1536.

110. Cf. J. Etienne, *Spiritualisme érasmien et théologiens louvanistes: un changement de problématique au début du XVIe siècle* (Louvain, 1956).

illumination of the Holy Spirit leading nowhere and engaging one to nothing, is only a new form of Christian Gnosticism such as we have described earlier.

Calvin follows Luther on most essential points concerning grace and freedom,[111] and in bringing the Lutheran doctrines into France rendered them both more logical and more radical.[112] However, where for Luther the denial of free will was a critical point in the development of his doctrine, in Calvin's writings the emphasis on predestination was arrived at slowly as a result of other considerations.[113] His primary interest is in justification, a word which is much used in this period and by which Catholics and Protestants mean something rather different. Calvin distinguishes justification from sanctification or regeneration: justification is by faith alone and is the imputation of Christ's justice to us; it is not a gradual process, but takes place instantaneously at conversion, and, once justified, a man remains so forever. Regeneration is the process begun by justification, and, although we continue to sin in this state, nevertheless through a life of faith and the imputation of Christ's justice to our works, we advance toward sanctification. This process is never completed in this life, and our lives remain basically corrupt even after our justification.[114] Now the Catholics recognize no such distinction—the two terms are taken as equivalent by the Council of Trent; justification means to them the whole process, and the first light of faith is neither privileged nor definitive in the way it is for the Reformers.

Again, although Calvin and the Catholics both distinguished prescience and predestination, it was for different reasons. For

111. See J. Rivière, art. "Justification," in *DTC,* VIII, cols. 2136 ff.

112. Cf. A. Renaudet, *La France de 1559 à 1650* (Paris: Les Cours de Sorbonne, n.d.), p. 73.

113. It is instructive to follow this development through the successive editions of the *Institutes*; the edition of the text of 1650 by J.-D. Benoit: Jean Calvin, *Institution de la religion chrestienne,* 4 vols. (Paris, 1957–61), indicates what was added in each edition.

114. See F. Wendel, *Calvin: sources et évolution de sa pensée religieuse* (Paris, 1950).

the Catholics, this distinction was part of a traditional way of softening the implications of predestination and preserving the free will. Neither Calvin nor Luther had any interest in saving the free will; for them God forewilled (predetermined) everything; quite naturally, then, He knew that what He had willed would take place. This is the only meaning they will allow to the word prescience, regarding all subtleties about God first foreknowing our actions and merits, and then adjusting His will to suit them, as sophistry or worse. God's will is primary and absolute, and so, therefore, is His predestination.[115] This means that grace is both gratuitous and irresistible, as it was also for Augustine;[116] but the person who receives it knows that he has it and that he cannot lose it, and that he is justified thereby, which is certainly not Augustinian.[117] And damnation (or reprobation, as it is usually called) is equally irresistible, though it is not gratuitous but justified by Adam's sin; yet God also has willed that Adam sin in order to damn those that He would damn, so His justice remains perfectly inscrutable. This too is close to the doctrine of St. Augustine, except that Calvin allows no distinction between God's willing and his permitting evil, which St. Augustine insists upon.[118] The result of this is to make God the cause not only of Adam's sin but of all sin, though Calvin insists that man is responsible for his sin in a mysterious way. Another result is to deny God's will—antecedent or otherwise—to save all men, and although Calvin is here again close to Augustine's own doctrine,[119] we have seen that the Catholic position has moved away from this denial, starting with St. Augustine's own disciples.

The Sixth Session of the Council of Trent, meeting in

115. Wendel, *Calvin,* p. 207.

116. Cf. G. Bavaud, "La Doctrine de la prédestination et de la réprobation d'après s. Augustin et Calvin," *Revue des études augustiniennes,* V (1959), no. 4, 431–38.

117. Cf. Wendel, *Calvin,* pp. 208–10.

118. *Enchiridion,* 95–103; cited in Bavaud, "Doctrine de la prédestination," pp. 433–34.

119. See *Enchiridion,* 97, 103.

1546–47, undertook to deal with these same questions under the heading of Justification, and made it plain in its preface that it was addressing itself to the new heresies.[120] It is a witness to the enduring strength of the Augustinian doctrine that in combating the predestinarianism of the Reformation, the Council was not forced into an exaggerated libertarianism; in fact, the declaration of the Sixth Session is a model of balance, including all that was most traditional on both sides of the scale, but avoiding, even to the point of sustaining apparent contradictions, any attempt to endorse a particular system for resolving the difficulties. The declaration opens with a description of our fallen state in which, "slaves of sin" that we are, our free will is weakened but not destroyed (chap. 1); Christ's Passion is our only salvation (chap. 2) but it is available only to those who receive its benefits through grace (chap. 3), and specifically through Baptism (chap. 4). The necessity and gratuity of grace are maintained, but our free "consent and free cooperation" are also affirmed (chap. 5). The progress of the justified man from faith to hope to charity is considered, and the necessity of the other virtues besides faith are insisted upon (chaps. 6 and 7); yet in listing the causes of our justification, our own action or merits are nowhere mentioned (chap. 7), and the importance and gratuity of the grace of faith are reaffirmed (chap. 8). But faith is not certitude and does not bring certitude: "No one can know for certain whether he has received God's grace" (chap. 9). Works are part of our continual justification (chap. 10) and although even the justified man sins at least venially, nevertheless, the commandments are not impossible to him, and God will not abandon the justified man unless He has first been abandoned by him (chap. 11). Still, one is always capable of abandoning God by any serious sin—not just by the loss of faith, as the Reformers claimed (chap. 15). No one knows whether he is among those predestined to election (chap. 12), nor whether he will persevere to the end (chap. 13); but if he falls from grace he may still be justified again by the sacrament of penitence (chap. 14). And finally, the role of merit is admitted: our good works

120. Denz., No. 792a.

really are good and satisfactory to God and are rewarded by eternal life (chap. 16).[121]

However loyal and adequate an expression of doctrine this may be, it was nonetheless clearly inadequate to the exigencies of its era; the theological battles of the next hundred years are ample proof of that. The new Humanism, with its increasing naturalism and enthusiasm for man's possibilities, could find nothing in these traditional formulas to satisfy its aspirations, and the newly founded Jesuit order would be most keenly aware of this. Yet the movement of reform, which moved the Catholic Church from within as well as from without, was also eager to throw off the shackles of Scholasticism and return to the positive exegesis of Scriptures and the Church Fathers, but for rather different motives, namely the condemnation of all natural human effort. These two movements, which seem so characteristic of the Renaissance and give it its peculiar vibrancy, correspond fairly well to the two poles of our problem of grace and free will, and it seems inevitable that this problem, which had already had a long and difficult career, should have become in the sixteenth century the theological ground for the expression of an age.

One of the more convenient battlefields had been prepared at Louvain by the establishment in 1542 of a Jesuit College close by the august and Augustinian Faculty of Theology of the University of Louvain. Tensions were present even from the Council of Trent during which the future General of the Jesuits, Diego Lainez, attacked the General of the Augustinians, Girolamo Seripando, who had prepared one of the versions of the decretal on Justification presented to the Council.[122] Nothing much came of this incident at the time, but the opponents had shown their colors and drawn up the lines for a battle which, although officially called a draw, was only an armed truce and broke out again soon enough. It is this struggle within the Church which eventually developed into the Jansenist quarrels of the mid-seventeenth century and with

121. Conc. Trid., sess. VI; see Denz., Nos. 793–810.
122. See Rondet, *Gratia Christi,* p. 275; and L. Cognet, *Le Jansénisme* (Paris: coll. "Que sais-je," 1961), pp. 9–10.

which we shall find Pascal deeply concerned. Before the Jansenist disputes were over (if indeed they are yet) not only would virtually every ecclesiastic of any importance in both France and the Low Countries be implicated, but the whole intellectual life of those countries and indeed of all Europe would be profoundly affected.

In the 1560's, Michel de Bay (Baius), Augustinian of Louvain, taught a doctrine which he claimed to be pure St. Augustine, unadulterated by Scholasticism.[123] Consequently, the famous distinction of the Schoolmen between natural and supernatural, which is nowhere to be found in St. Augustine, was rejected by him. Now the Thomists spoke of man's nature as being neither guilty and vicious, nor, on the other hand, fit for beatitude or union with God: he was simply one of God's creatures, his nature was good in itself without any consideration of his supernatural destiny. But Adam was given supernatural gifts in order to enable him to achieve beatitude in obedience to God; through one of these gifts—his freedom— he lost all the supernatural gifts. Yet he was left by the Fall not merely natural but something worse; he is guilty, stained by Original Sin. Baius could not see the point of postulating a hypothetical "natural" man who has after all never existed, neither in ourselves nor in Adam; but if one must use the term "natural" then it surely applies to man as he was created by God, namely Adam with his freedom and his beatific destiny. Man since the Fall is clearly unnatural and is so enslaved to concupiscence that he needs supernatural graces to elevate him to what was his original "natural" state. In this system, then, all that Pelagius would attribute to human nature —the freedom, the capacity to merit sanctification, etc.—Baius attributes to Adam's nature. Thus, although it is true that St. Augustine never uses the term "nature" in the Thomistic

123. For Baius' doctrine: Rondet, *Gratia Christi,* pp. 287–93; N. Abercrombie, *The Origins of Jansenism* (Oxford, 1936), pp. 87–92; X. Le Bachelet, art. "Baius," in *DTC,* II, cols. 38–111. Concerning both Baius and Jansenius, H. de Lubac's famous *Surnaturel* (Paris, 1946)— the first part has been revised and reissued as *Augustinisme et théologie moderne* (Paris, 1965)—has interesting insights but is too impressionistic and tendentious to serve as a reliable guide.

sense, Baius, by rejecting this Thomistic concept does not altogether manage to free himself from it. By applying it to Adam, as he believed St. Augustine would have, he obscures the whole Augustinian doctrine concerning God's justice: how can we justify the election of only some men to a destiny that is properly that of all men?

Again, although Baius insists on the actuality of grace as charity acting in us, and is as little inclined as was St. Augustine to speak of the habitual graces and various states of grace of the Scholastics, still the doctrine of merit he draws from this is peculiarly Pelagian in its emphasis on the accumulation of merit and recompense; but since all merit comes from God (for Baius, it is measured by the reward, rather than the reverse), then all the supposed merits of the pagans are in fact sins. Sixty-seven propositions of Baius concerning these questions were condemned by Pius V in 1567; but (as later in the case of the condemned propositions of Jansenius and of Quesnel) a purely negative censure, unaccompanied by any positive statement of doctrine, is bound to be ambiguous. In many cases, for instance, a compound statement is condemned with no indication as to which of its parts are heretical or whether each part is heretical taken separately or only taken in conjunction with the others.[124] Further, some of the condemned propositions could certainly be interpreted in a perfectly orthodox Augustinian sense,[125] and one has to suppose that they are condemned in some meaning peculiar to Baius. And to add to that, the lack of punctuation of the original Bull allowed of two possible interpretations, one of which considerably weakened the condemnation.[126] These ambiguities were taken up by Baius' many disciples, one of whom, Jacques Jansson, was later to have as his student another Louvain theologian named Cornelius Jansen, who in his turn would seek to defend at least certain of Baius' positions against the charges of heresy in a lengthy work entitled *Augustinus*. Meanwhile, however, a

124. E.g., Denz., Nos. 1004, 1011, etc.
125. E.g., Denz., Nos. 1016, 1025, 1027, etc.
126. Denz., No. 1080; see La Bachelet, art. "Baius," in *DTC*, II, col. 48.

Jesuit at Louvain named Lessius, instrumental in the second censure of Baius (1580) and eager to confound the Calvinist theories on predestination, found the doctrine he was looking for in the teachings of the Spaniard Molina.

Molina had his precursors among the Jesuits, but did not hesitate to claim originality for his system, which he frankly thought superior to that of St. Thomas or St. Augustine. Even before his work on free will and grace appeared in 1588,[127] his theories were attacked by the Dominicans, Bañez in particular (1584), and as taught by Lessius they were censured by the Faculty of Louvain (1587). Even among the Jesuits, Suarez and St. Robert Bellarmine had their doubts about Molina's system, although they thought it could be adapted to an Augustinian view with very little modification; Lessius, however, continued to teach a Molinism that smacked strongly of Pelagianism and aroused an important controversy within the Jesuit order, as well as being the cause of the famous *De Auxiliis* quarrels in Rome.[128] Without attempting to follow the sinuosities and detours of these controversies, which led only to another impasse, we must try at least to see what Molina's doctrine was, and how the doctrines of Lessius, on the one hand, and of Suarez and Bellarmine on the other, differed from it.

Molina's system, complex and subtle, is essentially a means of harmonizing God's knowledge and man's freedom. To do this, he invented, or claimed he did,[129] the *scientia media*. Rejecting the Thomistic notion of a grace intrinsically efficacious, he allowed only for one that was effective *ab extrinseco;* that is, God's will does not act directly on ours but has its effect by

127. *Concordia liberi arbitrii cum gratiae donis, divina praescientia, providentia et reprobatione ad nonnullos primae partis divi Thomae articulos* (Lisbon, 1588). For Molina's doctrine: Rondet, *Gratia Christi,* pp. 294–307; X. M. Le Bachelet, *Prédestination et grâce efficace,* 2 vols. (Louvain, 1931), I, 23–44; E. Vansteenberghe, art. "Molinisme," in *DTC,* X, cols. 2099–2100.

128. See Le Bachelet, *Prédestination, passim.*

129. Some authors attribute the system to Fonseca; see Rondet, *Gratia Christi,* p. 298, note.

means of circumstances known to God through the *scientia media,* the science whereby God knows all possible future contingencies (sometimes called "futurables"). Thus He knows what any man in any possible circumstances would do with whatever grace he might be given. So, in speaking of prevenient grace, Molina says that two men may be given identical graces, and one will choose salvation while the other will not; but if the grace is efficacious it will be so proportioned to the circumstances and to the individual's inclinations that he will infallibly choose salvation. Now, so far this theory seems not very different from that of St. Augustine or St. Thomas, and Bellarmine and Suarez found no difficulty with it up to this point. But Molina defined efficacious grace entirely in terms of its result (*ab effectu*) rather than of anything intrinsic to it; for him, there is no real distinction between means and ends when speaking of God—both are part of the divine intelligence. So our free action and the merits of our good works are part of the means through which God works His providential scheme of salvation.

Now this rather obscure doctrine was interpreted by Bellarmine and Suarez in an Augustinian sense: God, foreseeing what use a man *would* make of a particular grace in particular circumstances, apportions His grace to produce the effect He wishes. Thus, to use an example sometimes cited at the time, God foresaw how St. Peter and Judas would react, each of them, to temptation, and gave to St. Peter a grace adequate to make him choose (infallibly) to be faithful to Christ, while Judas was not given a grace sufficient to overcome his inclinations and so betrayed Christ. It was God's will to save one and not the other, and His knowledge of the way they would react to the graces offered them was merely an accessory to His will, which did not in any real sense depend either on the individuals' consent or on their merit; they were predestined *ante praevisa merita*—before any foreknowledge of their merits.

Lessius interpreted Molina's system quite differently. For him, God foresees the use a man *will* make of the grace offered him in given circumstances and carries out His divine election accordingly. So, St. Peter and Judas are offered the same grace, and God, foreseeing that Peter will use his faithfully, predestines him to salvation, and foreseeing that Judas will betray Christ, predestines him to damnation; but it is their free response to grace that determines their destinies—*post praevisa merita.*

Molina's work was vague enough to permit either interpretation. But as his doctrine was avowedly a system for reconciling prescience and freedom, much depends on his notion of freedom. St. Augustine, as I have mentioned, followed Aristotle in using "free" primarily in the sense of "free from constraint"; so, for him, the will was free by nature and the fact that it did not necessarily have freedom of choice did not alter this essential freedom. For St. Thomas, there had to be a *potestas ad opposita,* i.e., the possibility of choosing the opposite course of action, but in our present state the will was nonetheless drawn toward evil unless assisted by grace. But for Molina, freedom was always a freedom of indifference or indetermination: unless there was the real possibility of another choice, or at least choosing not to do something, there was no real freedom. Now this kind of freedom is maintained only if his system is interpreted in the direction of Lessius, and so in general Lessius' version is usually called "pure" Molinism and the modifications of Bellarmine and Suarez are usually known as "congruism."

The controversy involving Bañez and Molina was convoked to Rome in 1598 and the so-called *De Auxiliis* congregations were held, neither party willing to concede, and both arguing in a manner little conducive to producing a synthesis of their views. The vogue for positive theology—and the accompanying suspicion of Scholasticism—although it had its good side in the direction of simplifying doctrine and referring it to a common source in Scripture and the Early Fathers, also encouraged a form of argument in which the quotation of texts was one of the chief weapons, often with little regard for the context of the quotation and little knowledge of the historical circumstances that produced it.[130] In 1607, Paul V put an end to the congregations by declaring that the question was not at present soluble, allowing for the interpretation of grace as either a physical premotion with the Thomists, or a moral one with the Jesuits, and asking all parties to refrain from polemic.[131] The same questions, however, were raised again in 1610 (in a slightly different form) when Lessius attacked the congruism of Bellarmine and Suarez. This quarrel, which remained with the Jesuit order, centered around the question as to whether efficacious and sufficient grace were to be distinguished only by their results (*ab effectu*), thus leaving the way open to Lessius' interpretation, or were initially different (*in actu primo*). The General of the Jesuits, Aquaviva, decided against Lessius and again ordered silence.[132]

But the controversies of course continued, sometimes thinly disguised as discussions of other problems. When in 1640 the laborious *Augustinus* of Jansenius appeared, it was only another work in a long series, but it (or even more importantly, the attacks on it in France) brought the whole quarrel into the open once more, with renewed acrimony on both sides. Before looking at Jansenius' doctrine in that work, however, it is well to remind ourselves that the movement which henceforth bore his name already had a long history.[133] The origins

130. See *ibid.,* pp. 296–97; and Henri Gouhier, "La Crise de la théologie au temps de Descartes," *Revue de théologie et de philosophie,* IV (3ᵉ serie, 1954), 19–54.

131. See Rondet, *Gratia Christi,* p. 297.

132. See Le Bachelet, *Prédestination,* II, 236 ff.

133. The whole history of Jansenism is in the process of being rewritten; indispensable for a study of the early history are the works of Jean Orcibal (notably the series *Les Origines du jansénisme,* of which some six volumes have appeared since 1947); of Lucien Ceyssens, notably the *Sources relatives aux débuts du jansénisme et de l'anti-jansénisme 1640–1643* (Louvain, 1957) and his many volumes of *Jansenistica minora,* from which I have drawn especially from such articles as "Le Jansénisme: considérations historiques préliminaires à sa notion" and "Le Drame de conscience augustinien des premiers jansénistes"; and finally, of Louis Cognet, whose concise "Que sais-je" volume, *Le Jansénisme,* is most useful. Also still useful is the thesis of A. de Meyer, *Les Premières controverses jansénistes en France (1640–1649)* (Louvain, 1919).

of Jansenism as a movement are to be sought in the Renaissance, perhaps most importantly in the general renewal of Patristic studies at Louvain and other centers of learning in the sixteenth century, and especially in the new interest in St. Augustine as opposed to his Scholastic interpreters. Accompanying this interest was the tendency toward positive theology as opposed to rational or speculative theology. Alongside these developments, however, there was a growing tendency among some theologians (most notoriously the Jesuits) to reject the Augustinian view. There were many forces at work here: the so-called Humanism of the Renaissance with its emphasis on man's natural powers and his freedom to realize them; the voyages of discovery, which led to a new concern with pagans and their salvation, and to a renewal of the old question of pagan virtues. To face up to these things, the Jesuits—missionaries both at home and abroad—felt they had to accommodate Christian doctrine to society as they found it. The exclusivistic nature of the Augustinian doctrine of election, the apparent denial of freedom, the supposed "pessimism" of Augustine, all seemed incompatible with the aims of the Counter-Reformation, and for that matter too close to the doctrine of the Protestant Reformers. Theologians like Molina and Lessius, then, offered ways to circumvent these doctrines: by offering new doctrines to replace them, but also by achieving condemnations of extreme Augustinians and thereby casting suspicion on Augustinianism generally. Baius was one of these Augustinians, but only one among many; his importance lies in the fact that his condemnation brought the other Augustinians to his defense—not out of a desire to save his particular interpretation, but because they saw the doctrine and authority of Augustine himself threatened. These were the first "Jansenists": these Augustinians of the late sixteenth century who saw their beloved Augustine's doctrine, which they held to be official Church doctrine, being undermined not just by hostile theological views, but by official condemnations from Rome. Their anxiety at the prospect of the Church's denying the doctrine of grace it had previously hallowed, and shrugging off the Doctor of Grace himself, became extreme with the condemnation of Jansenius, whose work was taken by them to be a true compendium of the Augustinian teaching. So the term "Jansenism" is not inept: it was on his work that many of those Augustinians took their stand. There was, in a sense, a Jansenist movement before Jansenius' work appeared; yet even more important to bear in mind is that "l'antijansénisme préexistait au jansénisme," as one author put it;[134] Jansenism was a reaction to the movement described above, usually referred to as "Molinism." With this in mind, we can now look at the work that triggered the debate in France in which Pascal would become involved.

The *Augustinus* is a work in three volumes, the first being a history of Pelagianism, the second dealing with grace before the Fall and related matters, and the third with the grace of Christ.[135] Its originality lies much less with the doctrine exposed there than with its method, which is outlined in a preface to the second volume; it is not meant to be a doctrinal book in the usual sense, and even less a system of Scholastic theology, but rather an historical work.[136] But Jansenius, following certain passages in St. Augustine, claims this is the only proper way to write theology, which is not a philosophical system but a matter of Scripture and tradition; not a subject for rational lucubrations, but for faith and memory.[137] This

134. Cognet, *Le Jansénisme,* p. 35.
135. I have used as sources primarily the summaries of Abercrombie, *Origins,* pp. 126–53, and of J. Carreyre in his article "Jansénisme," in *DTC,* VIII, cols. 318–529; as ballast for these, I consulted the commentaries of Arnauld in the *Apologie pour Jansénius* (1643) and the *Seconde apologie pour Jansénius* (1645) in his *Oeuvres* (Paris, 1778), XVI, 39–323; XVII, 1–637. Cf. also J. Laporte, *La Doctrine de la grâce chez Arnauld* (Paris, 1922). If one looks at Y. de la Brière, "Le Jansénisme de Jansénius: étude critique sur les cinq propositions," *Recherches de sciences religieuses,* VI (1916), 270–99, one is mostly struck with how little progress has been made in the debate in nearly three centuries.
136. Barcos tried to defend Jansenius from charges of doctrinal error on the grounds that "il n'y avait aucune proposition dogmatique dans son livre"; supposedly everything in it was purely a matter of historical fact. Cf. H. Gouhier, "Crise de la théologie," p. 32.
137. Jansenius discusses two ways to elaborate the truths of faith:

explains why the whole first book has been taken up with a history of Pelagianism. However, this explanation is only half the story: the doctrines and errors of the Pelagians and semi-Pelagians are frequently said to be identical with those of certain neo-Scholastic thinkers, and in Book VIII of Volume I, Molina is finally named. The doctrinal intent is plain, even if the method is not dogmatic, and Jansenius in fact says his work is intended to bring back theology to the true Augustinian doctrines from which it had been wandering for several hundred years; the great Scholastics are thus indicted along with the Molinists. So when the errors of the semi-Pelagians are listed, we are to understand that they are in fact the errors of the Molinists, namely: (1) that predestination was *post praevisa merita* and therefore not gratuitous; (2) that this prevision was not only of some *initium fidei* but of final perseverance as well, thereby making God's will even further dependent on ours; and (3), the affirmation of this very dependence on the pretext that an irresistible grace would destroy human freedom. So in showing St. Augustine's refutation of these errors, he means also to refute Molinism. There is no question that he also wishes, as was mentioned earlier, to defend Baius, which he does explicitly in certain passages, but his defense is always Augustinian and he nowhere takes up any notions of Baius that cannot be justified from St. Augustine. The final claim is always to wish to reproduce the Augustinian doctrine, and he thus entrusts his work to the judgment of the Church. That judgment, in the form of the notorious five condemned propositions, was ambiguous and inept; yet in spite of its inadequacy, there is still no thorough study of the *Augustinus* that does not take those five propositions as its point of departure.

The main influence of Baius on Jansenius would seem to be in the rejection of the notion of "pure nature" and of the correlative distinction between natural and supernatural. Because

---

the first, by reason, leads either to error or to endless arid discussion; the second way, he says, is by charity: in some mysterious way, as one increases in charity, his understanding of the faith is thereby illuminated—a notion that had its influence on Pascal.

this question of the "nature" of man had reached a state of advanced confusion by this time, it might be well to attempt to show rather schematically the different views and what they represent. On one end of the scale, the Protestant Reformers, and according to many commentators also Baius and even Jansenius, believed that man's "nature" was as it had been created by God in Adam, that is, in God's image, just, whole; with the Fall, man's nature was ruined, he is now "denatured," capable of nothing by himself but concupiscence, sin. For the Pelagians—those of the Renaissance as well as those of the fifth century—man's "nature" is as we see it today; what Adam lost through the Fall was certain supernatural privileges: the immediate intuition of God and the possibility of eternal life with Him. But man retains his natural faculties intact, faculties by which he can (without the aid of grace) not only live the good life, but attain to the knowledge and love of God. Jansenists, Thomists, and Molinists in the sixteenth and seventeenth centuries all took positions somewhere between these extremes. But it is not hard to see that discussions of man's nature in this context are often obfuscations: they are a backhanded way of defending a particular notion of grace. Thus, for example, the Molinists claim to uphold man's need for grace in his present state; but if that grace is always and automatically given to man, how is it to be distinguished from his "nature"?

Now, for Jansenius, as for Baius, all this talk of a "pure nature" of man was nonsense. Man was created to love God, which was his one end and goal from the beginning. Adam at his creation was *sanum*, able to obey the commandments and to see that that was where his beatitude lay. He was also given a special grace, which Jansenius calls, after St. Augustine, the *adiutorium sine quo non*; but Augustine saw this grace of Adam as necessary because man, as a finite being, needed additional help toward an infinite end: Jansenius seems to feel that Adam, created out of nothing, needed grace even to keep from falling back into nothingness.[138] The analogy used by both writers for the *adiutorium sine quo non* is that of a man

138. Cf. Abercrombie, *Origins,* pp. 136–37.

with healthy eyes capable of seeing, but still needing light (God's grace) if he is in fact to see anything. Along with this grace, Adam also possessed a complete freedom to use it for good or evil, or in other words the freedom of indifference. His sin, the sin of concupiscence, or desiring something other than God, was transmitted to the rest of mankind by concupiscence and is the cause of our concupiscence.

With the Fall, Jansenius insists, again with St. Augustine, man did not lose his *libre arbitre,* but only his *liberté d'indifférence.* Fallen man's will is still free, though now under the domination of concupiscence; it is no longer free to choose between good and evil. So the Fall did more than merely withdraw the *adiutorium sine quo non.* If man was created not like other creatures but with God as his goal, to take away his means to that goal is not merely to reduce him to the level of other natural beings but to vitiate his nature in a radical way. Man without God is not an animal but a monster, and needs a radical cure; he no longer needs only light to see, but a cure for his blindness.[139] So in our present state, our free will is really capable only of evil,[140] and if an infidel does a good act we may say it is good in an objective way, but as its goal was not God it is still evil—this is the distinction between *officium* and *finis.* The grace of Christ which will free us from this necessity of sin (*necessitas peccandi*) is thus very different from that of Adam; it is an *adiutorium quo,* that is, not only necessary for all good acts but the very source of the acts, the means by which we do them. For Jansenius, the "sufficient grace" of the semi-Pelagians (i.e., the Molinists) is an absurdity: owing to our helpless state it could not be sufficient unless it actually and effectively cured our wills, in which case it would be efficacious. And God does not owe man any such grace to complete his "nature," as that nature is only a fiction and man's present state is the consequence of his own sin. Jansenius also rejects all the Scholastic types of graces—he

139. *Ibid.,* pp. 147–48.

140. This is not only thoroughly Augustinian, but was endorsed by the Council of Orange (Denz., No. 195); the same notion was condemned in Baius (Denz., No. 1027).

never mentions and seems to have no place for the habitual grace so much discussed by the Thomists; the only distinction he makes is between prevenient and subsequent (or consequent) graces, the latter following upon the first movement of grace and merited by it, as our concupiscence was merited by Adam's.

How then is such a completely determinant grace to be reconciled with free will? Jansenius does not have nearly so much trouble with this question as might be imagined. His definition of freedom since the Fall excludes the freedom of indifference or indetermination. An action is free as long as it is in our power to do it free from constraint. Now since nothing is more in our power or more free from external forces than our will itself,[141] it is especially free: we can always will what we want to even when other forces prevent our carrying out our intention. By this definition, Jansenius rejects not only the Molinist view, but also the traditional Thomist view in which the will to be free had at least to have a potential ability to choose otherwise (*potestas ad opposita*): that which is voluntary is by definition free, and in this Jansenius rejoins another condemned notion of Baius.[142] Since the Fall, man is necessarily either under the domination of sin or of grace, but neither of these forces acts against his will. He is attracted to sin by his own concupiscence and chooses and wills the sins he commits because he takes pleasure (*delectatio*) in them. If, on the other hand, he is moved by grace, it is through an even stronger delight in virtue which is victorious over the forces of concupiscence (*victrix delectatio*). In both cases we act voluntarily and therefore freely, but in the second case only are we truly free, for choosing the good is the proper aim of the will and such choices are by definition more truly voluntary.

With this theory of the will, predestination poses no great problem either. Jansenius equates predestination and predetermination: the elect are predetermined to salvation and so also are the means of their election. In the case of reprobation,

141. Cf. St. Augustine, *Retractationes,* I, 22; *BA,* XII, 408: "Nihil tam in potestate quam ipsa voluntas est."
142. See Denz., No. 1039.

he distinguishes two kinds: positive and negative. Positive reprobation is the decree of damnation and eternal punishment pronounced by God in His justice as a result of Original Sin. Negative reprobation is simply God's decision not to choose some men for salvation, and this decision is prior to Original Sin but by prevision of it. So the elect are chosen, and the damned not chosen, from all eternity, but the positive damnation of the damned is consequent upon Original Sin. This view corresponds to that of the so-called infra-lapsarian Calvinists and is more difficult to attribute to St. Augustine, except perhaps by implication.

Finally, what many modern Catholic critics regard as Jansenius' gravest error is his denial of God's "universal salvific will"; this error is condemned in the fifth proposition in the form of implying that Christ died effectively only for the elect, rather than for all mankind.[143] There is little doubt that this was Jansenius' view; there is no doubt at all that it was also the teaching of St. Augustine.[144] It was condemned as a doctrine by the Council of Quiercy but with qualifications,[145] and that particular Council was a local one gathered to combat Gottschalk and predestinarianism. The Council of Trent's statement on the subject is more cautious and conservative.[146] Yet, as I have said, opinion within the Church was increasingly scandalized by such exclusionist doctrines, and in the period since the Reformation, the Catholic Church has moved almost steadily toward a more universal theory of redemption, and away from any rigorist notions concerning election, primarily because of the problems posed by the discovery of whole worlds of pagans untouched by the Church and therefore presumably by grace. Outside of and after the Jansenist controversies, the problem is often posed in terms of these very pagans, and for most modern Catholic theologians it is no longer a question of whether God wishes to save all men, but only of how he distributes the graces by which he will do so.

143. See *ibid.*, No. 1096.
144. Cf. n. 119 above.
145. See Denz., No. 318.
146. Conc. Trid., sess. VI, chap. 3; Denz., No. 795.

We may bring this brief historical survey of the question of grace, free will, and predestination to an end with the *Augustinus* of Jansenius: the attacks on this work and apologies for it are approximately contemporary with Pascal's beginning to take an interest in these matters. Our purpose has been to give the main outlines of the problem as Pascal inherited it, and, for reasons which Jansenius himself has so well examined, that outline must be historical: the history of a theological doctrine is not incidental to it but of its essence. Our next chapter takes up the relatively unknown *Ecrits sur la grâce* of Pascal, in which we shall see him examining these questions free from the polemical needs of the *Lettres provinciales* and from the apologetic demands of the *Pensées*. But it has also seemed necessary to situate Pascal's views in the context of the history of the problem in order that we may examine his position free from certain traditional biases concerning Jansenism.

Starting from the first speculations of the Church Fathers, we have seen that the arguments on one side and the other have not varied greatly. Those arguing strongly for free will have tended to use two basic arguments, both philosophical in origin: one from moral responsibility, with certain texts from Scripture used only to prove the minor premise, that man is morally responsible; and one from the presence of evil in the world, again with a minimum of scriptural reference. The arguments for predestination, on the other hand, are mainly scriptural, although they were undoubtedly aided by a certain traditional fatalism inherited from Greek and oriental religious thought. It is consequently true in a general way throughout the history of the problem, that when rational or philosophical theology is dominant, free will is strongly affirmed and predestination ignored or deprecated; and when positive theology, or a more literal attention to revelation is in the ascendancy, then predestination takes over and free will is either greatly restricted or denied altogether. For this reason, the way in which Pascal sees the relation between reason and revelation will be seen to be intimately bound up with his views on free will and predestination.

We have also seen that in the course of history there has been considerable variation in the views of orthodox Christians on these matters. The position of most of the Church Fathers before Augustine is quite different from the doctrine he would formulate; and although his doctrine received about as much official support as could be given to doctrines by the post-Nicene Church, nevertheless it was possible for his doctrine to be radically undermined and his authority questioned by theologians of the sixteenth and seventeenth centuries. In fact, although the views of the Molinists undoubtedly resemble those of the Pelagians or semi-Pelagians (as the Jansenists claimed), historical parallelism suggests quite a different comparison: the Jansenists will be seen to be more like the semi-Pelagians and Molina more like St. Augustine. For, as we have seen, the semi-Pelagians were only trying to defend and conserve a doctrine which had been that of most great Christian writers up to that time against the apparent innovations of Augustine; this is exactly the position of the Jansenists with respect to the doctrines of Molina and others, however difficult it may be to see such a mediocre theologian as Molina in the role of an Augustine boldly formulating the new mind of the Church. But the truth is that whatever else the Jansenists were, they were not dangerous innovators: they were, one and all, theological conservatives, forced into the position of reactionaries by the "aggiornamento" of the Church which took place in the sixteenth and seventeenth centuries. I have already mentioned some of the factors favoring the new theology in the Renaissance: the new Humanism, the discovery of, and concern with vast pagan societies, as well as certain changes in later Medieval theology; but the attempt to accommodate these into a new synthesis was not the only reform movement within the Church. There was also a "conservative reform" in France,[147] closely allied with developments in Spain and the Netherlands, which owed

147. Recent studies of Bérulle and others are shedding new light on this movement; an excellent introduction to it is J. Orcibal, *Jean Duvergier de Hauranne, abbé de Saint-Cyran, et son temps (1581–1630)*, in Orcibal, ed, *Les Origines du Jansénisme*, Vol. II (Louvain, 1947).

most perhaps to Bérulle and Saint-Cyran. This reform was of course the spiritual source for Jansenism, and ought to be mentioned even though our concern is only with the theological manifestations.[148]

Finally, one might say that if some of the Augustinian theologians who came to be known as Jansenists were in fact guilty of heresy in the sense of actually departing from essential Augustinian views, they undoubtedly did so out of an excess of reaction: their conservatism was not always very enlightened concerning historical changes in the meaning of terms and in the historical and philosophical contexts of theological statements. A much more interesting question, therefore, than that of Pascal's supposed Jansenism or anti-Jansenism would seem to be whether Pascal did not see the dangers of a too rigid and literal conservatism and consequently seek ways of expressing a traditional Augustinism that were more modern and more precise than were the writings of his contemporaries. This question, too, we may hope to find answered by the *Ecrits sur la grâce*.

148. Nor will I be concerned with Jansenism as an ideology, such as it is presented by Lucien Goldmann in *Le Dieu caché: étude sur la vision tragique dans les "Pensées" de Pascal et dans le théâtre de Racine* (Paris, 1955), and in the introduction to his edition of the *Correspondance de Martin de Barcos* (Paris, 1956). M. Goldmann's schematization, which seems to me (and to other of his critics) to be based on a misreading of the *Pensées,* may help him to understand the sociological forces at work in this period, which are none of my concern, but his analysis only obscures, when it does not actually falsify the theological issues.

Pascal's *Ecrits sur la grâce* are among the least read, least studied of his works.[1] It is not difficult to imagine why: they are largely fragmentary, often repetitive, and deal matter-of-factly, and sometimes with considerable technical detail, with those very aspects of the doctrine of grace that have always seemed abstruse or sterile even in the more genial presentation of the *Lettres provinciales*. In addition, although no one doubts that these *Ecrits* are by Pascal, scholars have so far been unable to come up with conclusive evidence regarding the most basic questions about them: when they were written, and for whom or for what purpose;[2] also, being mostly frag-

1. *"Ecrits sur la grâce"* is the title given by Gazier to the fifteen fragments published in the GE, XI, 95–295. Gazier knew of the existence of a sixteenth fragment, summarized by Dom Clémencet from another MS in his *Histoire littéraire de Port-Royal* (see GE, XI, 128). This MS was recently rediscovered by Louis Lafuma and published under the title *Deux pièces imparfaites sur la grâce et le Concile de Trente* (Paris, 1947); it consists of the two pieces Chevalier calls the *I*er *Ecrit,* giving a few variants for the first piece, and being the only source for the second. Further remarks on the history of the *Ecrits* can be found in Lafuma's introduction (*Deux pièces*, pp. 16–19) or in that of Chevalier (*OC*, p. 947). Chevalier's edition thus gives all the known fragments; his text is also the one used in the edition "L'Intégrale" of the *Oeuvres complètes* (Paris, 1963) edited by Lafuma. As long ago as 1951, Jean Mesnard, in his *Pascal* (Paris, 1951), stressed the importance of the *Ecrits sur la grâce,* and recent books have begun to pay more attention to them: see Jean Steinmann, *Pascal,* 2d ed. (Paris, 1962), and especially J. H. Broome, *Pascal* (New York, 1965).

2. For a detailed discussion of the dating of these fragments, see Appendix A.

ments, they, like the *Pensées,* pose problems for editors as to how to order or group them.[3] Yet M. Jean Mesnard has called them "une des clefs de toute l'oeuvre de Pascal," [4] and has lamented the lack of serious study they have received. We shall examine them in this chapter, therefore, with two primary purposes in mind: first, we shall want to see just what was Pascal's opinion in writings relatively free of polemics on these much debated questions concerning grace, free will, and predestination; and then we shall look at his method of dealing with the problems, for insight into the workings of Pascal's

3. The best order, of course, would be chronological; this is at present impossible. Certain faults should be noted in existing editions, however, which future editions should take into account. First, in Chevalier's edition, the fifth fragment in the *IVe Ecrit (OC,* pp. 1041–44; that is, B.N. 12449, fols. 710–12) is manifestly a part of the letter and so belongs in the *IIIe Ecrit* (as it is in the GE, viz. part ii of the *IIIe Ecrit*). Again, Chevalier's III, 3 *(OC,* pp. 986–87; B.N. 12449, fols. 694–95) is followed immediately in the MS by Chevalier's III, 6 *(OC,* pp. 995–1006; B.N. 12449, fols. 696–704) and as there is no break in the reasoning, the two fragments should be rejoined (Chevalier here follows the GE, which notes, although with an error, the absence of a break; see GE, XI, 213, n. 1). Chevalier's III, 6 *(OC,* pp. 995–1006; B.N. 12449, fols. 696–704) is followed in the MS by his III, 5 *(OC,* pp. 991–95; B.N. 12449, fols. 704–707), but here the continuity is by no means clear. The order of the *IVe Ecrit* must remain arbitrary, though after the removal of Chevalier's fifth fragment *(OC,* pp. 1041–44) to the *IIIe Ecrit,* the last fragment (p. 1044) should be rejoined to the fourth fragment *(OC,* pp. 1036–40). In all these matters, the Lafuma edition (L'Intégrale) follows Chevalier.

Finally, future editors of the *Ecrits* should note that in the *IIIe Ecrit (OC,* p. 1000; B.N. 12449, fol. 700) the GE and all subsequent editions have accepted a correction of Bossut's which is in fact incorrect. The passage reads, in the MS, "La qualité essentielle de prochain est telle qu'elle met l'homme dans une incertitude absolue de la réduction à l'acte." Bossut has emended "incertitude" to "certitude"; however, this not only makes the immediate statement false, but also a close reading of the whole paragraph shows that such a reading is contrary to the argument Pascal is presenting. The gist of that argument is that since, if one has a "pouvoir prochain" to persevere, it is *un*certain whether one will use it; it is therefore "moralement impossible" and "impertinent" to assert with certainty that that "pouvoir" is *never* translated into action except when there are also "grâces efficaces."

4. *Pascal* (Paris, 1951), p. 105.

mind—and also for whatever new insights into these questions his particular approach seems to offer us.

The so-called *IIe Ecrit* is fortunately a completed and quite admirable little treatise on the true Augustinian doctrine—sometimes referred to as "that of the Church" or of the "disciples of St. Augustine." [5] It is admirable in several ways: not just for the quality of the reasoning and the language, but for its succinctness, the perfect balance of its parts, and especially for its fairness toward the positions of the Molinists and Calvinists with relatively little polemic. It sets forth the Augustinian doctrine with great care and completeness, followed by an exposé of the doctrine of the Molinists (called here "les restes des Pélagiens" [6]), and finally by a résumé of the opinion of Calvin; these last two sections follow the same order as the first and at each point it is shown where they differ from, or are similar to the Augustinian view. In the *Ier Ecrit,* part 1,[7] there is a similar presentation, though less well organized; and in the second part of that *Ecrit* are found variant versions of the same material.[8] Further similar material is found in a fragment of the *IIIe Ecrit.*[9] Let us follow this doctrine in its essentials, depending primarily on the *IIe Ecrit.*

For Pascal, the key to the Augustinian doctrine is the distinction between the two states of man: that of Adam before the Fall, and that of Adam and the rest of mankind after the Fall. This distinction is so important that it can be said that it is the failure to distinguish these two states which is the source of error for both Molinists and Calvinists.[10] The pre-lapsarian Adam, then, represented humanity as it issued from the hand of God, "juste, sain, fort. Sans aucune concupiscence. Avec le libre arbitre également flexible au bien et au mal. Désirant sa béatitude et ne pouvant pas ne pas la désirer." [11] Adam's free

5. *OC*, pp. 951, 954, etc. The entire first section of the *IIe Ecrit* is translated in Appendix B.

6. *OC*, p. 967.

7. *OC*, pp. 951–54.

8. *OC*, pp. 955–57.

9. *OC*, pp. 1002–1006.

10. *OC*, p. 957.

11. *OC*, p. 964.

will before the Fall is thus free of any pull in either direction, yet, desiring its beatitude, it is not an empty or gratuitous freedom, but one faced with a choice in order to secure that beatitude. Adam in this state also had a "grâce suffisante et nécessaire pour accomplir les préceptes" without which his transgression would not have been sinful, and which properly used would have enabled him to persevere in justice and merit the glory of the Angels, and to pass on this grace and freedom to his children.[12] God, in creating men thus, did so with a "volonté conditionnelle de les sauver tous généralement s'ils observaient ses préceptes." [13]

Now concerning this state of man before the Fall, Pascal finds that the Molinists (or Pelagians) are in complete agreement with St. Augustine. The free will, sufficient grace, and universal but conditional will of God to save all men—all are elements of the Molinist view; their error of course is not to see that Adam's sin changed these conditions. The Calvinists, on the other hand, are seen by Pascal to differ from St. Augustine in important ways concerning Adam before the Fall. For Calvin, God had no conditional or ambiguous ideas about man at his creation: he intended to damn some and save others absolutely.[14] Adam's sin, also, was essentially the same for the Augustinians and the Molinists: a free act of man, even though inspired by the Devil, in which he revolted against God and wished to be "indépendant de Dieu et égal à lui." [15] But for the Calvinists, Adam's sin was not permitted to his freedom, but decreed, ordered by God so that He could in justice damn those he had already determined to damn.[16] Pascal insists on this difference between permitting Adam to sin and forcing him: "Dieu a . . . non seulement permis, mais causé sa chute"; for Calvin, "Il n'y a aucune différence en Dieu entre *faire* et *permettre*." [17] The distinction is a traditional one, but

12. *OC,* pp. 964–65.
13. *OC,* p. 964.
14. *OC,* p. 969.
15. *OC,* p. 965; cf. p. 968.
16. *OC,* p. 969.
17. *OC,* p. 951.

was usually also applied to man after the Fall, in which case Pascal does not himself distinguish between *faire* and *permettre*.[18]

In his insistence on the importance of distinguishing the pre- and post-lapsarian states of man, Pascal is in complete accord with Arnauld's and Jansenius' interpretations of St. Augustine, following fairly consistently the account in Augustine's *De Correptione et gratia*. Concerning the vexed question of a natural or supernatural state of man, Pascal generally avoids the word "nature" in his discussions, being well aware of its ambiguities and even skeptical of the whole concept of nature.[19] However, as some writers have seen in this question the key to the Jansenist interpretation,[20] we should look closely at Pascal's version of Adam's state with this in mind. So Pascal says that Adam, although strong, healthy, and just, could not obey God's commands without God's grace (presumably superadded to his human nature), and since Adam's whole happiness, the beatitude which he could not help desiring, depended on his obeying God's commands, "Dieu ne pouvait avec justice

18. In a similar manner, Pascal has used the old argument (found in Philo and the early Fathers) that it is unjust for God to command unless his commandments are possible, but applies it only to "innocent man" before the Fall, to show the necessity for Adam's sufficient grace; cf. *OC*, p. 964.

19. Cf. *Pensées*, Br. 91–94, 121, 35c.; *OC*, pp. 1121–23.

20. Most notably among recent writers, Henri de Lubac, *Augustinisme et théologie moderne* (Paris, 1965), esp. chaps. II and III (cf. also his *Surnaturel* [Paris, 1946]). In his efforts to maintain the coherence of Augustine's doctrine—and in a polemical tone hardly justified by the subject—Lubac lashes out at Baius, Jansenius, Arnauld, and others for their use of Augustine's phraseology out of the context of his total doctrine; yet Lubac has no compunctions about doing the same to Jansenius et al.: so, for instance, he fails to see that the grace which triumphs over the will does so only over the will as dominated by concupiscence, not in opposition to the will itself or by doing violence to it. All Lubac seems to establish against Jansenius is that his analyses of the psychology of grace are meager by comparison with Augustine's; as to the theology of grace, Jansenius's version seems to remain intact as at least a possible interpretation. See J. Chéné's *Note complémentaire* no. 11 to the *De Correptione et gratia, BA*, XXIV, *Aux moines d'Adrumète et de Provence*, 787–97.

imposer des préceptes à Adam et aux hommes innocents sans leur donner la grâce nécessaire pour les accomplir." [21] Now one could argue that, since God in some sense "had to" give Adam the "grâces suffisantes et nécessaires" to obey God's commands, then these so-called graces are really part of man's nature as God created him, and so for Pascal (as for Luther and perhaps for Baius) pre-lapsarian Adam was the natural state of man, and the Fall has vitiated and destroyed that nature. However, Pascal's text renders this interpretation impossible. For what defines man, both before and after the Fall, as supernatural is his supernatural goal or destiny: he was created not just to enjoy the fruits of God's creation but, by persevering in justice to achieve the eternal glory of the Angels; and God gave him the graces necessary to that end not because He owed it to man's nature to do so, but because, having set man a supernatural goal, He had for the sake of justice to give him the means also. The means, like the end, are supernatural and arise out of man's unique relation to God. However, "Dieu laissa et permit au libre arbitre d'Adam le bon ou le mauvais usage de cette grâce," [22] which allowed Adam to revolt against God, to refuse the means offered, though never altogether to blind himself to the supernatural end for which he was created; in his sin itself, Adam wished to be like God. The very simplicity of the language of Pascal's version perhaps makes it possible to impose a variety of interpretations on it; but to suppose that there is a disguised naturalism underlying its terms would be to misunderstand both Pascal's concept of nature and his concept of the will (which we shall come to later).

Concerning Adam before the Fall, as also concerning the nature of the Fall itself, Pascal, then, sees the Augustinians and Molinists as in agreement. It is not even in the consequences of the Fall that they differ, for Jansenists and Molinists alike agree that Adam's sin was passed to his posterity, bringing man not only guilt but ignorance and concupiscence. It is rather, as Pascal notes with precision, concerning "la conduite

21. *OC,* p. 964.
22. *OC,* p. 965.

de Dieu envers les hommes après le péché" that they differ, that is, in the concept of grace. In the *IIe Ecrit,* Pascal maintains on the other hand that the Augustinians differ from the Calvinists "en toutes choses depuis le commencement jusqu'à la fin." [23] But in the *Ier Ecrit* he allows that the Calvinists

> *nous sont conformes de paroles en la volonté absolue de Dieu en la rédemption, mais différents en sens, en ce que nous entendons que le décret de Dieu est postérieur à la prévision du péché d'Adam et donné sur les hommes criminels, et eux prétendent que ce décret est non seulement prieur, mais cause du péché d'Adam et donné sur les hommes encore innocents.*[24]

Before going on to consider the grace required for fallen man, it might be well to point out the significance of Pascal's position on the grace of Adam. For Pascal, as for Augustine, the precise definitions of Adam's freedom and of the grace given him are not revealed truths from which one then can deduce the consequences of the Fall. They are rather attempts through speculative theology to account for man's present state —his ignorance and concupiscence, his inability to save himself, and his need for an unmerited grace as stated by St. Paul —while at the same time preserving God's essential attributes of goodness, justice, mercy, omniscience, and omnipotence. It is for this purpose, of course, that the Augustinians insist on Adam's very real freedom and on his having a grace sufficient to choose either good or evil, so that his sin, which introduced evil into the world, is entirely his fault—so God's justice is preserved; the grace God grants to the elect after the Fall must then be an effect purely of God's mercy. The Calvinists, however, allow their respect for God's omnipotence to obscure the need for His justice, and Pascal insists that for them God

23. *OC,* p. 969.
24. *OC,* p. 957. This difference in attitude toward the Calvinists in the two passages is probably not significant; in the *Ier Ecrit,* Pascal is developing a symmetrical argument in which the error of the Calvinists is opposed to the error of the Molinists; in both *Ecrits,* however, he is consistently harsh on the Calvinists and lenient toward the Molinists.

caused Adam's sin and thus damned man while he was still innocent. The Molinists, on the other hand, see God's grace after the Fall as still a function of His justice (rather than of His mercy), and as given in response to man's efforts. Pascal sums it all up in this way: "Ainsi les Molinistes posent la volonté des hommes pour source du salut et de la damnation. Ainsi les Calvinistes posent la volonté de Dieu pour source du salut et de la damnation. Ainsi l'Eglise [i.e., les Augustiniens] pose que la volonté de Dieu est la source du salut, et que la volonté des hommes est la source de la damnation." [25] Of course, I am not suggesting that Pascal sat down and worked this all out in a way that turned out to coincide with the system of St. Augustine: for him, as for all the Augustinians, that system had already been ratified as the official doctrine of the Church and was scarcely less binding than Scripture itself. But one must certainly assume that it appealed to him so decidedly (and in all its implications) exactly because it seemed to accord with and explain the facts of human existence as he saw it, and not that he first adopted a dogmatic view on Adam's grace and then adjusted his view of the human condition accordingly. This is particularly obvious in the *Ier Ecrit*, where the facts of our existence with respect to salvation are first laid down, then the possibilities for explanation set forth, and finally the reasons for the Augustinian solution are developed; this same movement from the observed facts of the human condition, through possible attitudes toward that condition, to the ultimate necessity of the Christian explanation will also of course be one of the main characteristics of Pascal's apologetic method in the *Pensées*.

To return to mankind after the Fall of Adam: "La concupiscence s'est donc élevé dans ses membres et a chatouillé et délecté sa volonté dans le mal, et les ténèbres ont rempli son esprit";[26] on this all are agreed. But for the Molinists, God in his justice wants to save all men and gives them the aids sufficient for that salvation; He cannot discern those worthy of salvation unless they give him occasion, and so it is left

25. *OC*, p. 957.
26. *OC*, p. 965.

to their free will to use these aids for well or ill. The grace of Christ was needed to counteract the effects of Adam's sin, but it is offered to all, and enables all to have faith in Christ and to pray for further help.[27]

For the Calvinists, on the contrary, there is no free will, "aucune flexibilité au bien, même avec la grâce efficacissime." God wishes to save only those He created for salvation; to them alone He gives the grace of Jesus Christ, which operates in them without any cooperation on their part, and they are saved not by any action of their own but by the merits of Christ, which are imputed or applied to them.[28]

For the Augustinians, however,

> le libre arbitre est demeuré flexible au bien et au mal; mais avec cette différence, qu'au lieu qu'en Adam il n'avait aucun chatouillement au mal, et qu'il lui suffisait de connaître le bien pour s'y pouvoir porter, maintenant il a une suavité et une délectation si puissante dans le mal par la concupiscence qu'infailliblement il s'y porte de lui-même comme à son bien, et qu'il le choisit volontairement et très librement et avec joie comme l'objet où il sent sa béatitude.[29]

And in like manner the grace of Christ "n'est autre chose qu'une suavité et une délectation dans la loi de Dieu," a "délectation" even stronger than that of concupiscence, and under its influence "le libre arbitre, charmé par les douceurs et par les plaisirs que le Saint-Esprit lui inspire, plus que par les attraits du péché, choisit infailliblement lui-même la loi de Dieu par cette seule raison, qu'il y trouve plus de satisfaction et qu'il y sent sa béatitude et sa félicité." [30] The vocabulary here is interesting. First, as regards the action of the free will, it is always free but necessarily follows the greater "délectation"; although this last term had become a technical theological one deriving for Pascal from Jansenius (and ultimately from

27. See *OC*, pp. 968–69.
28. See *OC*, pp. 969–70.
29. *OC*, p. 966.
30. *OC*, pp. 966–67.

Augustine), Pascal brings out its sensual meaning by the use of such words as "suavité," "félicité," "joie," "douceurs," etc. In this way he emphasizes the notion that neither concupiscence nor grace pushes or acts against the will, but rather solicits the will with irresistible attractions. And when the will embraces whatever "délectation" presents itself as most attractive, it does so "infailliblement"; by the use of this word, Pascal first avoids the notion of grace coercing or necessitating, an important point, since Jansenius' error has sometimes been thought to be that he allowed man to be free from coercion but not from necessity. But "infaillible" has almost exclusively intellectual connotations; in other words, the will under either concupiscence or grace infallibly acts accordingly—one might say it acts accordingly by definition. We shall see shortly what consequences this has for Pascal's overall conception of the will.

Interesting too are certain other terms used in the contrast between Molinist, Calvinist, and Augustinian theories of grace. For the Molinists, grace is something offered for their use: the verb "user" is virtually the only one Pascal employs in describing their theory.[31] For the Calvinists, on the contrary, it is grace which uses the will, "qui porte la volonté au bien (non pas qui fait que la volonté s'y porte, mais qui l'y porte malgré sa répugnance) comme une pierre, comme une scie, comme une matière morte";[32] in other words, grace acts on the will as gravity might on a stone, or as a builder might use a tool. For the Augustinians, however, since Adam's sin passed to his posterity "comme un fruit sortant d'une mauvaise semence,"[33] that is, naturally, organically, the grace of Jesus Christ must be a "grâce médicinale"[34] which will cure that nature, corrupt and ill as it now is. If there is a certain "naturalism" implied here in the position of the Jansenists, it is important once again to see that it is also a supernaturalism: man's true nature is always to attain a supernatural goal, a goal for which he always needs special help from God, whether before or after the

31. See *OC*, p. 968.
32. *OC*, p. 970.
33. *OC*, p. 965.
34. *OC*, p. 966.

Fall, and even after having received the initial grace of Christ, which is only the grace to believe and to pray for further aid. Secondly, the naturalism suggested here is organicist and is contrasted with the inherent mechanism of both Molinists and Calvinists: grace, for the Augustinians, operates in and through nature and the will, much as the principle of life itself; for Molinists and Calvinists grace is related to the will as is a tool, the only difference between the two being as to who is on which end of the stick.

The extent to which Pascal rejects a mechanistic view of nature, and the way in which his naturalism is in fact a supernaturalism, can also be shown regarding the question of perseverance. Of course Pascal recognizes that the question of perseverance is only an extension of the question of grace versus the "pouvoir prochain"; so in one passage, having noted that the Council of Trent condemned the proposition that the just man can persevere without a special aid from God, he goes on to say:

Remarquez donc que toutes ces questions ne sont qu'une même: si les justes, au premier instant de la justice, ont le pouvoir prochain d'accomplir les préceptes dans l'instant suivant. Si tous les justes, dans le premier instant de leur justice, ont le pouvoir prochain d'y persévérer (car accomplir les commandements à l'avenir et persévérer n'est qu'une même chose).[35]

Implied in this passage and elsewhere in Pascal's writings[36] is the notion of continuous creation such as is implied also in the works of Saint-Cyran;[37] that is, Pascal believed that the universe must be continually recreated by God from one moment to the next. There is thus an absolute discontinuity in time: each instant does not arise from the preceding instant in any

35. *OC*, p. 1043.
36. E.g., in the letter of November 5, 1648; see *OC*, pp. 487–88.
37. Cf. Georges Poulet, "Saint-Cyran et le temps," *Studies in Romance Philology and French Literature Presented to John Orr* (Manchester, 1953), pp. 233–44.

necessary way, but is a whole new creation; and the same must be true for each instant of grace. A passage from the *IIIe Ecrit* shows the implications of this notion for the question of perseverance:

Il est vrai que Dieu s'est obligé de . . . donner [les secours actuels] à ceux qui les demandent: et c'est pourquoi ils ne sont jamais refusés. Et qu'on ne pense pas tourner la chose en un mauvais sens, en disant qu'on demandera la persévérance dans la prière, et qu'ainsi on l'obtiendra; et qu'ainsi en demandant dans l'instant présent la grâce de prier dans l'instant futur, on l'obtiendra; et qu'ainsi on s'assurera de la persévérance; c'est se jouer des paroles. Car Dieu donne à ceux qui demandent, et non pas à ceux qui ont demandé, et c'est pourquoi il faut persévérer à demander pour obtenir; car il ne suffit pas de demander aujourd'hui avec un esprit pur la continence pour demain, car si ensuite on entre dans l'impureté, qui ne voit que le changement du coeur détruit l'effet de la prière précédente, et que pour avoir la continence demain, il ne faut point cesser de la demander? Et ainsi, si, dans l'instant présent, on demande le don de prière pour l'instant suivant, n'est-il pas clair qu'on ne l'obtiendra pas si l'on ne continue à le demander? Or dire qu'on aura l'esprit de prière dans l'instant suivant, si on prie dans cet instant suivant, n'est-ce pas dire qu'on l'aura si on l'a, et ainsi se jouer des paroles? [38]

Perseverance, then, is not a special grace which one can pray for: it is the continuance of present graces. Grace, for Pascal, as for Saint-Cyran and the other Augustinians, must be continually renewed; it is almost always actual grace that they speak of, the term "habitual grace" being for them almost a contradiction in terms. But, in addition, the nature through which grace acts is seen as so radically and continuously dependent on God that the word "nature" can be applied to it only by extension.[39]

As we emphasized in the first chapter, time plays an im-

38. *OC*, pp. 1010–11; translated in Appendix B.
39. Cf. in the *Pensées*, Br. 91–94, *OC*, p. 1121.

portant part in another way in the Augustinian theory of grace. The theory of the two states of man, before the Fall and after, cannot be reduced to two concomitant layers in man, or two ways of looking at man, without destroying the whole theory; the historical dimension is absolutely essential, as Pascal was well aware.[40] For, as he shows, if you make out God's will before the Fall to be the same as it is after, then you either assume with the Molinists that God has now a conditional will to save all men, in which case you ruin His omnipotence, or else you say with the Calvinists that even before Adam's sin God had an absolute will to save some and damn others, in which case you destroy God's justice. But the central event of history is of course the Incarnation of Jesus Christ, and in the *I*^{er} *Ecrit* Pascal sees the Incarnation not only as a figure of the mysterious cooperation between grace and free will (grace may be said to be incarnate in the will), but also as the stumbling block which is the source of all major heresies. He establishes a kind of dialectic of contrary heresies (of which the Molinists and Calvinists are excellent examples); and then adds that the Church is consoled in that "ces erreurs contraires éstablissent sa vérité; qu'il suffit de les abandonner à eux-mêmes pour les détruire." And yet,

Ce n'est pas en cette seule rencontre qu'elle éprouve des ennemis contraires. Elle n'a quasi jamais été sans ce double combat. Et, comme elle a éprouvé cette contrarieté en la personne de Jésus-Christ, son chef, que les uns ont fait homme seulement, et les autres Dieu seulement, elle en a senti presque en tous les autres points de sa créance. Mais en imitant son chef, elle tend les bras aux uns et aux autres pour les appeler tous et les embrasser ensuite ensemble pour former une heureuse union.[41]

It is on such a conciliatory note that the first section of the *I*^{er} *Ecrit* ends. There is, however, one further element in the

40. J. H. Broome, *Pascal* (New York, 1965), has emphasized this point well, pp. 92, 97, etc.

41. Both passages, *OC,* p. 955; translated in Appendix B.

contrast between the Augustinian, Calvinist, and Molinist doctrines which is worth noting and which bears on the question of Pascal's method in these writings. Concerning the Calvinist doctrine, he says it is "si horrible, et frappe d'abord l'esprit avec tant de force par la vue de la cruauté de Dieu envers ses créatures, qu'elle est insupportable." [42] But concerning the doctrine of the Molinists, he writes, "Cette opinion, contraire à celle des Calvinistes, produit un effet tout contraire. Elle flatte le sens commun que l'autre blesse. Elle le flatte en le rendant maître de son salut ou de sa perte." [43] And finally, concerning the doctrine of the Church (i.e., the Augustinian doctrine), he writes: "Elle n'est ni si cruelle que celle de Calvin ni si douce que celle de Molina. Mais, parce que ce n'est pas sur les apparences qu'il faut juger de la vérité, il faut les examiner à fond." [44] In other words the "sens commun" is not finally a reliable judge in these matters because it is itself at stake; the Molinist doctrine makes the "sens commun" (or reason as the deliberative faculty) the master of the individual's fate, while this faculty is considerably limited by the Augustinian doctrine and eliminated altogether (as a factor for salvation) in the Calvinist doctrine. The first part of the Ier Ecrit begins with an appeal to common sense by putting the whole question into terms reason can grasp and deal with: "Il est question de savoir si la volonté de l'homme est la cause de la volonté de Dieu, ou la volonté de Dieu la cause de la volonté de l'homme." [45] But since common sense cannot hope to give an unbiased verdict in a case where its own status is in question, the only sure rule will be the tradition of the Church; in the last part of the Ier Ecrit Pascal sets out to demonstrate the continuity of this tradition not only back as far as Augustine, but through the Fathers to the Apostles and ultimately to Jesus Christ himself. He begins with the illustrious defenders of St. Augustine's doctrine in the seventeenth century—defenders provided by a

42. *OC*, p. 956.
43. *OC*, p. 952.
44. *OC*, p. 956.
45. *OC*, p. 949.

special gift of God to His Church;[46] from them he moves backward in time through Thomas Aquinas to Peter Lombard, but the fragment breaks off there. The role of reason or common sense is thus precisely limited in the *I*er and *II*e *Ecrits*, subordinated finally to the weight of the tradition; but the "sens commun" is by no means eliminated from the discussion as long as it is kept within its domain, and we shall want to see how Pascal's method does in fact use the resources of reason in the examination of these theological issues.

Jean Mesnard describes Pascal's method in the *Ecrits sur la grâce* as consisting essentially of two steps:

> *La première démarche de cette méthode consiste à s'élever des points non contestés au points contestés. Sans cesser d'être exclusivement appuyée par l'autorité de la tradition, la doctrine se présente donc dans un ordre tout rationnel, et dans la suite, Pascal ne craindra pas de faire souvent appel au sens commun.*
>
> *La seconde démarche . . . consiste à présenter la doctrine de saint Augustin comme essentiellement compréhensive, comme également éloignée de deux erreurs contraires, calviniste et pélagienne, qu'elle dépasse et concilie.*[47]

This is true enough of the *I*er *Ecrit*, but the first step is much less apparent in the *II*e *Ecrit*, and in the *III*e and *IV*e *Ecrits* the method follows rather different lines, although one of the other fragments does begin much like the *I*er *Ecrit*.[48] In the *III*e *Ecrit* the first step is rather to analyze the terms of the problem before proceeding to quote texts or to show the reasonableness of the doctrine he wishes to prove. The *IV*e *Ecrit* begins with an explicit outline of the means he will use:

> *1. Le premier sera d'examiner par les termes de la proposition, quel est le sens qu'elle exprime, et que l'on en forme naturellement.*
>
> *2. Le second, d'examiner par l'objet qu'ont eu les Pères et*

46. *OC*, p. 959.
47. His *Pascal*, p. 104.
48. *OC*, pp. 995 ff.

le Concile en faisant cette décision, lequel de ces deux sens
ils y ont eu.

3. Et le troisième sera d'examiner par la suite du discours
et par les autres passages des Pères et du Concile qui l'expli-
quent, lequel est le véritable.[49]

In short, linguistic analysis, followed by an analysis of the
context and aims of the pronouncement, and finally the test
of its consistency with related writings and doctrines.

There are then broadly two methods in force in these writings: the one outlined by Mesnard, which applies to the two
finished expositions of the whole Augustinian doctrine of the
Fall and Redemption (the *Ier* and *IIe Ecrits*); and the method
of linguistic and contextual analysis used in the discussion of
certain quotations and propositions. Let us now look more
closely at this latter method and see how Pascal uses it, especially in the *IIIe* and *IVe Ecrits*.

One must keep always in mind that the greater part of the
material in these writings belongs to the science that came into
being in the sixteenth century and was known as positive
theology. Having its origins both in the standards of historical
and textual criticism made fashionable by the new Humanism,
and in the need to combat the heresies of the Reformation,
positive theology took for its goal the proving of the validity
of dogma by citation of scriptural and traditional texts. It
differed from Scholastic theology primarily in its methods,
which were textual rather than rational, and from that other
branch of theology, apologetics, in that it was aimed not at
the unbeliever, but at the believer who might be somewhat
confused about what he believed.[50] Pascal's method in these
writings is primarily textual: the main sources of evidence are
biblical, patristic, or canonical texts. His theological point of
view, his choice of texts, show him only as a clever, though not
really professional disciple of the Louvain theologians and of
his Port-Royal friends. He shows little sign of either great
humanistic erudition or theological originality. What is more

49. *OC*, pp. 1012–13; translated in Appendix B.
50. Cf. Yves Congar, art. "Théologie," in *DTC*, XV, cols. 426–30.

original with him is a keen awareness of the possibilities of verbal equivocation, and an even greater keenness at analyzing the sources of ambiguity; his awareness of the "intentionality" of language, expressed in step number two of the statement of method he outlined, seems quite modern, and yet it is a consequence of the very vision of man's condition he wishes to expose here and which we shall take up again.

Verbal identity is not logical identity: a single statement may have more than one logical interpretation. It is with this in mind that Pascal proceeds to analyze, in the *IIIe* and *IVe* *Ecrits*, the statement of the Council of Trent: "Les commandements ne sont pas impossibles aux justes." [51] Several of the fragments are analyses of this statement;[52] the other texts are on either problems raised by this statement (e.g., discussions of the meaning of "possibilité"), or the correct interpretation of certain other definitions of the Council regarding justification, especially the question of whether man first forsakes God, or God, man. Although the four texts on the above statement offer many parallels, and may seem rather dull and repetitious reading, they include many interesting variations. Each is in a slightly different form, and each shows certain new ideas or rhetorical inventions.

The trouble with this canon of the Council of Trent, then, was its ambiguity; "les commandements ne sont pas impossible aux justes" can be taken as meaning: (1) "les commandements sont toujours possibles à tous les justes"; or, (2) "il n'est pas impossible que les justes accomplissent les commandements" (when, that is, they are aided by God's grace).[53] One striking difference between the first fragment of the *IIIe Ecrit* and the other texts is that it allows that (1) is the more natural interpretation of the words, and that (2) "ne s'offre pas avec tant de promptitude." [54] In the other fragments, Pascal insists that (2) is the only meaning that even a "simple intelligence de la langue" will admit, because it is self-evident and "tellement

51. Conc. Trid., sess. VI, chap. 11, can. 18.
52. See *OC,* pp. 970–80, 1012–24, 1035–40.
53. See *OC,* p. 1012.
54. *OC,* p. 971.

clair qu'il est étrange qu'on entreprenne de l'éclaircir exprès." [55]
Perhaps this is mere rhetoric—Pascal would not have wished
to deny to his correspondent the modicum of intelligence
needed to see this truth—but it is also possible that his own
logical analyses led him to the point where (1) did seem
absurd and perverse. In any case, from the text in the *IIIe Ecrit*
to the fragments of the *IVe Ecrit,* there is a definite progression
in analytical keenness.

Another more striking difference between these texts is the
occurrence of a serious logical error in the *IIIe Ecrit,* which is
detrimental to his argument and which is not repeated in the
fragments of the *IVe Ecrit.* In the *IIIe Ecrit,* Pascal takes "les
commandements sont possibles aux justes" as the equivalent of
"les commandements ne sont pas impossibles aux justes." [56]
Now all that the Council of Trent has stated is that "les commandements sont impossibles aux justes" is anathema, i.e.,
is false. But, as the Port-Royal *Logic,* following Aristotle,[57]
makes clear, the falsity of a statement implies the truth of
the contrary statement only when the statement is particular
rather than universal; so, for example, the negation of "quel-
ques commandements sont impossibles aux justes" implies not
only the subcontrary, that some commandments are possible,
but also the contradictory, that all the commandments are possible to the justified. Whereas the negation of "tous les commandements sont impossibles aux justes"—which is the meaning Pascal wishes to attribute to the Council—implies only that
all the commandments are not impossible, or in other words
that some of them are possible, or, as he will put it, that they
are sometimes possible.[58] So in the first section of the *IVe Ecrit,*
he says, "Il n'y a point de règles de grammaire par lesquelles

55. *OC,* pp. 1013, 1035, 1036–37.
56. *OC,* p. 971.
57. *La Logique, ou l'art de penser,* ed. P. Clair and F. Girbal (Paris,
1965), part II, chap. 4, pp. 116–18; cf. Aristotle, *De Interpretatione,*
chap VII.
58. I use "some" rather than "sometimes" to adhere to the model
given in the Port-Royal *Logic;* but the same reasoning applies to
"toujours" and "quelquefois" as they are used by Pascal; the transfer
from quantity to time does not alter the logical structure.

on puisse prétendre que dire qu'une chose n'est pas impossible, soit dire, *qu'elle est toujours possible du plein et dernier pouvoir,* puisque'il suffit qu'elle soit possible quelquefois pour faire qu'elle ne soit pas impossible, sans qu'il soit nécessaire qu'elle le soit toujours." [59] And later in the fourth fragment, he asserts that either the word or the notion of "toujours" has been inserted in the canon, "non seulement contre les règles de la grammaire mais encore contre l'intention du Concile," by certain "personnes" (that is, the Jesuits).[60]

Now the word "impossible" used in the canon of the Council of Trent, and the related words "possible," "pouvoir," and "puissance" offer certain difficulties in themselves, as Aristotle showed in the *De Interpretatione*.[61] The problem is referred to in fragments in the *IIIe* and *IVe Ecrits*,[62] and dealt with in a systematic and relatively finished *opusculum* in the second section of the *IVe Ecrit*. A comparison with Aristotle is instructive, especially from the point of view of philosophical method: Aristotle is chiefly concerned with problems of logical necessity, contradiction, and finally with potency and contingency as basic ontological categories; Pascal, on the other hand, rejects Aristotelian essential definitions and accepts only nominal definitions and what he calls "mots primitifs" which are incapable of definition.[63] Such categories as contingency and potency, then, are of no interest to Pascal; what is of primary importance is ambiguity and the abuse of it by equivocation, as explained in the *De l'Esprit géométrique,* and the elimination of these faults by the method outlined there.[64] Parts of

59. *OC*, pp. 1013–14.
60. *OC*, p. 1037.
61. Chaps. XII–XIII.
62. *OC*, pp. 980–86, 1012–24.
63. See the *De l'Esprit géométrique, OC*, pp. 577 ff.
64. *Ibid.*, p. 578: "Il faut seulement prendre garde qu'on n'abuse de la liberté qu'on a d'imposer des noms, en donnant le même a deux choses différentes.

"Ce n'est pas que cela ne soit permis, pourvu qu'on n'en confonde pas les conséquences, et qu'on ne les étende pas de l'une à l'autre." The remedy for this vice is, in doubtful cases, to substitute the definition for the word it defines; Pascal continues: "Rien n'éloigne plus prompte-

these *Ecrits* form excellent examples of this method at work, and the resemblance of this approach to the analysis of "ordinary language" that has been developed recently in Anglo-Saxon philosophy is striking.[65] Some examples from the *Ecrits:*

> *Et, cependant, qui ne voit que le mot de* puissance *est tellement vague, qu'il enferme toutes les opinions? Car enfin, si l'on appelle une chose* être en notre puissance, *lorsque nous la faisons quand nous voulons, ce qui est une façon de parler très naturelle et très familière, ne s'ensuivra-t-il pas qu'il est en notre pouvoir, pris en ce sens, de garder les commandements et de changer notre volonté, puisque, dès que nous le voulons, non seulement cela arrive, mais qu'il y a implication [i.e., contradiction] à ce que cela n'arrive pas. Mais si l'on appelle une chose* être en notre pouvoir, *lors seulement qu'elle est au pouvoir qu'on appelle* prochain, *ce qui est aussi une façon fort ordinaire d'employer le mot de pouvoir, en ce sens, nous n'aurons plus ce pouvoir que quand il nous sera donné de Dieu. Ainsi cette expression de saint Augustin [i.e., les commandements sont possibles aux justes] est catholique au premier sens, et pélagienne au second.*[66]

Some examples of this distinction taken from ordinary language are cited:

> *N'est-il pas véritable qu'il n'est pas impossible aux hommes de faire la guerre? Et cependant il n'est pas toujours au pouvoir de tous les hommes de la faire.*
>
> *Il n'est pas impossible qu'un prince du sang ne soit roi, et*

---

ment et plus puissamment les surprises captieuses des sophistes que cette méthode, qu'il faut avoir toujours présente, et qui suffit seule pour bannir toutes sortes de difficultés et d'équivoques."

65. The distinction Pascal uses in these sections parallels rather closely that developed by Wittgenstein in the "Brown Book," pars. 43–49; see *The Blue and Brown Books* (New York, 1964), pp. 99–104. One need seek a reason for this resemblance no further, perhaps, than certain texts of St. Augustine which have been a source for the meditations of both Wittgenstein and Pascal.

66. *OC*, p. 983; translated in Appendix B.

cependant il n'est pas toujours au plein pouvoir des princes du sang de l'être.

Il n'est pas impossible aux hommes de vivre soixante ans, et cependant il n'est pas au plein pouvoir de tous les hommes d'arriver à cet âge, ni de s'assurer seulement d'un instant de vie.[67]

The short treatise on the relation between "la possibilité et le pouvoir" which forms the second section of the *IVe Ecrit* is much more Aristotelian in tone at the outset; it seems to take these two terms as faculties or qualities and to discuss whether their relation is necessary or not. The distinction drawn between "possibilité" and "pouvoir" is the same as that suggested above, and two of the same examples are used—the "prince du sang" and the possibility of living sixty years—to which is added that of a man healthy and free who has it "en son pouvoir" to run when he wishes; yet, "il ne répugne point de dire tout ensemble qu'un homme sain, mais enchaîné peut courir, puisque la rupture de ses fers est possible, sans qu'on puisse dire qu'il soit toujours en son pouvoir de courir, puisque la liberté ne dépend pas toujours de lui." And so it is with the commandments: one can say "que les commandements soient possibles aux hommes, et que néanmoins les hommes n'aient pas toujours le pouvoir de les accomplir." [68] Pascal then proposes a rule for discerning when something is in the power of the agent, namely when the cause of the effect in question is "présente et soumise au sujet." [69] The rule is a feeble one, ponderous and redundant—Aristotelian, in the worst sense; up to this point, one would scarcely recognize the mind of Pascal. But suddenly we discover that, according to his own rule, "comme la cause immédiate de l'observation des préceptes est la volonté de l'homme . . . cette cause résidant toujours dans l'homme, et dépendant de lui, on ne peut refuser de dire . . . qui l'observation des préceptes ne soit toujours au pouvoir de chacun des hommes." So his rule has served him badly it

67. *OC*, p. 1014; translated in Appendix B.
68. *OC*, p. 1025.
69. *OC*, p. 1026.

seems, proving in fact the Pelagian position to be correct. But of course this is only half the story: "Ce qui est étrange est que, selon cette même règle, l'observation des préceptes n'est pas toujours au pouvoir des hommes." [70] For the will of man is only a second cause (sometimes called a contingent or proximate cause) and the "première, dominante, maîtresse" cause is the will of God, which of course is not in man's power. Now we see where Pascal's imitation of a traditional philosophical method has been leading: "Il est donc évident que les qualités de *possible* et d'*impossible* conviennent ensemble à beaucoup de sujets selon les divers sens qu'on leur donne";[71] these so-called qualities are not in any sense inherent but are merely predicates and equivocal ones at that. So the man in chains, as a biped in good health and presumably capable of being released, has the power to run; and yet, "si l'on considère ce captif comme captif," [72] he hasn't the power to run in any sense, since his freedom is not in his power.

St. Thomas is then mentioned as having expressed such a case with the word "incompossible," that is, it is possible for a man to run and for a man to be in chains, but incompossible for him to be both. And so it is incompossible for a man to be both predestined to salvation and killed in a state of mortal sin.[73] Another comparison is made to a man who can see as

70. *Ibid.*
71. *OC*, p. 1027.
72. *Ibid.*
73. This reference to St. Thomas is problematical. No edition of Pascal's works gives a source for the reference, and the word "incompossibilis" is not a common one in St. Thomas. The *Lexicon of St. Thomas Aquinas*, ed. R. J. Deferrari et al. (Washington, D.C., 1948), s.v., gives no occurrence at all in the *Summa Theologiae*. The word is not used in *S.T.*, I, 23, a. 6. where Pascal's example of a *prédestiné* killed in mortal sin is discussed. But the word does in fact occur in the Leonine and earlier editions of the *S. T.* at Ia-IIae, q. X, a. 4, ad 3um, where the sense of the word is the same, though the application is different. (It is also used in St. Thomas' commentary on Aristotle's *De Caelo*, I, 29, and in the *Quaestiones disputatae: De veritate*, q. 6, a. 3.) It seems unlikely that Pascal had any of these passages at hand while writing. But as he refers to the section on predestination (i.e., *S. T.*, Ia, 23) in the *IIIᵉ Ecrit* (*OC*, p. 979) he had probably read both it and

long as his eyes are good and there is light. Finally, Pascal shows that the Council of Trent has in fact anathematized two contrary errors: that of supposing that a man is able to perform the commandments without a special grace, and that of supposing he cannot perform them with grace.[74] Thus the ability of man to perform the commandments depends absolutely on God's grace, and words like "possible" must be used with this in mind. In other passages this same distinction is made in a slightly different way: it is explained that when the Council says "les commandements sont possibles" they cannot mean that the just have "le pouvoir prochain d'observer les commandements à l'avenir" because that is equivalent to saying they have "le pouvoir prochain d'observer les commandements à l'instant suivant," and this latter is a definition of what is meant by "avoir le pouvoir de persévérer dans la justice," which canon 22 expressly denies.[75] Or again, a "pouvoir prochainement suffisant" is contrasted with a "pouvoir éloigné." [76]

What Pascal saw clearly, then, is this: if the commandments are not impossible to the justified, it is exactly insofar as they are justified, i.e., insofar as they are (as the canon states) "constitués sous la grâce";[77] in this condition they are fully able ("ont le plein pouvoir") to accomplish the commandments. But if, in the next moment, they should cease to be justified (that is, cease to be aided by God's grace), then canon 18 no longer applies and the commandments may very well be impossible to them, or possible for them only in the same way we would say it is possible for a man in chains to run.

Pascal goes on to deal with another attempt to evade this conclusion. It could be argued that the Council says that the justified haven't the ability to persevere without grace, but it

---

the section on the voluntary (*S. T.*, Ia-IIae, qq. 6–10) and remembered the example from the former and the term incompossibilis" from the latter.

74. *OC*, p. 1028; cf. Conc. Trid., sess. VI, cans. 18, 22.

75. *OC*, p. 975; cf. also the second version of this passage, *OC*, p. 1043.

76. *OC*, p. 998.

77. Conc. Trid., sess. VI, can. 18; cf. *OC*, p. 974.

doesn't say anywhere that they may lack this grace; consequently, it is fair to assume that they always have the grace necessary to perform the commandments, and thus the commandments are never impossible. In a rather polemical passage, reminiscent in tone of the *Provinciales,* Pascal shows the "vaine subtilité de leurs raisonnements." Imagine, he says, another party who would say:

Nous nous soumettons au Concile, et anathématisons les Luthériens et tous ceux qui disent qu'on ne peut accomplir les commandements quand on est secouru par la grâce; mais comme le Concile ne fait que défendre la possibilité des commandements, avec la grâce nécessaire pour les observer, sans déclarer qu'elle soit jamais présente, il nous laisse la liberté de dire qu'elle ne l'est jamais, et de soutenir dans cette supposition, sans blesser sa définition, l'impossibilité continuelle des préceptes.[78]

Such an opinion would be considered "extravagante" and yet it has just as solid a basis as the notion that the commandments are always possible. To clinch the argument, Pascal points out that those who have never even heard of the commandments are certainly incapable of performing them; he argues further that justified Christians are more able than the unjustified to do so, as they are free of dominant passions. But, he goes on, citing St. Augustine, even though an eye may be quite healthy, unimpeded, and capable of seeing in one sense, "[il] ne peut voir s'il n'est secouru de la lumière"; so also a man, "quoiqu'il soit parfaitement justifié ne peut vivre dans la piété s'il n'est assisté divinement par la lumière éternelle de la justice." [79] Pascal is led then, in a manner reminiscent of Thomas Aquinas, to describe the varying degrees of grace or divine light that correspond to various uses of the words "possible" and "pouvoir." [80]

In the *IIIᵉ Ecrit*, once Pascal has shown his correspondent

78. *OC*, pp. 1030–31.
79. *OC*, p. 1033; cf. Augustine, *De Natura et gratia*, chap. 26.
80. *OC*, pp. 1034–35.

that the contradiction between the Augustinian doctrine and certain statements of the Fathers and the Councils, and even Scripture, is only an apparent one based on the ambiguities inherent in the word "possible" and its related words, he turns next to the question that most bothers his friend.[81] It is a question that arises naturally out of the preceding problem—and is in a sense identical with it—and concerning which also many statements can be found contradicting the Augustinian doctrine: the question of the "délaissement des justes," that is, whether God forsakes the justified before they have abandoned Him.[82] There are several passages in which Pascal affirms that the reply to this question follows logically from the preceding,[83] but in the *IVe Ecrit* (quoted above, p. 73)[84] he shows that the two questions are really the same.

He shows there that the Council having stated that it is false to say that the justified can persevere in the way of justice without a special grace,[85] and the Gospel assuring us that what we ask will be given, it follows that we cannot persevere even in asking without the special grace of God. But, Pascal continues, "cette question aussi n'est point différente des précédents: Si Dieu ne laisse jamais un juste sans la grâce nécessaire pour prier dans l'instant suivant, sans que ce juste ait auparavant laissé Dieu par quelque péché pour le moins véniel?"[86]

Thus if we maintain with the Council of Trent that God does not abandon the justified man unless He is first abandoned by him, it follows that the justified has the power

81. Apparently the author of the letter to which Pascal is replying has sent a list of quotations to the effect that the commandments are possible: "Certains passages . . . dont votre petit papier est rempli: *Dieu ne commande point des choses impossibles,* et les semblables." This is followed by: "Je viens donc maintenant à la question qui vous touche le plus." *OC*, p. 990; see also p. 995.

82. Cf. Conc. Trid., sess. VI, chap. XI: "Deus namque sua gratia semel iustificatos non deserit, nisi ab eis prius deseratur."

83. E.g., *OC*, pp. 976, 990.

84. *OC*, p. 1043.

85. See Conc. Trid., sess. VI, can. 22.

86. *OC*, p. 1043.

to persevere without any special aid from God, which is directly contrary to the Council.[87] Pascal regards it as logically inevitable that if we accept that the commandments are sometimes impossible to the just, we must accept also that God abandons man before being abandoned by him;[88] apart from a few quotations from St. Augustine and his disciples, and a reference to a recent Jansenist work that treated the matter extensively,[89] he does not devote much effort to proving the latter statement. But the fact remains that such a statement seems once again to be in contradiction to the Council of Trent and various passages from the Fathers and the Scripture. So he must again show that the contradiction is only apparent, and if possible dispel some of the Calvinist harshness that seems implied in the Jansenist position.

This time, however, ordinary language does not yield an easy way out: "abandon" does not seem as rich with possibilities as "possible" was—we don't normally say that someone has abandoned someone and mean it in a limited or conditional way. So Pascal's method here will not be to refer to ordinary usage, but to show that in theological language we do use many words in such a special way. And his demonstration will start at the source of these theological double meanings, namely, Scripture itself. In the *IIe Ecrit*, for example, he juxtaposes two scriptural meanings of the same words applied to the elect and the abandoned:

> *Que les élus de Dieu font une universalité, qui est tantôt*

87. "Car si Dieu ne refuse jamais cette grâce de prier dans l'instant suivant, aux justes qui n'ont pas encore péché, il est visible qu'on peut dire de chaque juste qu'il est en son pouvoir de persévérer à prier, puisque Dieu lui donne toujours la grâce prochainement suffisante pour la prière future, et partant, par les promesses de l'Evangile, il obtiendra toujours l'effet de sa prière. Donc, le pouvoir de persévérer dans la prière, enfermant le pouvoir de persévérer dans la justice, chaque juste a le pouvoir de persévérer dans la justice sans un secours spécial, mais par un secours commun à tous les justes, ce qui est directement contre le concile." *OC*, p. 1044.

88. *OC*, pp. 976–77.

89. L'Abbé de Bourzeïs, *Lettre d'un Abbé à un Président;* see *OC*, p. 991.

appelée monde *parce qu'ils sont répandus dans tout le monde,*
tantôt tous *parce qu'ils font une totalité, tantôt* plusieurs *parce*
qu'ils sont plusieurs entre eux, tantôt peu, parce qu'ils sont peu
à la proportion de la totalité des délaissés;

Que les délaissés font une totalité qui est appelée monde,
tous *et* plusieurs *et* jamais peu.[90]

So when Christ says, "I did not come to judge the world
but to save the world" (John 12:47), he means the elect, but
when he says, "If you were of the world, the world would
love its own, but because you are not of the world . . ." (John
15:19), we must understand "world" to mean the unsaved, the
abandoned. And when St. Paul says, "For there is one God
. . . who gave himself as a ransom for all" (I Timothy 2:5–6),
we read "all the elect," but when he says, "so that all may be
condemned who did not believe the truth" (II Thessalonians
2:12), we read "all the damned." And again, we read "the Son
of man came . . . to give his life as a ransom for many" (Matthew 20:28) and on the other hand, "for many . . . will seek
to enter and will not be able" (Luke 13:24). And finally,
"Many are called but few are chosen" (Matthew 22:14), that
is, the elect are few, but, as Pascal points out, the damned are
never referred to as few.

Further in such statements of St. Paul as: "J'ai travaillé
plus qu'eux tous, non pas moi, mais la grâce qui est avec moi"
(I Corinthians 15:10) and "Je vis, non pas moi, mais Jésus-
Christ en moi" (Galatians 2:20)[91] contradiction is insisted
upon, and it is on statements such as these that Pascal will
build his theory of theological contradiction. So, in reference
to the problem of the "délaissement des justes," Prosper says,
"Dieu ne quitte point si l'on ne le quitte, et il fait bien souvent
qu'on ne le quitte point"; and Pascal analyzes this as follows:
"Donc quand on le quitte, c'est parce qu'il ne fait pas qu'on
ne le quitte pas; c'est parce qu'il ne retient pas; donc il arrive
premièrement que Dieu ne retient pas et ensuite on le

90. *OC*, p. 966; this is part of the passage from the *IIᵉ Ecrit*, which
is translated in Appendix B.

91. *OC*, pp. 949–50, 981–82. The translations are Pascal's.

quitte." [92] And St. Augustine is quoted to the same effect with the following rather astonishing summary:

Il paraît donc que Dieu ne quitte que parce qu'il a été quitté, et que l'homme ne quitte que parce qu'il a été quitté; et qu'ainsi il est absurde de conclure que, dans les sentiments de saint Augustin, Dieu ne quitte jamais le premier, parce qu'il a dit que Dieu ne quitte point le premier; et que l'un et l'autre est ensemble véritable et qu'il quitte, et qu'il ne quitte point le premier, à cause des différentes manières de quitter. [93]

But there are not only different ways of "abandoning"; there are also "deux manières dont l'homme recherche Dieu; deux manières dont Dieu recherche l'homme; . . . deux dont l'homme persévère; deux dont Dieu persévère à lui faire du bien, et ainsi du reste." [94] A single example will clarify all these cases: "La persévérance à prier et à demander simplement les forces dont on se sent dépourvu, est bien différente de la persévérance dans l'usage de ces mêmes forces et dans la pratique des mêmes vertus." [95] In short, there is a perseverance in prayer which is a direct result of God's predestinatory grace, and then there is a perseverance in practice which is a result of the auxiliary grace given us as a result of our prayers. These different "stages" of grace are reminiscent of the Schoolmen, and in fact Pascal refers to St. Thomas (Ia, q. 23, a. 5) in this section; but, as is also true of St. Thomas, the multiplication of these varieties of grace is never used as a means of evading the question of a necessary, predestined grace which first moves the will and precedes all of its subsequent cooperation and even precedes the prevision of merits. We may note also Pascal's reluctance to assign Scholastic labels to these different graces, even though he accepts the distinctions.

But what is the basic distinction Pascal is making here?

92. *OC*, p. 984.
93. *OC*, p. 985; translated in Appendix B.
94. *OC*, p. 977.
95. *OC*, p. 978.

I have spoken of "stages"; in a rough way it would seem that stages in time are implied—whether God forsakes man *first.* But God's grace precedes man's will in a larger sense; a relationship that Pascal discusses several times as the relation of two causes, a first cause, "première dominante et maîtresse," [96] and a second cause, which concurs or cooperates with it. In this he is still following St. Thomas, though his manner of seeing the relationship between them seems new.

The matter is discussed in three separate fragments: in the section on "possibility," which we have already discussed, but also in the *Ier* and *IIIe Ecrits.* In these latter two fragments we can see further evidence of Pascal's linguistic approach and logical subtlety. In the *Ier Ecrit,* a very specific argument is set up: there are two wills, that of God and that of man; one is the cause of the other. Which is it—is God's will the cause of man's, or vice versa? Again the presentation is in terms not of essences or real causes, but of how we talk about such matters: "Si donc on demande pourquoi les hommes sont sauvés ou damnés, on peut en un sens dire que c'est parce que Dieu le veut et en un sens dire que c'est parce que les hommes le veulent." [97] And again:

Il est question de savoir si la volonté de l'homme est la cause de la volonté de Dieu, ou la volonté de Dieu la cause de la volonté de l'homme. Et celle qui sera dominante et maîtresse de l'autre sera considérée comme unique en quelque sorte: non pas qu'elle le soit, mais parce qu'elle enferme le concours de la volonté suivante. Et l'action sera rapportée à cette volonté première et non à l'autre. Ce n'est pas qu'elle ne puisse être aussi en un sens rapportée à la volonté suivante: mais elle l'est proprement à la volonté maîtresse, comme à son principe. Car la volonté suivante est telle qu'on peut dire en un sens que l'action provient d'elle, puisqu'elle y concourt, et en un sens qu'elle n'en provient pas, parce qu'elle n'en est pas l'origine; mais la volonté primitive est telle qu'on peut

96. *OC*, p. 1026.
97. *OC*, p. 948; cf. p. 981.

bien dire d'elle que l'action en provient, mais on ne peut en aucune sorte dire d'elle que l'action n'en provient pas.[98]

This way of putting the problem makes it clear that Pascal is not at all interested in cause as a physical principle, nor in reconciling God as first cause with any physics, Aristotelian, mechanistic, or otherwise: he is interested in squaring our way of speaking about these things with Scripture and the tradition (the passage immediately following these remarks takes up the statements of St. Paul quoted above, p. 90), and showing also its internal consistency. For his first purpose we have seen passages and could find many others in which man's salvation is attributed to man's free will and also to God's will; and we have seen it denied to man's will—"it depends not upon man's will or exertion, but upon God's mercy" (Romans 9:16)—but we will not find it denied anywhere that man's salvation comes from God.

The more important point, however, is the sharp distinction drawn between such concepts as "will," "seek," "abandon," "help," etc., when they are used of God on the one hand, and when they are used of man on the other; or even when they are used of God the Omnipotent, Creator, and Predestinator, as against the case of God the Father, after He has already entered into an interpersonal relationship with man through the mediation of Christ.[99] Man's will, then, in a sense precedes this "second" will of God and is the cause of it, for by the New Covenant, "whatsoever you ask in prayer, you will receive it, if you have faith" (Matthew 21:22): this is the area in which good works and their merit operate, and eternal salvation can be seen as their reward. But the first will of God precedes man's will and includes it in such a way that it causes man's will and all its effects, and is in a sense even the primary cause of those effects; man's will, as also his justice, might be called a metonymy of the Divine will and justice. Pascal quotes St. Augustine to the effect that "on peut dis-

98. *OC*, p. 949; this and the preceding quotation are translated in Appendix B.
99. This is brought out most clearly in the *IIIᵉ Ecrit, OC*, p. 978.

tinguer la foi d'avec les oeuvres comme on distingue dans le royaume des Hébreux Juda d'avec Israël, quoique Juda fût d'Israël." [100] So we commonly distinguish the human will and the Divine will, but the former is really a part or effect of the latter, and is itself a cause only by participation in the primary cause. This explains the words of St. Paul quoted above which Pascal analyzes in two different places,[101] and which apply this principle to life itself and to the Ego: "Je vis, non pas moi, mais Jésus-Christ vit en moi." It is true that we are alive, but only insofar as that life is given us through Jesus Christ; therefore if we attribute life to ourselves alone, we are in error. This ambiguity even of the first personal pronoun is something we shall wish to return to when we look at Pascal's analysis of the "moi." The notion is carried so far as to apply to Christ himself when he says, *"Ce n'est pas moi qui fais les oeuvres, mais le Père qui est en moi,* et néanmoins, il dit ailleurs: *les oeuvres qui j'ai faites"* (John 14:10, 12),[102] where one can see Christ distinguished in his humanity and in his divinity, a distinction of importance for interpreting the fifth of the condemned Jansenist propositions, concerning whether Christ died for all men. For, it can be said that the human Christ died in the intention or with the desire to save all men, although as God he knew that in the ultimate economy of salvation his death would bring salvation only to the elect.

In the discussion of theological problems, then, one must take into account not only the usual ambiguities of language but the special ambiguities inherent in theological statements, which arise ultimately from the mystery of God-in-man in Jesus Christ, and as extended by adoption to God in the men He touches by His grace, or as one might say to the dilemma of natural men with supernatural destinies. Instead of exploiting equivocal passages for one's purposes, one should endeavor to explicate them through reference to unequivocal ones;[103] for "les propositions qui sont contradictoires dans les paroles, ne

100. *OC*, pp. 978–79.
101. *OC*, pp. 949–50, 981–82.
102. *OC*, p. 950.
103. *OC*, p. 980.

le sont pas toujours dans le sens" but may be in fact "liées ensemble par un enchaînement admirable."[104] The rules Pascal gives for determining the exact meaning of propositions drawn from the Church Fathers or from the Councils[105] are of an admirable thoroughness. After examining the terms used in such a proposition, one must then go on to examine what was the Fathers' or Council's object in making such a statement, that is, to what problem or heresy they were addressing themselves and with what intention. One must look at the whole context of any given statement—the evidence they give in its favor as well as the conclusions they draw from it; in other words, one must examine the logical context, to see what meaning follows from the proofs given in support of a proposition, and also whether that meaning justifies the conclusions which in turn are deduced from it. Finally one must refer to other statements of the Fathers and the Councils to see if that meaning is supported or contradicted there.

Such a method, admirable in its rigor, is based on a particular notion about theological propositions and the language in which they are expressed. Clearly, for Pascal, no verbal formula, whether from Scripture or the Church Fathers, by Councils or Popes, has an absolute truth value but must always be understood in terms of its intention and its context—historical as well as textual. This is so not because of any "historical relativism" in the modern sense: the notion that what is true for one age may not be so for another was exactly what Pascal and the other Augustinians of the seventeenth century were combating. The sort of contextualism Pascal advocates is necessary rather because that is the only way in which one can establish the exact meaning of a proposition. The way in which Pascal uses such words as "objet" and "sens" (as when he says, "L'unique objet de l'Ecriture est la charité"[106]) shows that for him all language is "intentional" (in the phenomenological sense), even mathematical language, as the discussion of definitions in the *De l'Esprit géométrique*

104. *OC*, p. 977.
105. See *OC*, pp. 1012–13; cf. also pp. 973, 1038.
106. *Pensées*, Br. 670, *OC*, p. 1274.

shows.[107] Now Pascal makes clear in the *Pensées,* by his analyses of the ambiguities of prophecy and paradox and parable in the Bible, that Scripture, and by extension official doctrines of the Church, have a special object as they also have a special Author. But the revealed truths of Christianity reach us through verbal formulations[108] with all the possibilities for misunderstanding inherent in the nature of human language. Pascal's ideas on the relation between reason and revelation have already been much discussed [109] and are not the main subject of this book; however, the *Ecrits sur la grâce* show us one aspect of that relation which deserves to be emphasized, namely, the linguistic aspect. Actual languages, like theology,

107. *OC,* pp. 576–83. Pascal's refusal to allow any but nominal definitions restricts even geometry to a level of intentional discourse; whatever truth value might be thought to reside in the structure of the method itself is shown by him to depend ultimately on unproved propositions and undefined terms; so even the Q.E.D. of geometry is an affirmation and to be understood in terms of the object or intention of its author, though of course this is much less true of mathematics than of most other forms of human discourse.

108. One must always except, of course, the direct, mystical vision. It is interesting, in that connection, that Pascal's own "mystical" experience of the night of November 23, 1654, was apparently almost immediately put into a verbal formulation (see *OC,* pp. 553–54), and in fact not a single word in the text of the *Mémorial* (except perhaps the enigmatic "FEU") suggests that vision was involved. (Cf. the very interesting discussion of that text by J. Russier, H. Gouhier, and others, in the volume of the Cahiers de Royaumont on *Blaise Pascal, l'homme et l'oeuvre* [Paris, 1956], pp. 225–58, 296–341.)

109. The best work on the subject is of course Mlle Jeanne Russier's *La Foi selon Pascal,* 2 vols. (Paris, 1949). The only fault I find with her otherwise admirable exposition (aside from the questionable use of the *Discours sur les passions de l'amour*) is the tendency to assume that Pascal's Jansenist views on these matters are a direct result of his association with Port-Royal from the time of the writing of the *Provinciales.* Pascal's obvious debt to the *Augustinus* in the *Préface pour le traité du vide* (written at the latest in 1651) seems to me evidence enough that he had worked out his (Jansenist) views on this matter well before his collaboration with the "solitaires de Port-Royal." Moreover, as one reviewer pointed out (J. Dedieu in the *Revue d'histoire littéraire,* LI [1951], 489–91), most of the texts that Mlle Russier compares with those of Pascal date from after his death and may show more his influence on Port-Royal than theirs on him.

96   *Ecrits sur la grâce*

belong with history in a domain to which memory is the appropriate faculty and dogma and authority the appropriate recourse.[110] But the logical analysis of linguistic statements belongs to reason, and it is clear from Pascal's approach to theology in the *Ecrits sur la grâce* that the most important role to which reason can aspire in theological discussion is the logical and linguistic analysis of theological statements. For Pascal, the attempt to prove rationally what are properly articles of faith is an absurdity, a contradiction in terms.[111] But reason can go far toward removing the obscurities and ambiguities inherent in the language through which that faith must express itself, just as in Pascal's apologetic, reason (even mathematical reason) is put to the job of removing the obstacles to faith rather than of attempting to prove even such supposedly demonstrable notions as the existence of God or the immortality of the soul.

Let us finally try to see clearly just where the combination of linguistic analysis with a concise and rhetorically careful exposition of doctrine has got us in these *Ecrits sur la grâce* concerning some of the traditionally problematic aspects of the question of grace and free will. Pascal has managed to put aside certain old arguments on the ground that they are based on verbal misunderstandings, such as the question "Why should God command what is impossible?"—"impossible" is used equivocally here, as he has shown. Or again: "If the divine will is omnipotent, why does God command us at all?" —again, the omnipotent will and the commands of God are on different levels and there is equivocation if they are spoken of on the same level. And, "If we are predestined to salvation, why should we work to merit it?"—as Pascal shows, we are predestined to merit it also.

We have also seen God's justice and mercy preserved each in its place in a doctrine that depends on our recognizing the important difference between the pre-lapsarian and post-lap-

110. Cf. the *Préface pour le traité du vide, OC,* pp. 529–32.

111. At least from the time of the writing of the *Préface pour le traité du vide;* the case is less clear at the time of the conversations with M. de Rebours.

sarian states of man; for following the Fall (which was of course entirely the result of Adam's free will), God could with perfect justice damn all men: that He has chosen to save some is the work of His divine mercy and there is no injustice if He predestines those chosen before they have merited salvation, as in fact Scripture tells us He does. We have seen further that this doctrine is necessarily involved in a linear notion of historical time; the history of a person and of his salvation makes sense only when seen in the light of sacred history—the eternal predestination of souls is expressed through the individual destiny.

We may doubt, however, that Pascal has done much to resolve the old dilemma of the freedom of the will under an infallible, a victorious grace. As we have seen, the "libre arbitre" in Pascal's view contains its own principle of motion; it is nevertheless infallibly determined. It is determined, however, not "from behind" by a God who pushes us against our will, but in a sense from in front, that is, by its object. The theory of the "délectation" of the will comes under discussion in several places in the *Ecrits* and deserves our attention. The best exposition of this theory is found in the *IIIe Ecrit*.[112] There, having proved that in our corrupt state we no longer have the "indifférence prochaine aux opposites" which the Jesuits would claim for us, but which was in fact found only in Adam before the Fall, Pascal goes on to define Adam's state: "Le libéral arbitre d'Adam n'était attiré par aucune concupiscence." Since the Fall, however, "la concupiscence . . . a rendu l'homme esclave de sa délectation," [113] that is to say, "ce qui le délecte davantage l'attire infailliblement." [114] There follows one of the finer paragraphs in the *Ecrits,* typically Pascal and on a level with some of the best passages in the *Provinciales*:

Car qu'y a-t-il de plus clair que cette proposition, que l'on fait toujours ce qui le délecte le plus? Puisque ce n'est autre

112. *OC*, pp. 1002–1006.
113. *OC*, p. 1002.
114. *OC*, p. 1003.

chose que de dire que l'on fait toujours ce qui plaît le mieux, c'est-à-dire que l'on veut toujours ce qui plaît, c'est-à-dire qu'on veut toujours ce que l'on veut, et que dans l'état où est aujourd'hui notre âme réduite, il est inconcevable qu'elle veuille autre chose que ce qu'il lui plaît vouloir, c'est-à-dire ce qui la délecte le plus. Et qu'on ne prétende pas subtiliser en disant que la volonté pour marquer sa puissance, choisira quelquefois ce qui lui plaît le moins; car alors il lui plaira davantage de marquer sa puissance que de vouloir le bien qu'elle quitte, de sorte que, quand elle s'efforce de fuir ce qu'il lui plaît, ce n'est que pour faire ce qu'il lui plaît, étant impossible qu'elle veuille autre chose que ce qu'il lui plaît vouloir.[115]

So, "esclave de la délectation," man's will must follow "infailliblement celle de la chair ou celle de l'esprit, et il n'est délivré d'une de ces dominations que par l'autre." [116] Pascal disposes of any possibility of the "liberté d'indifférence" in our present condition: even if the attractions of flesh and spirit were exactly equal, we should not be free to choose, but rather paralyzed and unable to choose. He develops at length various metaphors involving a man in chains, pulled from two sides, but adds that such metaphors are not accurate, "parce qu'il est impossible de trouver dans la nature aucun exemple, ni aucune comparaison qui convienne parfaitement aux actions de la volonté." [117] The reason, as we might have guessed, is that, while one is being dragged off by a chain, he may well wish to go the other direction, but when the will itself is being infallibly drawn, it is because that is what it wants: that is why it is called a "délectation" rather than simply a force; and the word, as well as the doctrine, comes to Pascal, of course, from Jansenius.

Now, considering these points, as well as those brought out in the *Ier* and *IIe Ecrits* concerning the Fall of Adam, can we arrive at any clearer idea of how Pascal envisages the human will in its present state, and how grace operates on or through

115. *Ibid.;* the whole passage is translated in Appendix B.
116. *Ibid.*
117. *OC,* p. 1005.

it? One essential point that must be emphasized is what it seems proper to call the "intentionality" of the human will since the Fall: to put it simply, "I will . . ." or "I want . . ." and all the related verbs (choose, decide, etc.) require a complement—I want . . . something, I will that . . . something, I choose to do . . . something. In short there is no such thing as pure willing; every act of willing has a content, and that content is what defines it and, in a sense, also defines the subject.

At this point, a comparison with some of the early Fathers might be helpful, in particular with Origen, whose concept of the "phantasia" might seem to coincide with this content of the will. Yet, as we have seen in Chapter I, virtually all these pre-Augustinian Fathers follow Philo in maintaining that God gave man a free will to choose, and, as Origen says, "The rational animal, however, has, in addition to its phantasial nature, also reason, which judges the phantasies and disapproves of some and accepts others." [118] Now Pascal's "délectations" are by no means representations or attractions that we can draw back from and deliberate upon; yet it is not that we are totally incapable of reason or deliberation, but rather that if we do pause to deliberate on a course of action it is because we choose to do so, and if we choose to do so it is because we have already a "délectation" in the use of our reason, that is, it pleases us to use our reason—otherwise we should follow our animal nature. And of course if we do have a "délectation" in the right use of reason, it is because God has given it to us by a "secours special." Now what both Origen and the Jesuits seem to want us to believe is that even the most sensual sinner has at least a glimpse of what is right and therefore when he chooses to follow his fleshly desires he does so freely, having been offered the possibility of choosing good. Pascal finds such a notion not only contrary to St. Augustine but "contraire . . . aux lumières du sens commun," and he goes on to explain:

car comme l'homme change à toute heure et ne peut jamais

118. Origen, *De principiis,* trans. F. Crombie, in the Ante-Nicene Christian Library (Edinburgh, 1869), X, 159.

demeurer en même état, il faudrait qu'à mesure qu'il s'attache
ou détache des choses du monde (ce qu'il est toujours dans son
pouvoir de faire, plus ou moins, quoique non pas entièrement),
il faudrait que cette délectation de la grâce, qui le mettrait
toujours dans ce pouvoir prochain, changeât ainsi à toute heure
pour suivre son inconstance, et (ce qui serait monstrueux à
la grâce) qu'elle augmentât à mesure qu'il s'attache plus au
monde, et qu'elle diminuât sa force à mesure qu'il s'en dé-
tache.[119]

This passage could lead to a misunderstanding of Pascal's position if wrongly interpreted, especially the first parenthetical
remark, which might seem to give to man considerable freedom outside of the action of grace. But the whole passage is an
attempt to show the ridiculous consequences of just such a
notion and should be understood as follows: man is seen to be
very changeable and even to be able at times to detach himself
to some extent from the things of this world; now if one takes
God's grace as being an attraction toward good which is given
all men even as they turn to sin, and which makes their act a
refusal of that good and consequently a free choice, then it follows, first, that this grace is extremely variable, having to
accommodate itself to the variability of man, and, second, that
grace becomes stronger as man is more strongly drawn toward
sin, which is ridiculous. I think that Pascal found the notion
unacceptable on the grounds of common sense because it made
of grace not something acting in the world, but a "phantasy,"
a mere postulate introduced to save a philosophical dogma.
Grace must operate in and through man's will and not be external to it.

But we can conclude further that the "délectation" is not in
any real sense something external to the will. When we want
an apple, or decide to build a fence around our house, our
"délectation" is not the apple or the fence; we could at most
say that it is something we project onto the apple or fence.
"Délectation" then is more akin to appetite or desire,[120] and its

119. *OC,* p. 1006; translated in Appendix B.
120. Cf. the expression "appétit prévenant," *OC,* p. 965.

seat—the "libre arbitre" or "volonté" or "coeur"—is the source of all our actions whether spontaneous or rationalized. And this will is concupiscent, that is, "esclave du péché" and "ne peut pas être délivré de l'esclavage du péché que par une délectation plus puissante qui le rende esclave de la justice"; this is in strong contrast to Adam's pre-lapsarian will, which was "entièrement libre et dégagé";[121] ours is "engagé" and so decidedly so that even grace does not disengage it, but merely draws it irresistibly in the right direction. The will before the Fall, then, had a genuine "liberté d'indifférence" but with the peculiarity that one of the two choices available to it involved the loss of that very liberty. The will since the Fall is a slave to evil or to grace; but it is nevertheless called free, not because it is absolutely free, but because, being "charmé par la concupiscence,"[122] it believes that its felicity lies in evil and so chooses it "volontairement et très librement et avec joie comme l'objet où il sent sa béatitude."[123] In other words we do not choose evil or good "against our will": "on veut ce que l'on veut." Or, to put it another way, "free" is taken as equivalent to "voluntary"; so the will is free by definition.

Perhaps one will find Pascal's definition of the will a mere tautology and hardly worth stating. Here we might apply the same contextual method he applied to the Council of Trent and ask ourselves what conception of the will he is combating. If the will for him is affective and intentional, he must be aiming to contradict conception of the will as rational or nonintentional. Now he doesn't seem particularly concerned with the first in these writings, although his insistence on the primacy of the heart or will over reason in the *Pensées* in fact follows directly from what we see here, and becomes a cornerstone for the projected apology. As for the nonintentional will, we may find it difficult to conceive even of what that would be: pure will or volition, exalted for its own sake, perhaps, or in other words, the will as power. That this tendency to exalt the will as power was current at the time and indeed was part of a

121. *OC*, p. 1002.
122. *OC*, p. 965.
123. *OC*, p. 966.

larger current descending from Duns Scotus and pervading not only the Jesuits but much of the spirituality of the Counter-Reformation, this has already been discussed and hardly needs to be insisted upon. And in fact this is exactly what Pascal devotes passage after passage to denouncing: the notion that free will implies power; and he shows that in marking its power, the will is doing nothing really but marking its impotence to be anything other than what it is, namely an enslaved appetite. As to the way in which grace actually operates in and through the will, Pascal is apt to turn to similes (or "figures" as Professor Mesnard calls them[124]), the most significant of which is the Incarnation itself. Allusion is also made to the Eucharist:[125] the Calvinists' denial of the Real Presence of Christ in the Eucharist is akin to their inability to allow both grace and freedom to reside together in the will.

Finally, the will, like language, being what I like to call "intentional," one can see certain similarities between them. For, just as divine Truth must be expressed in languages, which are in a sense corrupt, subject to decay, full of ambiguities, so God's grace must find expression through human wills; even if Pascal's Jansenist views seem rather severely to limit the freedom of the will, they do not detract from either its importance or dignity.

Finally, we have not so far seen much to satisfy that old moral argument which has many forms, but which is probably best known to us today from the Erasmus-Luther controversy. Roughly it is this: perhaps one can make a good logical and theological case for predestination, but isn't such a doctrine the ruin of the moral life? Not only can the individual justify past sins on the ground they were predestined, but it will seem futile for him to strive in the future as nothing he can do will change his destiny. Now this kind of argument is in part a sophism, as was seen by St. Augustine when similar points were presented to him by the monks of Hadrumetum. When

124. J. Mesnard, "L'Invention chez Pascal," in *Pascal présent*, Conférences prononcées à Clermont-Ferrand au Tricentenaire de la Mort de Pascal (Clermont-Ferrand, 1962), pp. 39–58.

125. *OC*, p. 958.

Augustine is asked, "What is the use of reprimands, exhortations, etc., if all is predestined?" his answer is that if the sinner takes the reprimand to heart and is converted to God then its usefulness is obvious, even though his heart had also to be touched by grace.[126] So if one wishes it otherwise, one presumably wants one's reprimands or exhortations to be effective independently of God's grace, in other words, one wants to be independent of God and equal to Him, which, as Pascal says, was exactly Adam's sin. A similar principle can be applied to such a question as "Why should I be blamed for my sins?" This question really turns out to mean "Don't remind me or accuse me of my sins." And the person who says it is in fact actively resisting recognizing his own sinfulness, and so is resisting God's grace.[127] One could go on to say that when dealing with a thoroughgoing predestination like Augustine's, the argument from morality (à la Erasmus) is completely invalid. Questions such as "Why exert myself?" are only further instances of the predestined response, and really mean "I don't wish to exert myself," or in other words are simply a sophistical expression of the lack of grace. One might even argue in a general way that when any thorough determinism, psychic or physical, is involved, if one assumes that an abstract solution to the problem is possible, one is also presupposing the possibility of getting outside the determinism, for otherwise one would have to assume that the solution was itself predetermined; and yet to make this assumption is to prejudice the solution in advance. Thus the problem cannot even be posed in a purely rational context without paradox.

But Pascal makes other points on the moral implications of the Augustinian doctrine. The main point, on which he insists in several passages, is that the discernment of the elect from the damned, when all have merited damnation, "n'est pour aucune raison qui puisse nous être connue, puisque c'est par un jugement occulte; ce qui est d'une si grande force, que je vous le laisse à exagérer."[128] This is especially important in dis-

126. *De Correptione et gratia*, VI, 9; *BA*, XXIV, 287.
127. *Ibid.*, V, 7; *BA*, XXIV, 279.
128. *OC*, p. 992; cf. p. 966.

tinguishing the Augustinians from the Calvinists, for the latter believe that the elect are saved once for all, "indubitablement, infailliblement," and that the damned are damned in the same manner, which Pascal calls a cruel and insupportable doctrine.[129] But for the Augustinians, not only are the reasons for the judgment hidden (which the Calvinists admit), but the judgment itself is also. That is, one never knows even to the very end whether one is among the elect or not, and so:

tous les hommes du monde sont obligés sur peine de damnation éternelle et de péché contre le S. Esprit irrémissible en ce monde et en l'autre de croire qu'ils sont de ce petit nombre d'Elus pour le salut desquels J.-C. est mort et d'avoir la même pensée de chacun des hommes qui vivent sur la terre quelque méchans et impies qu'ils soient, tant qu'il leur reste un moment de vie, laissant dans le secret impénétrable de Dieu le discernement des Elus d'avec les réprouvés.[130]

Pascal is obviously aiming at (his understanding of) Calvinism here and laying waste to the separation of faith and works, the despair of those who think themselves damned, the self-righteousness of the elect, and in short all the moral hypocrisy that goes with such a doctrine. But this same moral doctrine is turned against the Jesuits. For Pascal shows that if one actually had the certain and continual power to perform the commandments and so to persevere to the end, why should one be told to believe or to fear? "Work out your own salvation with fear and trembling," says St. Paul (Philippians 2:12), and it is only silly to say one is afraid that one will not persevere to the end when one has this power to do so. Further,

leur crainte ne serait pas seulement détruite, mais leur espéance, car puisqu'on n'espère pas des choses certaines, ils n'espé-

129. *OC*, pp. 951, 956, 970.
130. Cited from Lafuma's text in *Deux pièces imparfaites sur la grâce et le concile de Trente*, p. 31; cf. *OC*, p. 954. I have quoted the earlier version on the theory that the additions and corrections represented by Chevalier's text may possibly not be by Pascal. The passage is translated in Appendix B.

reront pas la continuation de ce secours puisqu'il leur est certain. . . . Quel sera donc l'objet de leur espérance, sinon euxmêmes, desquels ils espéreront le bon usage d'un pouvoir qui leur est assuré? [131]

So both a holy fear and Christian hope depend on ignorance of our election: ". . . tous doivent être dans la crainte, puisqu'il n'y a point de justes qui ne puissent à toute heure tomber; comme il n'y a point de pécheur qui ne puisse à toute heure être relevé, la grâce de prier pouvant toujours être ôtée et donnée." [132] The same reasoning is shown to hold for humility, and for poverty of spirit. [133] So the doctrine that was supposed to be the ruin of the moral life is shown to be the only sound foundation for the Christian virtues of faith and fear, hope and humility.

Many, of course, have felt that such a doctrine of grace still somehow destroys a freedom which we feel is, or ought to be ours. Does such a doctrine supply a basis not only for hope and fear but for effective human action? Clearly it did for Pascal, who not only undertook various scientific and practical projects even to the end of his life, but devoted his main efforts to the writing of an apology, which some have thought particularly paradoxical as it attempts to be effective in the very area of salvation where God's power is most certainly sovereign. [134] The arguments just cited show that there is no contradiction involved. It seems even that Pascal's unmistakable enthusiasm for his project was based on his precise knowledge of its limitations; his great discovery—especially apparent in the so-called wager—was a way of writing about our human choice without going outside the determined human situation in which that choice has to be made. So one could say that his theology, so far from turning him away

131. *OC*, p. 1007; translated in Appendix B.
132. *OC*, p. 1011.
133. *OC*, pp. 1006, 1011–12.
134. J. H. Broome, for example, goes to some trouble to reconcile what are for him apparently contradictory positions; see his *Pascal*, pp. 94, 141–42.

from the project of an apology, actually suggested the form it would take. But that is a matter for discussion in a later chapter when we take up the notes for that apology, which we nowadays call the *Pensées*.

Chapter III   The *Lettres provinciales*
                and Shorter Works

Having analyzed and assessed Pascal's theology in the *Ecrits sur la grâce*—writings whose primary purpose was to set forth that theology—we are now in a better position to inspect the role of theology in works written for other purposes. In this chapter and the next we shall look at these other works. Our aim will be twofold: to see what role Pascal's theology of grace plays in the development of his ideas; and to see also what light these developments shed on his understanding of the theological problems. We shall not need to concern ourselves with other influences, such as the polemical or apologetical background, or the social-intellectual context so brilliantly analyzed by M. Paul Bénichou;[1] not, of course, that these aspects are unimportant, but simply because we are looking for something different. So, when I discuss a tirade against "l'honneur" in the *Provinciales*, or statements about the "moi" in the *Pensées,* it will be understood that Pascal's views on these subjects were partly defined and motivated by his position in the society of his time; but I shall also assume that there are at least "two sources of morality and religion," and that Pascal's basic attitudes are part of a vision, the most profound expression of which had to be theological. His psychology and anthropology will be seen to be, in the traditional way, part of his theology, and I shall not attempt to explain his theology in psychological or sociological terms, but rather to explain his various comments on man and society in theological terms. This may seem a peculiar bias, but it is also quite clearly that of Pascal himself.

1. *Morales du grand siècle* (Paris, 1948).

Before turning to the *Lettres provinciales,* and in the next chapter to the *Pensées,* let us look first at some of Pascal's shorter works and at his correspondence. Some of these works[2] will naturally not offer any great interest from our point of view. The *Trois discours sur la condition des grands,* for example, relates to some of the *Pensées,* but not in any direct way to the problem of grace and free will. Also the *Comparaison des Chrétiens des premiers temps avec ceux d'aujourd'hui,* although it shows Pascal's concern with the reform of the Church, has only a distant relationship with the theology of grace. Already more interesting for our purposes is the eloquent *Prière pour demander à Dieu le bon usage des maladies.* The concurrence of freedom and necessity operating in the will for instance is invoked: "Oh! qu'heureux sont ceux qui avec une liberté entière et une pente invincible de leur volonté aiment parfaitement et librement ce qu'ils sont obligés d'aimer nécessairement."[3] And the necessity for God's grace to make the initial movement toward faith gives the following passage the paradoxical twist which seems so characteristic of Pascal:

bien loin de prétendre que mes prières aient du mérite qui vous oblige de les accorder de nécessité, je reconnais très humblement . . . [que] je ne puis attendre aucune grâce que de votre miséricorde, puisque . . . tous les mouvements naturels de mon coeur, se portant vers les créatures ou vers moi-même, ne peuvent que vous irriter. Je vous rends donc grâces, mon Dieu, des bons mouvements que vous me donnez, et de celui même que vous me donnez de vous en rendre grâces.[4]

2. I shall not devote any attention to the *Discours sur les passions de l'amour,* as it seems to me fairly certain it is not by Pascal. Without entering into the details of the controversy on this problem, I should say that the presence of undeniably Pascalian "pensées" in that work is far more plausibly explained by supposing it to emanate from a *salon* at which Pascal put forth his ideas, or more simply that it was written after the publication of the *Pensées* and made use of them, than to suppose such a frivolous hodgepodge—which resembles nothing else in his entire *oeuvre*—could have been written by Pascal.

3. *OC,* p. 609.

4. *Ibid.*

And the problem of the perseverance of the just is alluded to when Pascal speaks of the duty of the Christian to "faire pénitence des fautes qui se commettent tous les jours, et qui même sont ordinaires aux plus justes, de sorte que leur vie doit être une pénitence continuelle sans laquelle ils sont en danger de déchoir de leur justice."[5] All this is very straightforward and demands no further commentary, except perhaps to note that here already we can see that the Augustinian theology of grace, however arid or schematic it may seem to some, was the source for Pascal of the most profound meditations and fervent prayers.

Two of Pascal's shorter works show his direct use of Jansenius' writings. In the *Préface pour le traité du vide*, Pascal uses notions about theology and science, reason and revelation, which he undoubtedly derived from Jansenius' *Augustinus*, and which we have already discussed in the preceding chapter. The *Abrégé de la vie de Jésus-Christ* is also based on a work of Jansenius in Latin,[6] and amounts to little more than a selection and translation from that work. It was probably done as a spiritual exercise of a kind practiced at Port-Royal; its main merit is in its conciseness and in the elegance of the translations from the Vulgate.

Turning to Pascal's correspondence, we find a particularly valuable source for our purposes in the spiritual letters he wrote to his sister Gilberte and to Mlle de Roannez. In these two cases, Pascal evidently took on himself the role of spiritual director—just as his sister Jacqueline acted as his director in the crisis of 1654.[7] These letters, then, are uniquely valuable in showing us Pascal's conception of the Christian life, a concep-

5. *OC*, p. 610.

6. The *Tetrateuchus, sive commentarius in Sancta Jesu Christi Evangelia*, 4 vols. (Paris, 1643). The *Abrégé* is modeled on the "Series vitae" section.

7. Cf. J. Mesnard, *Pascal et les Roannez* (Paris, 1965), I, 504–506. It should be noted that in this discussion I use the terms "first conversion" and "second conversion" to refer to the changes in Pascal's religious life that occurred in 1646 and 1654 respectively. I hope my use of these traditional terms will not prejudice the reader's understanding of the significance I wish to attach to these periods in Pascal's life.

tion which is often lost sight of by interpreters of the *Pensées*
and the *Lettres provinciales*. One outstanding fact about them
is the almost total lack of moralism;[8] this lack of moralism is
particularly important to note given the tendency to equate
Jansenism and moral rigor. The letters are based on, and
recommend rather a spiritual doctrine which is essentially that
of Port-Royal: the principles of the direction of souls are those
of Saint-Cyran and Singlin, and the theology of grace is that
of Augustine as understood by Jansenius. It is also most clear
in the correspondence that Pascal adopted this doctrine fully
from the time of his first conversion; the letters to his sister
Gilberte from as early as 1648 do not differ in doctrine from
the letters to Mlle de Roannez written in 1656.

To bring out certain themes in these letters which most
directly relate to the theology of grace, let us go back first to
the state of Adam before the Fall. In the beautiful letter on
the death of his father, there is a passage which forms a bridge
between the theology of the *Ecrits sur la grâce* and certain of
the *Pensées:*

*Dieu a créé l'homme avec deux amours, l'un pour Dieu, l'autre
pour soi-même; mais avec cette loi, que l'amour pour Dieu
serait infini, c'est-à-dire sans aucune fin que Dieu même, et que
l'amour pour soi-même serait fini et rapportant à Dieu.*

*L'homme en cet état non seulement s'aimait sans péché, mais
ne pouvait pas ne point s'aimer sans péché.*

*Depuis, le péché étant arrivé, l'homme a perdu le premier de
ces amours; et l'amour pour soi-même étant resté seul dans
cette grande âme capable d'un amour infini, cet amour-propre
s'est étendu et débordé dans le vide que l'amour de Dieu a
quitté; et ainsi il s'est aimé seul, et toutes choses pour soi, c'est-
à-dire infiniment.*

Voila l'origine de l'amour-propre.[9]

And there also is the essence of Pascal's understanding of the

8. *Ibid.*, p. 538.
9. *OC*, p. 496. The ideas here are of course Augustinian in origin, by
way of Jansenius.

human condition; as he says in the same passage, what was just and natural for Adam in his innocence has become immoderate and criminal in our present state and this is the origin of all our sins and vices.

The question then is how to escape from this predicament and focus our love on God instead of ourselves. The theory of the "délectation" is invoked just as in the *Ecrits sur la grâce*, for the reason that "on ne quitte les plaisirs que pour d'autres plus grands."[10] In the letters to Mlle de Roannez, however, we see the theory of the "délectation" used not in order to resolve the dilemma posed by grace and free will, but to point to the very real "délectation" of the Christian life. He emphasizes the joy of the Christian life, the many satisfactions that accompany a life of piety, the "lumière éclatante" that enlightens everything once one has turned toward God.[11] There is nothing here of any supposed Jansenist pessimism. But at the same time, the joy of the Christian can never in this world be unmixed: "Les Chrétiens ont cette joie mêleé da la tristesse d'avoir suivi d'autres plaisirs, et de la crainte de la perdre par l'attrait de ces autres plaisirs qui nous tentent sans relâche."[12] And the reason that one must fear losing that joy is because, as we saw in the *Ecrits sur la grâce*, God may at any time withdraw His grace, abandoning us to our sinful desires. This continuous flow of grace which can always be cut off is described by Pascal as follows:

Ainsi la continuation de la justice des fidèles n'est autre chose que la continuation de l'infusion de la grâce, et non pas une seule grace qui subsiste toujours; et c'est ce qui nous apprend parfaitement la dépendence perpétuelle où nous sommes de la miséricorde de Dieu, puisque, s'il en interrompt tant soit peu

10. *OC*, p. 515; cf. p. 507. Mesnard has pointed out that the same text from St. Augustine is used in the letter to Mlle de Roannez as in the *Ecrits sur la grâce*; see his *Pascal et les Roannez*, I, 513–18.

11. In the seventh letter to Mlle de Roannez, *OC*, pp. 515–16.

12. *Ibid*. This mixture of joy and sadness is developed in the letter on the death of his father, *OC*, pp. 594–99. Cf. also the "créance mêlée de crainte" of the *Ier Ecrit sur la grâce*, *OC*, p. 954.

le cours, la sécheresse survient nécessairement. Dans cette né-cessité, il est aisé de voir qu'il faut continuellement faire de nouveaux efforts pour acquérir cette nouveauté continuelle d'esprit, puisqu'on ne peut conserver la grâce ancienne que par l'acquisition d'une nouvelle grâce, et qu'autrement on perdra celle qu'on pensera retenir, comme ceux qui, voulant renfermer la lumière, n'enferment que des ténèbres.[13]

This necessity for continuous striving means that the Christian in his spiritual life cannot be satisfied with a limited perfection, as Pascal says later in the same letter, but must take very seriously the commandment of Christ to be perfect as his Father in Heaven is perfect.[14] But this striving of the Christian for perfection in the spiritual life is the very opposite of ordinary ambition, which looks to future accomplishments. For it is this same fluid and ever-present nature of grace that undoubtedly determined another of the notions Pascal puts forward in the letters to Mlle de Roannez: that of the necessity of living in the present, an idea that will be echoed in the *Pensées*. "Le présent est le seul temps qui est véritablement à nous, et dont nous devons user selon Dieu," writes Pascal; "cependant le monde est si inquiet, qu'on ne pense presque

13. From a letter to Gilberte in 1648, *OC*, p. 498. Cf. a similar passage from the sixth letter to Mlle de Roannez, *OC*, p. 514: "Car c'est un flux continuel de grâces que l'Écriture compare à un fleuve et à la lumière que le soleil envoie incessamment hors de soi, et qui est toujours nouvelle, en sorte que, s'il cessait un instant d'en envoyer, toute celle qu'on aurait reçue disparaîtrait et on resterait dans l'obscurité." Marcel Raymond has pointed out the relation between the doctrine of grace in the letters to Mlle de Roannez and the texts of the *Mémorial* and the *Mystère de Jésus* ("La Conversion de Pascal," *Revue de théologie et de philosophie*, 1963, no. 1, pp. 24–40; see especially pp. 29–30); what I should like to emphasize is the continuity of the doctrine from the time of the first conversion as evidenced by the passage from the letter of 1648. The dependence of Pascal's letters to Gilberte on the *Lettres chrétiennes et spirituelles* of Saint-Cyran has been sufficiently documented by Sister Marie-Louise Hubert, *Pascal's Unfinished Apology* (New Haven, 1952), pp. 38–40.

14. *OC*, pp. 485–86.

jamais à la vie présente et à l'instant où l'on vit; mais à celui où l'on vivra."[15] And here once again the correspondence bridges a gap between the theology of the writings on grace and the analyses of man's condition in the *Pensées*: the whole meditation on "divertissement" is based on this notion of man's inability to live in the present.

Another theological theme related to these is that of the *Deus absconditus,* to which most of the fourth letter to Mlle de Roannez is devoted.[16] This letter makes it plain how wrong it is to interpret Pascal's notion of the hidden God as being equivalent to an absent God.[17] Pascal does insist here

15. *OC,* p. 517.

16. *OC,* pp. 509–11. The best commentary on this letter and related texts is that of Henri Gouhier in his *Blaise Pascal: Commentaires* (Paris, 1966), chap. IV; I have drawn on his remarks in this discussion.

17. It is M. Lucien Goldmann in his *Le Dieu caché* who is most notoriously guilty of this error. In a way that is characteristic of his method, Goldmann develops a whole theory of a "Dieu toujours absent et toujours présent" from one enigmatic "pensée" (Br. 599; *OC,* p. 1282; see Goldmann, pp. 45 ff.), and never refers to the letter to Mlle de Roannez in which Pascal's notions on the "Dieu caché" are clearly developed and explained. Of course, M. Goldmann justifies such a procedure (which is actually in violation of his own announced method of totalization and integration) by postulating a radical break in Pascal's views around 1657 (see his chap. VIII). But the historical evidence for such a break is feeble in the extreme, and without such evidence Goldmann's argument becomes entirely circular: there *must* be such a rupture, he argues, because the *Provinciales* are "rationalist," while the *Pensées* are the first example of "la philosophie tragique"; on the other hand, it is only by postulating such a rupture—a rupture so severe as to require us to interpret the *Pensées* with reference to Marx, Engels, and Lukacs, instead of in the context of the author's other works—that Goldmann can proceed to analyze the *Pensées* so as to make them out to be an expression of "philosophie tragique." M. Goldmann should perhaps be excused on the grounds that he is a sociologist and not trained in the careful reading of texts; his work certainly abounds in misreadings, many of which have already been pointed out, e.g. by A. Blanchet, "Pascal est-il le précurseur de Marx?" *Etudes,* no. 292 (March 1957), pp. 321–37; L. Lafuma and Julien Eymard d'Angers, "A propos d'une thèse marxiste sur Pascal," *Etudes franciscaines,* VII (N. S. 17, Dec. 1956), 172–88; and in the discussion of Goldmann's "Le pari est-il écrit pour le libertin?" in *Blaise Pascal,* Cahiers de Royaumont, Vol. I (Paris, 1956).

that God must be hidden from most men most of the time if
faith is to have any meaning; but he goes on to enumerate the

---

There is one misreading, however, that underlies Goldmann's whole
thesis on the "Dieu caché" and Jansenist ideology which I have not
seen pointed out elsewhere: it is his reading of the word "monde" (see
the article just cited, also *Le Dieu caché,* and his introduction to the
Correspondance de Martin de Barcos). To simplify greatly Goldmann's
thesis, there are three positions involved: that of Arnauld and Nicole,
which defended at least some actions in the "world"; that of Barcos,
which called for a complete renunciation of the "world"; and that of
Pascal, uniting the two into a "refus intramondain du monde." Yet
this whole analysis is based on an equivocal use of the word "monde,"
of which Pascal was, incidentally, aware (see above, p. 90). The
meaning of "the world" in this spiritual tradition is not of course the
world in its totality, including social and intellectual activity; it is the
world in the scriptural sense—the world which Christ came to save and
which knew him not; and for Augustinians, that world is defined as
the world of concupiscence. Conversion of course involved turning
away from this world of concupiscence to the world of grace, but this
turning away took place in the heart: it did not consist in the act of
withdrawal from society; so on the need to renounce the world in this
sense, all Jansenists (if not indeed all Christians) would be in agreement. There remains the question of the subsequent attitude toward
society and the value of action in society. Barcos obviously saw the
world in this sense as a more futile and dangerous place than did the
others, and advocated withdrawal from the world in the sense of
removing oneself from normal society; but even such an act of withdrawal is itself a social act with implications not only for the individual
but also for the society as a whole. So there is no such thing as complete withdrawal from social action—what is involved is in fact withdrawal simply from those forms of society in which concupiscence
seems to be the governing force. In any case, all this is ultimately a
question of spiritual direction, not of basic theology. There were
various degrees of "retraite" at Port-Royal, from the "religieuses"
through the "solitaires" to such informal associations as those of Pascal
and the Duc de Luynes. But to call Pascal's renunciation of the world
and his continuation of social and intellectual activities in the world a
paradoxical or tragical "refus intramondain du monde" is, as Pascal
would say, "se jouer des mots"; it would be so only if the world of
concupiscence were identical with the world of grace, if the world of
the damned were coextensive with the world of the elect, which for an
Augustinian is definitely not the case. Unfortunately, a great deal of
M. Goldmann's analysis of Jansenism seems to rest on this point, which
is based finally on pure equivocation.

many ways in which God manifests Himself. The point of departure for the whole discussion is a recent miracle, in which God has precisely shown Himself to "those whom He wishes to engage in His service." Then going back over Sacred History, Pascal shows how, before Christ, God was first hidden in nature, accessible only to those few pagans capable of discovering an "invisible God in visible nature." He was also hidden in Scripture: hidden to those who could see only the literal sense, but available to those capable of seeing the mystical sense. Then He became visible in the Incarnation, but because of His humanity in Christ still unrecognizable to the bulk of mankind. And finally—greatest mystery of all—He is still visible (and hidden) in the bread of the Eucharist, a revelation so obscure that only the orthodox Catholic tradition has succeeded in sustaining it against the heretics. But in all these ways, God has appeared in history and continues to be visible to those capable of seeing Him.

Underlying this whole theory of the Hidden God (or as Pascal often puts it, the "Dieu qui se cache") is of course the doctrine of predestination; God, perfectly visible to Adam, hides Himself from Adam's descendants with perfect justice because of Adam's sin; out of pure mercy, however, He gives some men the grace to discover Him. These latter, the elect, see God everywhere, for, as Pascal says, in a letter of 1648, "les choses corporelles ne sont qu'une image des spirituelles." [18]

This attitude in turn leads to the perhaps more surprising affirmation that when God shows us His will through the course of events, it is a sin not to be reconciled to it,[19] or as Pascal puts it yet more strongly in the *Mystère de Jésus,* "Si Dieu nous donnait des maîtres de sa main, oh! qu'il leur faudrait obéir de bon coeur! La nécessité et les événements en sont infailliblement." [20] This same attitude is extended in an eloquent letter dating probably from 1661 in which submission to events is carried to the point where even in the fight for truth we must not expect the triumph of truth, but rather must

18. *OC,* p. 484.
19. Third letter to Mlle de Roannez, *OC,* p. 508.
20. *OC,* p. 1313.

recognize that the forces opposed to the truth have been permitted by God's justice, and so the real sign that we are on the side of Truth will be a lack of the desire to triumph, and the presence of peace of mind and soul even in the face of opposition and defeat.[21]

Such is the doctrine that one can extract from Pascal's correspondence. It is a truly spiritual doctrine, emphasizing always spiritual attitudes rather than moral rules or actions. It enjoins essentially a kind of alert serenity, attentive always to the present (for God is present to us only in the present) and to events (which are the direct expression of God's will) but aware also of our radical dependence on God, a dependence which means that our position is always to some extent precarious, and that we must strive for our salvation diligently, but which also means that our salvation is ultimately in the hands of God and so our striving must be without anxiety, marked by peace and joy.[22] Commentators have found varying degrees of mysticism in this doctrine,[23] but it also quite evi-

21. *OC*, pp. 524–26.
22. This doctrine as it is found in the letters to Mlle de Roannez is excellently analyzed by Jean Mesnard in his *Pascal et les Roannez,* I, 541–44. I might note here, however, what I take to be a misreading of a passage from the letter on the "Dieu caché." The sentence in the letter is as follows: "Cet étrange secret, dans lequel Dieu s'est retiré, impénétrable à la vue des hommes, est une grande leçon pour nous porter à la solitude loin de la vue des hommes" (*OC,* p. 510). Mesnard takes this to mean "Dieu, se cachant loin des hommes, il se trouve plus aisément dans la retraite" (*Pascal et les Roannez,* I, 532–34). However, the syntax and the use of the word "leçon" seem to me to indicate that Pascal means rather that since God saw fit to hide Himself from men's sight, let us imitate Him and do likewise. This mode of seeking a motive for imitation in every action of God was a common spiritual exercise in the period (cf. for example Jacqueline's *Mystère de Jésus,* GE, II, 447–73). The "leçon" which Pascal means for Mlle de Roannez to draw is something akin to Christ's commandment to pray in secret rather than with ostentation, to withdraw, as Christ did even from his disciples, for the purpose of prayer; this interpretation, of course, makes the passage less than ever an injunction to Mlle de Roannez to hasten to the cloister.
23. See the excellent discussion by Gouhier in his *Blaise Pascal: Commentaires,* pp. 49 ff. Cf. also his earlier essay on the subject and

dently depends in all its essentials on the Augustinian theology of grace which Pascal adopted. And just as Pascal did not alter his adherence to that theology from his first conversion to his death, so the letters from 1648 to 1661 give us a remarkably consistent spiritual doctrine.

One other group of texts deserves our attention prior to a discussion of the *Lettres provinciales*: the writings that surround the so-called second conversion of Pascal. The *Mémorial*, the *Ecrit sur la conversion du pécheur*, the *Entretien avec M. de Saci*, and the *Mystère de Jésus* would all seem to be relevant to this event and call for interpretation. These texts have all been well studied, and there is no need to comment on them in detail. But there is one theme that recurs in all but the *Entretien* which derives directly from the theology of grace: that is the notion of separation, or abandonment by God. As Marcel Raymond has pointed out, the idea of separation from God recurs no less than six times in the very short text of the *Mémorial*.[24] And the *Mystère de Jésus* has Christ "délaissé seul à la colère de Dieu," suffering "cette peine et cet abandon dans l'horreur de la nuit," and again "au milieu de ce délaissement universel."[25] This text probably dates from fairly soon after the experience of November 23, 1654, of which the *Mémorial* is a record, in a period when Pascal was still without a spiritual director, still seeking the way to "conserve" (as the *Mémorial* shows) the grace received. In it the agony of Christ is—like the anguish of Pascal—one of abandonment, an anxiety of separation. The eminent psychiatrist, Dr. Charles Baudouin, in a very interesting study,[26] has shown quite convincingly how Pascal suffered from the early death

the discussion of it in the Cahiers de Royaumont volume on Pascal, pp. 296–341; cf. also Mesnard, *Pascal et les Roannez*, I, 542 ff.

24. See "La Conversion de Pascal," *Revue de théologie et de philosophie*, 1963, no. 1, pp. 24–40.

25. Br. 553; *OC*, pp. 1312–13. As will be seen, I accept Raymond's arguments for dating this text (and Br. 555) in early 1655, while Pascal was still seeking a director, that is, before he met M. de Sacy.

26. *Blaise Pascal, ou l'ordre du coeur* (Paris, 1962).

of his mother, and to what a great extent his anxieties turn around this notion of separation (his opposition to Jacqueline's entry into Port-Royal is a repetition of this anxiety), and how his passion for salvation can be seen as a search for his lost mother. But Dr. Baudouin also cautions against any notion that this "explains" Pascal. And it is striking that an equally acute psychoanalyst, Louis Beirnaert, has shown the same separation anxiety in the conversion of Ignatius of Loyola.[27] As Dr. Beirnaert makes clear, the anxiety and fear of separation in such a state are usually accompanied by an obsession with the Law, the Pact that will guarantee that the mysterious (maternal) presence will not be withdrawn; as long as one remains in this state, the "conversion" is incomplete, for such an attitude is still a refusal to "enter into history." St. Ignatius passed through this state and found his freedom and his historical vocation in a broad acceptance of the world, and in a humanism strongly colored by a military and heroic ideal. How Pascal emerged from a similar state into a position so apparently opposed to this ideal is matter for speculation.

What seems clear to me is that the night of November 23, 1654, although an important event for his ultimate spiritual position, was not in fact the moment of his conversion: his true conversion came afterward—after a period of intense seeking (of which the *Mystère de Jésus* seems a particularly vivid and intimate expression). For one thing, the experience of the *Mémorial* did not fall into a vacuum; Pascal was already committed to a theology and a spiritual tradition, and the *nuit de feu* had somehow to be understood in the light of this tradition. This was not so easy as it might seem. One is aware at once that the concern with "conserving" rather than renewing a grace received, expressed in the *Mémorial,* is quite opposed to that tradition, and, as we have already seen, to Pascal's own opinions as expressed in letters in 1648 and again in 1656. Also, the word "certitude," repeated in the *Mémorial,* has

<hr>

27. "L'Expérience fondamentale d'Ignace de Loyola et l'expérience psychanalytique," *La Psychanalyse,* III (1957), 111–37 (reprinted in the author's *Expérience chrétienne et psychologie* [Paris, 1965]); cf. also Ernest Jovy, *Pascal et saint Ignace* (Paris, 1923).

already been singled out as peculiar for its intellectual connotations,[28] but it is also suspect theologically: certitude is exactly what Pascal in the *Ecrits sur la grâce* reproaches the Calvinists with thinking they possess, and is there said to be opposed to the true Christian faith and hope. If the *Ecrit sur la conversion du pécheur* is indeed by Pascal,[29] it seems to me to belong to

28. See Raymond, "La Conversion de Pascal," p. 28.

29. The attribution of the *Ecrit sur la conversion du pécheur* to Pascal remains problematic. The GE (X, 419 ff.) attributes it to Blaise or Jacqueline Pascal, and remains skeptical of evidence attributing it to the former. But Mesnard, in the "Introduction générale" to Vol. I of his edition of the *Oeuvres complètes* (Paris, 1964) seems to have eliminated the obstacles to this attribution as far as questions concerning the MSS are involved (see esp. pp. 102–103); however, the most that can be claimed from his evidence is that Louis Périer probably *thought* it was by Blaise Pascal. The main argument usually given in favor of the attribution to Pascal is that the *Ecrit* describes Pascal's condition at the time of the second conversion as we know it from a letter by Jacqueline of January 25, 1655 (cited, e.g., by Mesnard, *Pascal et les Roannez*, I, 394, who adds: "Or, le même état d'âme est analysé dans l'*Ecrit sur la conversion du pécheur*, dont l'attribution à Pascal s'impose"). However, there is another, more obvious explanation possible for this resemblance: that the *Ecrit* is also by Jacqueline. If the *Ecrit* in fact describes Jacqueline's conception of the state of a soul in process of conversion, it is natural that she would describe her brother's conversion in the same terms. One can ask further whether the *Ecrit* does really describe Pascal's state. "Car encore qu'elle ne sente pas ces charmes dont Dieu récompense l'habitude dans la piété . . ." (*OC*, p. 550) may describe the soul of Pascal before the first conversion, but surely not before the second. And how can the slowly growing conviction concerning the "véritable bien" described in the *Ecrit* be reconciled with the experience of the *Mémorial*? The *Ecrit* could, on the other hand, correspond to Jacqueline's own conversion or even to her conception of her brother's, since she presumably knew nothing of the *nuit de feu*.

Against attributing the *Ecrit* to Pascal are also, it seems to me, the several passages where God is described as a good "qui ne peut lui être ôté que par son propre consentement" or which "ne peut être ôté qu'à ceux qui le rejettent" (*OC*, pp. 550–51); such a notion is virtually incompatible with the theology of the *Ecrits sur la grâce* and indeed with Pascal's position as expressed anywhere else in his writings. Mesnard himself says, "C'est une habitude chez Pascal que de réserver toujours la possibilité d'une perte de la grâce, même chez ceux dont le salut paraît le plus solidement assuré" (*Pascal et les Roannez*, I, 528).

the same period (i.e., very soon after the second conversion), for the description of the soul after conversion is quite rudimentary and fragmentary compared with the analysis of the state leading up to it; in this work we find the very curious statement that God "ne peut pas être ôté qu'à ceux qui le rejettent, puisque c'est le posséder que de le désirer et le refuser c'est le perdre." [30] This is difficult to reconcile with the theology of the *Ecrits sur la grâce,* which set out to prove that God abandons man first. Can we find here a progression that will make sense of these texts with their apparent contradictions? It is clear that at the time of his first conversion Pascal embraced with enthusiasm a Jansenistic Augustinianism which he communicated to Jacqueline and even to Gilberte. Then, on the advice of his doctors, he lent himself more and more to worldly pursuits and, led on by his great success both in science and society, he became more attached to the world than his original spiritual position would have tolerated. So when Jacqueline went to Port-Royal, Pascal felt abandoned by her, and saw that he was also abandoned by God—and that he had himself abandoned Him. This state of which he was painfully

---

One can attempt a reconciliation of these passages from the *Ecrit sur la conversion* (as I have done) with certain passages from the *Mystère de Jésus,* e.g., "Tu ne me chercherais pas si tu ne me possédais." But these passages in the *Mystère de Jésus* are accompanied by the commands "Console-toi," "Ne t'inquiète donc pas," and can be read as a direct reply to the "Mon Dieu, me quitterez-vous" of the *Mémorial*; but can either of these texts be related to the "raison aidée de la lumière de la grâce lui fait connaître . . . qu'il ne peut être ôté qu'à ceux qui le rejettent, puisque c'est le posséder que de le désirer" of the *Ecrit sur la conversion?* The latter would seem rather to echo such a text as the following: "Les chrétiens ont cet avantage que s'il leur est défendu de s'abandonner aux plaisirs du monde, il leur est aussy défendu de s'attrister des malheurs qui y arrivent; et mesme il leur est commandé de s'en réjouïr; et comme les uns sont sans difficulté plus fréquents que les autres, leur joye est bien plus continuelle. Aussy, N. S. J. C. dit que personne ne la leur pourra oster . . ." (from a letter of Jacqueline's of March 24, 1649; GE, II, 396). So, although I try in this chapter to show how the *Ecrit sur la conversion du pécheur* could *possibly* be fitted in with other works of Blaise Pascal, the probabilities seem to me to point to its being by Jacqueline.

30. *OC,* pp. 550–51.

aware yet powerless to overcome was abruptly ended by a direct inspiration of some kind, felt as an influx of grace, on November 23, 1654, but which left Pascal in a state of anxiety: how to keep from being once again abandoned by God? In the text just quoted from the *Ecrit sur la conversion du pécheur* he would be still in that state, seeking assurance that God will not abandon him as long as he does not again turn away from Him. So he is still not altogether reconciled to the Augustinian theology of Port-Royal or of his own earlier views; much less is he on the way to being the author of the *Provinciales* or the Apology. Eventually this anxiety of separation—the need for assurance—was broken, perhaps through deep meditation: the formulas in the *Mystère de Jésus* show already the more paradoxical position of which the letter on grace (the *IIIe Ecrit*) is a more abstract and discursive development. "Tu ne me chercherais pas si tu ne me possédais" [31] may seem to echo the text on the conversion of the sinner, but can be interpreted without difficulty in the sense of the *IIIe Ecrit*, which the other text cannot. If this development is correct, then, the *Ecrit sur la conversion du pécheur* followed on the heels of the *Mémorial*, perhaps in December of 1654; it was probably, then, at Port-Royal des Champs while still without a spiritual director that Pascal, meditating on the agony of Jesus, arrived at that profound and paradoxical version of Christianity that is both thoroughly Augustinian and yet for us so peculiarly Pascalian.

The *Entretien avec M. de Saci* would then be the last in order of these texts, showing us a Pascal already on the way to devising his Apology.[32] Two points only need to be made regarding this text and Pascal's theology. The first is that the whole schema of opposing Montaigne and Epictetus, each

31. Br. 555; *OC*, p. 1315.

32. For a study of the authenticity of the *Entretien* and of the remarks attributed to Pascal and Saci, see Pierre Courcelle, *L'Entretien de Pascal et Sacy* (Paris, 1960). An analysis of the *Entretien* in terms of Pascal's projected apologetic is provided by Henri Gouhier, *Commentaires,* chap. II.

containing a half-truth, and each used to destroy the errors of the other, seems perfectly to parallel the notion of the contrary heresies destroying each other in the history of Christian doctrine which Pascal developed in the *Ier Ecrit sur la grâce*.[33] The method in the *Entretien* then seems a bridge between the dialectic of heresies and the "renversement du pour au contre" of the *Pensées*. The second matter of interest in the *Entretien* is the evidence it contains of Pascal's interest in and knowledge of theology. The passage quoted as an epigraph to this book seems evidence enough of his interest; but evidence as to Pascal's knowledge of theology at this time is mainly negative.[34] However, the evidence comes from people who did not really know Pascal and regarded him as essentially another newly converted "mondain"; and if for no other reason than the rebuff he received from M. de Rebours in the incident alluded to earlier, Pascal had no doubt learned that modesty was the best policy when talking with professional theologians. But Pascal, here as elsewhere, shows himself as having no doubt that he has something to offer in the realm of theology; so much so that his mood during this period when he is clearly thinking in terms of a projected Apology, is taken by his sister Jacqueline as far too exuberant, and she asks him, in a letter filled with irony, "comment M. de Sacy s'accomode d'un pénitent si rejouy." [35] The projected Apology, however, would before long give way to another project: Pascal was asked to come to the defense of the friends who had seen him

33. See especially *OC*, p. 955.

34. For example, Fontaine says, "M. Pascal est extrêmement estimable en ce que, n'ayant point lu les Pères de l'Eglise, il avait de lui-même, par la pénétration de son esprit, trouvé les mêmes vérités qu'ils avaient trouvées" (*OC*, p. 561); whatever there is beyond pure fatuity in this statement can be attributed to Fontaine's ignorance—just as he shows his ignorance on the same page concerning the affair of the cycloid. However, Pascal probably fostered such notions himself, partly out of a genuine recognition of the superior learning of some of his Port-Royal friends, and partly as a defense against the sort of presumption that got him into trouble with M. de Rebours.

35. Letter of January 19, 1655; GE, IV, 17.

through his crisis, and his newly found confidence and sense of vocation would be directed to the writing of the notorious *Lettres provinciales*.

The history and circumstances surrounding the writing of these letters is well known and the progress of the polemic which they sustain must of course be illumined by a knowledge of the various events and reactions that determined Pascal's tactics and shifts of emphasis. But this very necessary work of situating them into a narrow historical context may tend to reduce their ultimate import: they may appear as mere polemic dictated by the arguments of the moment with no real doctrinal or stylistic unity. The stylistic unity has already been adequately treated;[36] it is our job to try to establish a doctrinal unity, a task which at first seems doomed to failure.[37] A bewildering number of subjects are treated in these eighteen letters: there are the familiar theological questions of efficacious and sufficient grace, and of the power of the just to fulfill the commandments; there is the famous distinction of "fait" and "droit" with excursions on ecclesiastical (and even civil) authority; there is an attack on the natural and pagan morality of the Jesuits, with asides on the deists and "libertins"; there is also an attack on laxism within the Church and on "la dévotion aisée"; casuistry and probabilism, and the "direction of intention" are blamed; and various moral questions, from appetite and honor to usury and homicide, are discussed; the problem of penance and the contrition-attrition dispute are treated; philosophical distinctions concerning voluntary and involuntary, speculation and practice are brought in; the politics of the Jesuits are contrasted with Pascal's method in

36. See F. Brunetière, *Etudes Critiques* (9th ed.; Paris, 1932), IV, 73–110; J.-J. Demorest, *Pascal Ecrivain* (Paris, 1957).

37. The only extended study of the theological unity of the *Provinciales* that I know is the thesis of Mlle Paule Réguron, *De la théologie à la prière de Pascal* (Grenoble, 1934). Her view that Pascal arrived at Port-Royal "jusque-là ignorant en théologie" (p. 8), and that the *Provinciales* represent a "théologie d'emprunt" from Arnauld and Nicole, is quite opposed to my own and so therefore are her conclusions.

polemics; and even a theory of the stages of sacred history is introduced. To find in all this a central guiding body of doctrine either Pascalian or Jansenistic has usually seemed a hopeless task; it has been said that the unity of the Jansenists' doctrine consists in being against the Jesuits.[38]

A traditional approach to the *Provinciales* has been to divide the theological dispute from the attack on the Jesuits' moral views, a method suggested by divisions within the letters themselves, and perhaps justified by Pascal's own statement regarding the condemned propositions of Jansenius and the doctrines of the casuists: "Il n'y a aucun rapport d'une de ces matières à l'autre." [39] Now what Pascal means here is that even if the Jansenist theology of grace is condemned, that doesn't authorize the Jesuit morality—which is certainly true. I shall take it as a basis of my analysis, however, that most of the points touched on in the *Provinciales* are in fact related to each other precisely through their relation to the theological dispute. As I have already pointed out, the help that Pascal received in writing the *Provinciales* was primarily in the reading of the Jesuit casuists; he was presumably largely unaware of their books and doctrines before 1656. One will look in vain for any preoccupation with moral laxism in his private correspondence prior to that time: spiritual exhortation and theological interpretation are clearly his major interests. It seems to me perfectly accurate to say that Pascal became interested in the casuistry and moral laxity of the Jesuits only when he saw them as moral heresies[40] emanating from false theological doctrine.

Corresponding to the division between theological issues and moral questions in the *Provinciales* is an apparent disparity within Jansenism itself. Between the doctrine of grace and free will of Jansenius on the one hand, and the practices and attitudes of Port-Royal regarding penance, the Eucharist, and the conversion of the heart on the other, there is sometimes seen

38. Attributed to Cardinal Bona; see Cognet, *Le Jansénisme*, p. 124.
39. *Factum pour les curés de Paris,* presumed to be by Pascal, *OC,* p. 917.
40. Cf. the same passage, *OC,* p. 917.

to be little connection beyond the early friendship and mutual influence of Jansenius and Saint-Cyran. In fact, recent scholarship has tended to minimize even that connection: Jansenius' correspondence shows that his "discovery" of St. Augustine came after his period of close association with Duvergier de Hauranne, and the latter's Augustinianism is said to be more Bérullian than Jansenistic.[41] Beyond personal associations, the *Augustinus* and such works as *De la Fréquente communion* are said to be related only by a common spirit of conservative reform.[42]

Now the attitudes of Saint-Cyran, and of his disciple Arnauld, concerning the approach to Communion involve two points: the reality of Christ's presence in the Eucharist, and the sacrament of penance. In the sixteenth *Provinciale,* Pascal defends the writings of the two men on the Eucharist against the claims of the Jesuits that they were in accord with Geneva in denying the Real Presence. Pascal is justly indignant and scornful in this letter: it is clear that the Jansenists are far more devoted to the sacrament than are their attackers. Yet if the Jansenists believe in the presence and power of Christ in the Eucharist, why should they wish to limit access to it? Pascal distinguishes our present state from that of the Jews before Christ ("les Juifs n'ont possédé de Jésus-Christ que les figures et les voiles") and that of the blessed in heaven ("les bienheureux possèdent Jésus-Christ réellement sans figures et sans voiles"); but "les Chrétiens possèdent Jésus-Christ dans l'Eucharistie véritablement et réellement, mais encore couvert de voiles." [43] So this veiled presence of Christ is exactly proportioned to our faith, "parce que la foi . . . n'est pas des choses qui se voient." [44] The effect of the Eucharist depends

41. See Jean Orcibal, *Les Origines du jansénisme,* Vol. 1, *Correspondance de Jansénius* (Louvain, 1947), e.g., p. 55, n. 9, and *passim.* Cf. L. Cristiani, *L'Hérésie de Port-Royal* (Paris, 1955), pp. 14 ff. Also Cognet, *Le Jansénisme,* pp. 20–22.

42. See, for example, A. Gazier, *Histoire générale du mouvement janséniste* (Paris, 1923), Avant-propos, and chaps. I–III.

43. *OC,* p. 857. The thought here is very close to that expressed in the fourth letter to Mlle de Roannez, *OC,* pp. 509–11.

44. *Ibid.*

then on the state of the person who receives it, just as those who saw Christ in person were not all converted, and just as the bread at the Last Supper—the first Communion—was poison to Judas.[45] If this seems in some ways close to the Calvinist view, it still retains Christ present in person in the sacrament, even if the efficacity of that presence depends on the disposition of the recipient. The error of the Jesuits was to imagine that Christ was effective in the sacraments (and this applies to other sacraments besides the Eucharist) in a way in which he was not, even in his Incarnation: as a powerful purgative which if taken in frequent enough doses could assure the salvation of even the most hardened sinner. It is interesting that in the Jesuits' view the sacrament of penance loses much of its importance, and in this the Jesuits seem more in accord with the Calvinists, who abolished it altogether.[46] For the Jansenists, the degree of penitence determined the ability to receive the grace of the Eucharist and was of prime importance to the salvation of the individual. Here we rejoin another theological question, much debated since the Council of Trent, that of contrition versus attrition; it is the special subject of the tenth *Provinciale*.

Now the distinction between contrition and attrition was made even among the early Scholastics; the meaning of the terms remained vague, however, attrition being defined usually as a less perfect contrition. Luther brought discussion to a head by stating that contrition based only on the fear of hellfire, or of punishment in general, prevented only external, not internal sins, and thus led to hypocrisy and pharisaism, in other words to even greater guilt. The Council of Trent took a strong stand against this view, saying that when fear of punishment brought about a turning away from sin and the hope of pardon, it was a gift of the Holy Spirit, moving the sinner toward repentance even though not yet inhabiting him; the Council gave the name "attrition" specifically to the form of

45. Arnauld quoting St. Augustine; cited in Laporte, *La Doctrine de Port-Royal: La morale*, II, 31. My summary of these questions is largely based on Laporte's extensive discussion of them in that volume.
46. Cf. Laporte, *Doctrine de Port-Royal: La morale*, p. 42.

contrition based on the fear of punishment.[47] Now it appears that a number of the theologians at the Council felt that this attrition was sufficient to prepare for the sacrament of penance, and wished the Council to state this, but there was also opposition to such a view and for "sufficit" (ad sacramentum) was substituted the word "disponit," which could be taken to mean that it could dispose the sinner to prepare for true penitence but was not in itself an adequate preparation. This deliberate ambiguity opened the door to a quarrel that is not yet ended but was particularly heated in the late sixteenth century and in the seventeenth until 1667 when, after an investigation, Pope Alexander VII issued a decree enjoining silence on both sides. The main argument against attrition came, of course, from the Augustinians: Baius, and after him Jansenius, held that since the fear of Hell was certainly not a "délectation divine" it must arise from concupiscence or at least from a purely natural egoism; now this is not quite Luther's point, but it is close enough to it and was among the condemned propositions of Baius. The main proponents of the sufficiency of attrition were the Jesuit neo-Thomists, starting with Suarez.

The tenth *Lettre provinciale,* then, begins with a new attack on the "easy devotion," namely the various subtleties and deceits permitted to make confession and penitence easier. The author listens to the Jesuits' various ingenuities, then asks how they are to be reconciled with the doctrine of the Gospel, which seems to demand "une véritable conversion du coeur, qui fait autant aimer Dieu qu'on a aimé les créatures." [48] The Jesuit Father points out that this would be a genuine contrition and that the Jesuits all agree that only attrition is necessary and consider those who insist on contrition as heretics. He then points out further that the Jesuits accept an attrition "qu'on ne conçoit qu'à cause du seul mal temporel qui en arrive, comme d'avoir perdu la santé ou son argent." [49] The

---

47. Conc. Trid., sess. XIV, chap. iv. For this brief résumé of the question, I have used A. Beugnet, art. "Attrition," in *DTC,* I, cols. 2235–62, and Laporte, *Doctrine de Port-Royal: La morale,* pp. 35 ff.

48. *OC,* p. 772.

49. *OC,* p. 774.

author objects that this would seem to be a purely natural motivation excluding any supernatural grace and thus contrary to the Council of Trent; the Jesuit agrees and goes on to say that perfect contrition based on the love of God is seen by the Jesuits as usurping the power of the sacrament and thus in a sense to be an obstacle to the sacrament of penance; and finally he boasts that the Jesuits have delivered mankind from the "obligation pénible" and even "fâcheuse" of loving God.[50] At this point, the author of the *Provinciales* can no longer contain himself and delivers a tirade against the Jesuits and in favor of the love of God as taught in the Gospels and by St. Paul; and so it is at this point that Pascal breaks off the visits to the imaginary Jesuit, and abandons the series of ironic "mises en scène" to speak directly to the Jesuits in his own voice. This turning point in the letters marks also the central point of doctrine involved in Pascal's polemic.

It would be too easy and also misleading to say that Pascal's insistence on the love of God is a case of his claiming the rights of the "coeur" in matters of religion, especially if one takes this "coeur" in the sense of "sentiment." There is nothing "sentimental" in the passage in the tenth *Provinciale*: the appeal is to orthodoxy, to the weight and sanctity of the Gospels and the tradition. The question is a theological one and Pascal is outraged not at the heartlessness, but at the heresy of the Jesuits. Furthermore, the love of God, taken as a psychological question, is almost beyond definition and dispute. An example of the difficulties involved is suggested by this very passage, for Pascal quotes Christ as saying that "qui ne l'aime point, ne garde point ses préceptes," [51] yet John 14:24, of which he is presumably thinking, is preceded by the statement that "he who has my commandments and keeps them, he it is who loves me" (John 14:21), which seems to imply that keeping the commandments is sufficient evidence of the love of God— a position very close to that of the Jesuits.

But on a theological level the question is much more clear-cut. It is once again a question of grace: does the attrition

50. *OC*, p. 777.
51. *OC*, p. 778.

involved represent a supernatural grace or not, and if not, how can it lead to true penitence? Now the Council of Trent had defined a fear of punishment that banished the desire to sin as a gift of God and an impulse of the Holy Spirit, i.e., it is clearly supernatural. Jansenius maintained, however, that the fear of hell or of punishment cannot of itself lead one to true repentance because it arises out of a natural impulse and true penitence must result from a supernatural attraction.

This point is kept quite clear in the tenth *Provinciale*: Pascal lets pass a series of examples where the attrition involved seems less and less sincere; the sincerity of a repentant sinner is after all a difficult matter to judge and if it seems obvious that the Jesuits err in the direction of laxity, still it is hard to say just where to draw the line. But the Jesuits finally cross the line drawn by the Council of Trent, and Pascal clearly has caught them at it when they call sufficient an attrition that is purely natural.

The same line is drawn regarding other devotional practices. The passages in the ninth letter (regarding easy ways to hear the Mass or to procure salvation by reciting an occasional prayer to the Virgin, or simply by wearing a rosary bracelet) may seem at first to aim at the same kind of reform the Protestants were advocating: interior faith as opposed to exterior practices. We have only to think of the end of the "pari," where Pascal advises his potential convert to act as if he believed, "en prenant de l'eau bénite, en faisant dire des messes, etc.,"[52] to realize that his notions are quite far removed from such an attitude. He is careful in this letter not to scorn the practices under discussion, but points out rather that if such practices are taken as *assuring* salvation, they are "bien plus propre à entretenir les pécheurs dans leurs désordres, par la fausse paix que cette confiance téméraire apporte, qu'à les retirer par une véritable conversion que la grâce seule peut produire."[53] These practices, then, are valid only "quand elles partent d'un mouvement de foi et de charité"[54] and are the natural signs

52. Br. 233; *OC*, pp. 1215–16.
53. *OC*, p. 755.
54. *OC*, p. 754.

of a supernatural grace; when they are part of a purely natural impulse—as in the case of the young man who goes to Mass in order to look at the women—they have no relation to salvation, they are of a different order. If this seems still in contradiction to the text quoted from the "pari," it is perhaps the latter text which has not been properly understood; it will be discussed further in its place.

So far we have considered only the devotional side of Christian life: yet the same basic distinction and quarrel underlies the many moral questions treated in the other letters. The most common tactic of Pascal's polemic is of course simply to show the crimes permitted by the Jesuits, and to draw back in righteous horror. But when he descends to argue with their principles, it is not on the basis of rigorism versus laxism. He knew that the Jesuits had the advantage there: the power of concupiscence is such that many will rise to the defense of the Jesuits in the name of charity, not knowing that in fact their zeal "vient du déplaisir secret et souvent caché à nous-mêmes, que le malheureux fonds qui est en nous ne manque jamais d'exciter contre ceux qui s'opposent au relâchement des moeurs." [55] The real issue is this same question of natural versus supernatural. Now in the fifth *Provinciale* the Jesuits' laxism is said to be the cause of their doctrine of grace; this seems unfair, as Pascal would surely not have allowed that the Jansenist doctrine of grace was merely the justification of their moral rigorism. Yet the relation between morality and doctrine is clearly stated: for the Jesuits, ". . . tous les hommes ont toujours assez de grâce pour vivre dans la piété de la manière qu'ils l'entendent. Comme leur morale est toute païenne, la nature suffit pour l'observer." The Jansenists, on the other hand, insist on a supernatural grace for the only morality that is truly Christian: ". . . pour dégager l'âme de l'amour du monde, pour la retirer de ce qu'elle a de plus cher, pour la faire mourir à soi-même, pour la porter et l'attacher uniquement et invariablement à Dieu, ce n'est l'ouvrage que d'une main toute-puissante." [56]

55. *XIe Provinciale, OC*, p. 784.
56. *OC*, pp. 706–707.

What are the characteristics of this natural and pagan morality? Pascal shows that it permits such diverse crimes as usury, simony, bribery, larceny, adultery, and murder, such vices as lying and gluttony, ambition and laziness, lust and greed. Now, for the Jesuits such things can be justified provided that they are properly motivated, and the motivations that are considered legitimate can be reduced to a very few: the desire to acquire or defend worldly goods or honors, and the need to follow a natural appetite. So, for example, in the seventeenth letter we see that a man may kill another, not only in dueling, but for a blow received, or even for a "médisance" or even to "empêcher les médisances," and the justification is that "on peut tuer pour défendre son honneur."[57] Or again, in the ninth letter, the Jesuits permit one to "boire et de manger tout son saoul sans nécessité, et pour la seule volupté," and the reason is that "il est permis à l'appétit naturel de jouir des actions qui lui sont propres."[58] Yet even the Jesuits have their limits: one may not overeat if doing so might ruin one's health, or in other words a natural appetite may not go against nature. And in the case of homicide, one may not kill "par haine ou par vengeance,"[59] which would put the crime on a spiritual level rather than on a purely natural one. Even laziness is justified only as long as it is a natural laziness and cannot be defined as "une tristesse de ce que les choses spirituelles sont spirituelles."[60] In all these cases, it is not hard to see that a certain region is being delimited in which actions and desires are not motivated by charity nor directed toward salvation, but neither are they inspired by hatred or the desire to blaspheme: they are merely "natural," and if not positively good, they are at least legitimate. If it seems difficult to us today to put honor into this class of "natural" virtues, it did not seem so then, in the light of a Renaissance and feudal

57. *OC*, p. 735.
58. *OC*, p. 759.
59. *OC*, p. 733.
60. *OC*, p. 759.

heritage;[61] honor was the natural aim of the very "moi" of every man, and, as the Jesuit says, "plus cher que la vie." [62]

We have already seen how important was the question of "human nature" in the beginnings of Jansenism; let us now try to be more precise about the implications of those doctrines for the question of morality. One of the earliest sources of difficulty regarding a conception of nature is the confusion of the question of what is natural and what supernatural in the case of miracles with the very different question of what human nature is. St. Augustine, in discussing miracles, distinguished between those occurrences that seem to us normal because we are accustomed to them—we would say that they are in accordance with natural law—and events that seem totally unexpected and extraordinary, which we would call supernatural. In this he follows the Greeks and Philo. Yet he is always careful to point out that both natural and supernatural happenings are the work of the same creator, and the regularity of nature, the operation of natural laws, is no less miraculous, in a sense, than an extraordinary intervention on the part of God: both kinds of event are the direct result of the will of God.[63] Now if one applies this notion directly to man and for nature reads "human nature" and for supernatural reads "grace," one can say, as Pelagius does in effect,[64] that our human nature, our ordinary free will, is in its way also miraculous, and even though there may be special supernatural interventions of God in our lives which we call "grace," yet in another sense all is grace, human nature no less than anything else. Now St. Augustine specifically rejected such a view and held always to the view that there are two states of human nature: an integral nature, which was that of Adam at his creation (which included immortality and absolute freedom of the will); and a

61. See Bénichou, *Morales*; cf. *XIVe Provinciale, OC,* p. 831.

62. *OC,* p. 735.

63. See *De Gen. ad lit.,* VI, 13, 24, ed. Vivès, VII, p. 184; and *De Civ. Dei,* XXI, 6, 2 to 8, 5, *BA,* XXXVII, 400–21.

64. See E. Gilson, *The Spirit of Medieval Philosophy* (New York, 1940), p. 378.

133

fallen nature, vitiated by Original Sin and transmitted from generation to generation.[65] When Aristotelian naturalism invaded the Schools in the thirteenth century, the distinction between a natural order and a supernatural order seemed essential if the Greek philosophy was to be reconciled with Christian theology. Once again this distinction invaded the domain of human nature, and although the Schoolmen were largely faithful to St. Augustine and did not go too far in the direction of Pelagianism, the old confusion was reintroduced and endless subtleties invented to explain what "human nature" was, apart from the doctrine of the Fall. Had man ever existed in a purely natural state? If so, what were the characteristics of that state? And how did it relate to the various modes of supernatural grace? Such were the questions raised by the Scholastics in an attempt to reconcile the Greek notions of nature with the Christian doctrine concerning man.[66]

The Jansenist reform, then, consisted of a return to the Christian doctrine of human nature with no attempt to reconcile that doctrine with any given philosophy. To say that the Jansenists exaggerated the effects of Original Sin on human nature[67] is to miss a very important point: in fact they denied a human nature altogether. Man, having been created with a supernatural goal and the means to attain it, lost the means though not the goal. His state now could hardly be described as natural, as it is characteristic of other natures to fulfill their essences (or goals) in the normal course of things, while it is the condition of man to be incapable of that fulfillment without divine aid. Let us leave aside the philosophical issues involved: it is clear that this is exactly Pascal's theological position in the *Provinciales* and the source of his opposition to the Jesuit doctrine. Man has no natural good to which he can

65. Cf. for example, *De Natura et gratia* (written in 415), LXVII, 81, ed. Vivès, XXX, 245, where he points out also that his ideas on human nature had not been changed by the Pelagian controversy, but were essentially the same even in the *De Libero arbitrio* (written in 395); see III, 19, 54; *BA*, VI, 426.

66. Gilson, *The Spirit of Medieval Philosophy*, p. 379.

67. Bénichou, *Morales*, pp. 79–80.

aspire, nor any natural appetite he can safely follow: all that does not lead him toward his supernatural goal, which is the love of God, is a perversion of that love, that is, concupiscence. There is no middle ground of legitimate natural action, not for the individual nor for the human race: the so-called virtues of the pagans are really vices, and savages are no more "natural" than civilized men. One can see also, in the light of this doctrine, the particular danger of the idea of "l'honneur." For even though Jesuits admitted honor only as a natural goal of man, nevertheless, since the pursuit of honor could lead a man to sacrifice mere natural appetites, it was also a rival and substitute for man's true supernatural goal: "C'est cet honneur qui a toujours été l'idole des hommes, possédés par l'esprit du monde. C'est pour se conserver cette gloire, dont le démon est le véritable distributeur, qu'ils lui sacrifient . . . leur salut par le péril de la damnation auquel ils s'engagent"; and again: "L'honneur des Chrétiens consiste dans l'observation des ordres de Dieu et des régles du Christianisme, et non pas dans ce fantôme d'honneur que vous prétendez, tout vain qu'il soit, être une excuse légitime pour les meurtres." [68] Thus, although this particularly virulent attack on "l'honneur" has no doubt its sociological origins, it is also part of a coherent theology that underlies all of the *Provinciales*. It is difficult to see how anyone could read the seventeenth and eighteenth letters and miss this coherence, for there Pascal attempts specifically to resume his position and also to assume full responsibility for it. This is surely the meaning of his very strong insistence in the seventeenth letter[69] that he is not of Port-Royal. It is absurd to see here a dishonest ruse to throw his enemies off his trail. If there is any exaggeration in his statement (and there is little reason to think that there is), it is more likely to spring from his desire to protect Port-Royal than himself: the letters were considered by many at the convent itself to be too polemical and uncharitable. Pascal declares that the doctrines he has put forth are his own, not in the sense that he may not have

68. *XIVe Provinciale, OC,* pp. 831–32.
69. *OC,* pp. 867–68.

learned them from others, but in that he has adopted them himself and proposes them on their own merit and not as a declaration of policy of some imaginary Port-Royalist party.[70]

Finally, having seen the dependence of the Jesuit morality on their naturalistic theology, let us look at their methods for translating theory into practice, their casuistry. Two features of their casuistry fall especially under the scornful attacks of Pascal: the doctrine of probabilism, and the direction of intention. It is clear that Pascal regards both doctrines as not only detrimental to Christian morality but as containing serious intellectual errors.

The defenders of probabilism have even accused Pascal of hypocrisy or inconsistency in condemning probabilism in the *Provinciales* but using probabilistic methods in his scientific works and in the "pari." [71] Such an accusation contains two errors. The first is pointed out by Pascal himself in the fifth *Provinciale*: "La plaisante comparaison," he says, ". . . des choses du monde à celles de la conscience." [72] Using basically the same distinction as that between "le fait" and "le droit" exploited in the first letters, Pascal points out that though we often must accept only probabilities regarding matters of fact (e.g., in conflicting testimonies), matters of conscience are of a different order altogether. The second error is intimately connected with the history of probabilism itself. Questions of conscience were hardly discussed before the Scholastics. But St. Thomas and many following him formulated cases in which one is not sure whether a given action is permitted or prohibited; the answer given by St. Thomas is that if one has any doubts that the action is permitted, but does it anyway, there is grave sin just as if it were prohibited.[73] Others, following St. Thomas, modified this to say that if one opinion was far more probable than the contrary, one could follow it without

70. See the excellent article by Jean Mesnard, "Pascal et Port-Royal," *Revue de théologie et de philosophie*, 1963, no. 1, pp. 12–23.

71. E.g., E. Baudin, *La Philosophie de Pascal* (Neuchâtel, 1946), III, 112 ff.

72. *OC*, p. 710.

73. See Th. Deman, art. "Probabilisme," in *DTC*, XIII, cols. 417–619; for St. Thomas, cols. 424–26.

grave risk. But in the late sixteenth century, a Dominican, Medina, of the School of Salamanca, formulated the view that if an opinion is probable, it is permissible to follow it, even if the contrary opinion is more probable.[74] It is this view that founded modern probabilism in the usual definition,[75] and which is under attack by Pascal. The doctrine includes a crucial equivocation, for in the traditional sense, a probable opinion implied one that was as certain as it is possible to be on a given matter; to speak, then, of a contrary opinion as "more probable" is properly to deny the probability of the first.[76] Yet in this ambiguous soil sprouted a whole "science," which flourished under the Jesuits of the late sixteenth and early seventeenth century, and was not seriously questioned until the Jansenists exposed its abuses; the *Provinciales* were of course of prime importance in bringing the whole matter before the general public, both lay and clerical.

It is perfectly clear, then, that the doctrine Pascal is attacking is not any traditional or ordinary use of probability; he would have accepted not only St. Thomas' view, but even the more indulgent view of many later Thomists, sometimes called "tutiorism," that one can follow an opinion that is truly probable.[77] And even if we allow the dubious comparison between the factual and the moral, it is only this kind of probability that Pascal uses in the "pari" or anywhere else. But the probabilism which he turns to scorn is not only a pernicious moral doctrine: it is a logical absurdity that would be intolerable in any domain. And if Pascal has no desire to attack probability in general, but only a modern distortion of it, still less does he condemn the whole science of casuistry, but again only "ces nouveaux casuistes"; Brunschvicg saw this clearly enough, and those who have ignored it have invariably been led into a

74. *Ibid.*, col. 466.

75. *Ibid.*, col. 417.

76. See M.-M. Gorce, art. "Medina," in *DTC*, XX, cols. 483–85.

77. Cf. for example this statement from the *Ecrit des Curés de Rouen*, usually assumed to have had Pascal's collaboration: "La question n'est pas s'il y a des opinions probables dans la morale, personne ne doutant qu'il y en ait . . ." (cited in Deman, art. "Probabilisme," in *DTC*, col. 516).

serious misunderstanding regarding Pascal's whole theology.[78]

Once again it is worth noting that it is not here a question of rigorism versus laxism, unless this last term is clearly defined; for if it is taken simply as the opposite of rigorism, the real issue is again obscured. A notion which occurs again and again in the *Lettres* on probabilism is that of "en conscience" and "en sureté de conscience," [79] and in the *IVe Factum pour les curés de Paris* probabilism is defined as the doctrine "qui consiste à tenir pour sûr en conscience le vrai et le faux." [80] The whole matter is precisely stated in the first *Factum*: "C'est un mal bien moins dangereux et bien moins général d'introduire les déréglements en laissant subsister les lois qui les défendent, que de pervertir les lois, et de justifier les déréglements." [81] So it is not laxism in the sense of indulgence that is attacked—the Church has always been indulgent toward avowed and repentant sinners—but only in the sense of a corruption of the moral law itself. Laxism, in this sense, is not an indulgence toward sinners, but a means of removing sin altogether, and so also eliminating repentance and the need for

78. Brunschvicg, introduction to the *Provinciales* in the GE, IV, pp. li–lii. Baudin, who even quotes Brunschvicg on this matter (*Philosophie*, III, 79–80), persists in this confusion and takes it as basic that the *Provinciales* are a general attack on casuistry. Yet one will look in vain for a passage in the *Lettres provinciales* in which it is not clearly stated or implied that it is the "nouveaux casuistes" or "les casuistes d'aujourd'hui" or "la société de leurs casuistes" (i.e., of the Jesuits) which are under attack. The only passage that might lend itself to a more general interpretation is none for the *Provinciales*: "Les casuistes soumettent la décision à la raison corrompue et le choix des décisions à la volonté corrompue, afin que tout ce qu'il y a de corrompu dans la nature de l'homme ait part à sa conduite" (Br. 907; *OC,* p. 1061); but again it is obviously only the probabilists who are indicated, for it is only their brand of casuistry that does in fact leave a choice to the corrupt will, traditional casuistry being exactly the science by which moral questions are decided by reason enlightened by revelation rather than by reason corrupted by the passions. See Baudin, *Philosophie*, III, 76 ff.

79. See *OC*, pp. 709, 724, 726, 728, 735, 739, 746, etc.

80. Cited by Baudin, *Philosophie*, III, 77, n. 1. This *Factum* either had Pascal's collaboration or was directly inspired by his ideas.

81. *OC,* p. 907.

a Savior: "Voilà celui qui ôte les péchés du monde!" had become more applicable to the Père Bauny than to Christ.[82]

Yet again the reason given for denouncing the danger inherent in this new laxism depends on a Jansenist-Augustinian theology:

Comme la nature de l'homme tend toujours au mal dès sa naissance, et qu'elle n'est ordinairement retenue que par la crainte de la loi, aussitôt que cette barrière est ôtée, la concupiscence se répand sans obstacle, de sorte qu'il n'y a point de différence entre rendre les vices permis, et rendre tous les hommes vicieux.[83]

The long passage in the thirteenth *Provinciale* on whether what is permitted "in speculation" is also permitted "in practice" has the same basis, and Pascal easily shows that the distinction is purely a ruse invented by certain Jesuits to keep from arousing the civil authorities against their more pernicious maxims, and that the distinction is expressly rejected even by Escobar.[84]

The theology expressed in the moral critique of the *Lettres provinciales* seems to be, then, a consistent Jansenistic interpretation of St. Augustine—Jansenistic in the sense that it is traditional and even reactionary. It is also more limited in its implications than is usually maintained: the attacks on the Jesuits center on precise points of doctrine more often than not and, if read attentively, bring a new precision to the analysis of those errors. There is a point, however, on which Pascal is not above reproach: satire is limited to condemnation and negative criticism, and as we have seen in the example of the condemnation of propositions by the Church, its object is not always well defined, even when its point of departure is a specific positive body of doctrine. Pascal's irony does not always lend itself to precise interpretation, and the less acute reader may often miss the subtle point and see only the scorn and its

82. *IVe Provinciale, OC*, p. 694.
83. *Factum pour les curés de Paris, OC*, p. 907.
84. *OC*, pp. 810–12.

target in a general way. So in bringing such questions before a less informed public, and treating them satirically, he lent support to various anticlerical, antiecclesiastical attitudes—which was certainly not his intention. Further, regarding one of his own arguments—that the Jesuits were corrupting the moral law itself—it is only fair to point out that the majority of the books he quotes were written in Latin and addressed to priests, and most of the maxims were certainly unknown to the public before Pascal translated them in the *Provinciales*. So the permission to perform these pernicious deeds was not proclaimed by the Jesuits to the general public, but distributed to "directeurs de consciences" for use in difficult individual cases. There were exceptions, of course, of which *La Dévotion aisée* and Bauny's *Somme des péchés* are prime examples, but it is worth noting that the book which the Priests of Paris wanted condemned as dangerous was the *Apologie pour les casuistes,* which was the Jesuits' first serious defense of their casuistry written in French, and which appeared only as a reply to the *Provinciales*. So it must be admitted that Pascal, in discovering the Jesuits' intentions to the general public, also altered them in a way that the sincere theologians in the Company must have found not only unfair but most unfortunate for the faithful.

There is one further topic treated at some length in the *Provinciales* which we have not yet discussed: the direction of intention. This method of the Jesuit casuists is explained in the seventh letter. First it is precisely delimited in its use: "Nous ne souffrons jamais d'avoir l'intention formelle de pécher pour le seul dessein de pécher; et quiconque s'obstine à n'avoir point d'autre fin dans le mal que le mal même, nous rompons avec lui; cela est diabolique." [85] Short of the diabolical, however, one may perform all sorts of actions not normally permitted, as long as one's intention is directed toward what is permitted. So, for instance, one may kill an enemy in a duel, or even from behind, as long as one's intention is not revenge but simply to defend one's honor. It is easy to see that the method is at the service of the same natural morality analyzed above and for which Pascal, of course, has no use; so his attack

85. *OC,* p. 728.

on this method is quite in order in those letters in which the more general subject is the Jesuits' morality. But there are also suggestions here regarding another theological and philosophical issue, namely, the nature of intention and its implications for a general view of the human will. To see the full implications of these notions, then, we shall have eventually to go beyond the *Provinciales* to the *Pensées*.

Within the *Provinciales,* however, certain interesting points can still be made. First, let us note that alongside the many examples in which crimes are permitted because of the purity of intention—"C'est l'intention qui règle la qualité de l'action," says a Jesuit author in the ninth letter[86]—Pascal shows us that the Jesuits also allow merit for actions that are good in themselves even though unintentional, or of bad intention. In the same ninth letter Vasquez is quoted as saying, "Qu'on satisfait au précepte d'ouïr la messe, encore même qu'on ait l'intention de n'en rien faire," as when one is taken to church by force, or even when one has a "méchante intention, comme de regarder des femmes avec un désir impur." [87] Besides catching the Jesuits in a blatant contradiction, Pascal seems to suggest that their whole notion of intention as separable from the act itself is ill founded. Certainly this last kind of case is specifically condemned in the Gospels (Matthew 5:27–28). And we normally recognize that one is not fully responsible for an act that is unintentional, but we usually have in mind doing something unwittingly or else under constraint; so we should say that someone who heard a Mass by accident or against his will, did so unintentionally and no one could seriously maintain that he deserved credit for doing so. But in the case of a person who says that his intention is one thing and proceeds knowingly and without constraint to do something else, we say either that he never had any intention of doing what he said, or at least that his intention was insincere. As Pascal puts it: "Et comment pouvez-vous concevoir qu'un homme qui demeure volontairement dans les occasions des péchés, les déteste sincèrement? N'est-il pas visible, au contraire, qu'il n'en est point touché

86. *OC*, p. 760.
87. *OC*, pp. 763–64.

comme il faut?" [88] So the Jesuits seem to allow and even encourage the grossest insincerity, to see as a way to Heaven those very "good intentions" with which, proverbially, the way to Hell is paved.

If this were all that the question implied, we should certainly be somewhat surprised to find in the eleventh letter that Pascal defends his own apparently uncharitable attack on the Jesuits on the ground that his intention is charitable: "L'esprit de charité porte à avoir dans le coeur le désir du salut de ceux contre qui on parle, et à adresser ses prières à Dieu en même temps qu'on adresse ses reproches aux hommes." [89] Even more striking is the juxtaposition of the passage in the ninth letter, in which Pascal exposes the Jesuits' method for avoiding lies by mental restriction and the direction of intention, [90] with the statement in the fifteenth letter, this time in all sincerity, that "la qualité de menteur enferme l'intention de mentir." [91] But in both these cases where Pascal seems to invoke a direction of intention, there is a difference: he then proceeds to give evidence for that intention, to show that his own charitable intentions and also the Jesuits' mendacious ones are "visible," to use Pascal's word. He does not in fact deny the existence of intentions nor even the validity of the Jesuit precept that the intention determines the quality of the act in certain cases. But it is important to distinguish these cases and once again we see Pascal as a linguistic analyst at work. For if lying consists not merely in saying a falsehood—one can simply be mistaken— but includes the intention to deceive, the same cannot be said of all actions. So the author of the *Provinciales* says concerning usury, "J'ai toujours pensé que ce péché consistait à retirer plus d'argent qu'on n'en a prêté." The Jesuit replies, "Vous l'entendez bien peu. . . . L'usure ne consiste presque . . . qu'en l'intention de prendre ce profit comme usuraire." [92] In another example, to kill a person is still homicide regardless of whether

88. *Xe Provinciale, OC*, p. 772.
89. *OC*, p. 787.
90. *OC*, pp. 760–61.
91. *OC*, p. 834.
92. *VIIIe Provinciale, OC*, p. 743.

the motive was revenge or something else; as Pascal puts it, "L'intention de celui qui blesse ne soulage point celui qui est blessé." [93]

One of the Jesuits' errors here is to have confused motive and intention. If we define motive as being essentially backward-looking, i.e., as depending on some previous act or event or state,[94] and intentions as essentially forward-looking, i.e., toward what one is going to do, we then see, for instance, that revenge is not an intention but a motive, though it may well arouse the intention to kill someone. So this first example of the benefits of the direction of intention is pure equivocation. St. Paul says, "Repay no one evil for evil" (Romans 12:17); the words "revenge" and "vengeance" hardly occur in the New Testament. But, the Jesuits say, as long as one does not have the intention to revenge oneself but only to defend one's honor, one may fight a duel, or even kill an enemy from behind. Now it is "visible" that to kill someone who has insulted or harmed you is to repay evil for evil—and is motivated by revenge— regardless of what other intentions, even perfectly sincere ones, you may adduce, such as defending your honor.

The Jesuits' equivocation can be even grosser than this, as in the case where they say that although dueling is forbidden it is not forbidden to take a walk in the place assigned for a duel with the intention of defending one's honor.[95] There is not much difference between this and saying that one only intended to drive a sword through an enemy's heart, but not to kill him; it is to pretend one can intend the means to an end without intending the end itself, which is contrary to the nor-

93. VIIe Provinciale, OC, p. 739.

94. This definition is suggested by the very illuminating discussion in G. E. M. Anscombe, *Intention* (Oxford, 1957), pp. 18 ff. "Motive," as Miss Anscombe points out, is also used in a larger sense to include both intentions and motives: as when one wants to know the motive for a crime, it is equally proper to invoke something in the past, e.g., revenge for a past hurt, or something in the future, such as financial gain from an inheritance. This use of "motive" may be called "interpretative motive" and applies to motivation in general, but is less useful for analysis of the very act of willing.

95. VIIe Provinciale, OC, p. 731.

mal Scholastic definition of intention.[96] In fact the whole notion of "directing one's intentions" is absurd and equivocal, implying as it does in fact that one can intend one's very intentions. In some cases the absurdity is so obvious that Pascal feels it is sufficient merely to quote the Jesuits' examples. The fact is, however, that intentions play an important part in the usual discussions of merit. Pascal, then, has no desire to ruin the doctrine of intention, which as we have pointed out is crucial to his own theology, but only to show the abuses of it by the Jesuits. The seventh *Provinciale* does not linger on the subject but returns to what is still the central issue, namely, morality. For in all Christian doctrine, man's ultimate intention must be his beatitude, and even though the Thomists maintained that man could not direct all his actions toward God, still they maintained that those which do not have beatitude as an immediate goal must depend on virtuous intermediate intentions with an underlying ultimate and habitual intention of salvation. But the Jesuits sought to justify sinful acts by ascribing to them permitted, natural intentions such as preserving one's honor or one's goods; as it is put in the *Factum,* they "font succéder aux préceptes de l'Ecriture qui nous oblige de rapporter toutes nos actions à Dieu, une permission brutale de les rapporter toutes à nous-mêmes." [97] So the doctrine of intention is just another ruse in the defense of the Jesuits' natural morality, and it is not the distinction of intentions to which Pascal objects, but the distinction of a class of just or natural intentions unrelated to sin or salvation. As he says, in a note for the *Provinciales,* "Comme s'il y avait deux enfers, l'un pour les péchés contre la charité, l'autre contre la justice!" [98]

The relation of these questions of intention and morality to the doctrine of grace is best brought out in the fourth *Lettre provinciale,* which forms the transition from the letters on grace to the letters on morality. The dialectic of this letter may make it difficult to see at first just what this relation is. It

96. See A. Thouvenin, art. "Intention," in *DTC,* VII, cols. 2267–68.
97. *Factum pour les curés de Paris, OC,* p. 908.
98. Br. 916; *OC,* p. 1062.

begins with the Jesuit defining actual grace as the knowledge in any given case of the good and evil involved, along with the desire to do good; without these conditions, sin cannot be imputed. The author of the *Provinciales* points out that by this definition those with the least thought of God are also the least sinful. The Jesuit counters that all men have these inspirations to know and do good (in other words a sufficient grace); the author and his Jansenist friend show that this is both manifestly false according to the facts of experience (and would thus be a scandal to nonbelievers), and also contrary to Scripture. The Jesuit rallies to say that Aristotle is on his side as he says that an action is involuntary and cannot be imputed to blame if it is done in ignorance; but an examination of the passage in Aristotle shows that the ignorance which renders an action involuntary and blameless is ignorance of the circumstances of an act such as would render it unwitting or accidental, as when one doesn't know that a pistol is loaded, etc. And finally St. Augustine is quoted to the effect that sins of ignorance are still sins, even when committed by "une volonté qui se porte à l'action et non au péché." [99]

This citation of St. Augustine, then, ruins the Jesuits' technique of direction of intentions right from the start, not by denying intentions nor even that they may be directed toward an action rather than at the sin which the action embodies, but by stating that such actions are still sins. The fact that this doctrine of St. Augustine's is preceded in the letter by the quotation from Aristotle is not merely fortuitous. Professor Wolfson has shown that Augustine's doctrine of free will depends on the Aristotelian definition of the voluntary. [100] For according to Aristotle, an action is voluntary as long as it is not performed against one's will, i.e., either unwittingly or through external compulsion. For an act to be voluntary and thus free, it is not necessary to have freedom of choice in any absolute sense, but only to do what one wills to do, regardless of

99 *OC,* p. 702.
100. Harry A. Wolfson, "Philosophical Implications of the Pelagian Controversy," *Proceedings of the American Philosophical Society,* CIII, no. 4 (Aug. 1959), 560–61.

whether that will is determined by concupiscence or grace. The necessity of grace (or concupiscence) is akin to a logical necessity: the actions of the will are necessary in the sense that they could not be otherwise (in the same way that God is necessarily eternal) but not in the sense that they are compelled or constrained. This doctrine of St. Augustine's was outlined earlier and is certainly also that of Pascal. The Jesuit doctrine, which we have discussed in the versions of Molina and Lessius, is that freedom implies an absolute freedom of choice, or freedom of indifference; the implications of this doctrine for morality are clearly seen here in the fourth *Provinciale*. The idea that Pascal's Jesuit will not give up, even when he retreats on the question of the distribution of actual graces, is that for there to be sin there must be this freedom which consists of a clear moral choice and at least sufficient motivation toward the good to counterbalance the effects of our original corruption and reestablish an indifference in our choice; then when we choose evil it really is evil. Now this is exactly what we have seen to constitute true evil in the exposé of Jesuit morality in the *Provinciales*: the choice of evil as evil. Anything less may not be good or meritorious, but it cannot be imputed as sin. This notion no doubt gained strength through its opposition to the Reformed doctrines of the gratuitous and inevitable imputation of sin from which even our virtues are no escape. But it also opened the way to this broad no-man's-land of unintentional sins which, so long as they conformed to the new notions of human nature and its rights and goals, were not to be considered as sins at all. It is not so hard to see, then, the coherence of the Jansenist attack as we have it in the *Provinciales*. The Molinists' views on grace and freedom were not merely new and opposed to the traditional Augustinian ones; they also encouraged the establishment of a new "natural morality"—a morality virtually without sin. Pascal never tires of pointing out that the Jesuits have taken it on themselves to do away with the sins of the world, and that in so doing they have weakened the priesthood, and the sacraments, and even rendered the Redemption unnecessary. It was not just the orthodoxy of Arnauld or Jansenius which was at stake, nor even the much more important doctrine of efficacious grace: it was the whole structure and conception of the Church that depended on this doctrine. So, although Port-Royal had theologians more professional than Pascal at its service, it is doubtful whether any of them saw more clearly than he the total implications of the new doctrines, or could attack them on so many different levels. The diversity of his attack was necessary and to some extent effective, but it rests nonetheless clearly on a solid doctrinal unity, traditional and Augustinian, and which involves much more than an abstruse notion of efficacious grace or a mere moral rigorism.

But this doctrine had its difficult points, its obscurities and paradoxes, such that mere outlines and reiterations of the doctrine, as we had for example in the second *Ecrit sur la grâce,* do not offer much illumination. Further, even as Pascal was writing the *Provinciales,* the Jansenists began to suffer a series of defeats that led to their almost definitive downfall. And if the spirit of the Renaissance and the new notions in science and philosophy did not justify the excesses of the Counter-Reformation, they surely obliged even the most traditional Christians to reevaluations and reinterpretations of traditional doctrines. Pascal's notions in science, mathematics, and even logic were distinctly progressive; can we believe that in matters of religion he was merely a rigid traditionalist? The *Pensées* clearly belie such a notion: they seem to many to be relevant to the twentieth century in a way that they were not to the eighteenth and nineteenth centuries. The modernity of the *Pensées* has perhaps been sufficiently emphasized; but we shall be closer to appreciating the true genius and originality of Pascal when we see to what extent his most "modern" insights are also the result of his reflection on a most traditional theology. This will be the main task of our final chapter.

Chapter IV   The *Pensées*

That the *Pensées* of Pascal are not the random jottings of a
tortured genius, but are notes toward an Apology for Christianity made by a man with an exceptionally well-ordered mind;
that the writing of that Apology was first postponed by other
projects—most notably, the *Lettres provinciales*—and finally
and definitively by illness and death; that Pascal had in mind
nonetheless a definite plan or outline for his projected Apology, a plan which he partly exposed in a lecture to his friends
at Port-Royal, and in accordance with which he himself sorted
and classified his notes in an order which has been largely
recovered: all this has been brought out and sufficiently demonstrated by recent scholarship.[1] The informed reader of a
modern edition of the *Pensées* can no longer read them as did
a Voltaire, a Chateaubriand, or an Unamuno. However,
Pascal's apologetic method is of only secondary relevance to
our purpose, which is the investigation of the theology of
grace in the *Pensées*. Our order, then, will be quite different
from that of the projected Apology. We shall look first at
those sections where the theology is most evident—at Pascal's
conception of biblical Christianity; from there we may proceed
to those elements in his analysis of the human condition which
may be illuminated by his theology, or which may in turn
shed light on his way of thinking that theology. I shall not, of
course, attempt to comment on the entirety of the *Pensées* in
terms of the theology of grace—though I am not sure this

1. The literature on this problem is too vast for citation here; a good
discussion with ample bibliography is Sister Marie-Louise Hubert's
Pascal's Unfinished Apology (New Haven, 1952).

couldn't be done—but shall center rather on those areas of Pascal's thought which through their paradoxical or controversial nature have seemed problematic to his interpreters, and which are thus most in need of illumination.

The fragments concerning religion amount to a very large portion of the *Pensées*, and are generally thought less interesting on the whole than his ideas on style, on human psychology, on the human condition generally. Two subjects in particular account for the bulk of Pascal's reflections on Christianity: prophecies and miracles; and given his apologetic purpose, this is not surprising. His interest in miracles was also undoubtedly inspired by the miraculous cure produced in his niece Marguerite by the application of the Holy Thorn, a miracle to which Pascal himself gave official testimony.[2] But he was especially admired at Port-Royal for his interpretations of the prophecies, concerning which he had what amounts to a theory of his own; I shall attempt only to summarize this theory, so as to relate it to his theology, rather than enter into the details of his views.[3]

A devoted reader of the Bible, Pascal saw a grand design uniting the Old and New Testaments. For him the Jews of the Old Testament were a unique and irreplaceable part of what he would call "la perpétuité de la foi": the faith of Christians is continuous with the faith of the prophets. But the essential role of the Jews was to prophesy; their prophecies were the necessary preparation for the coming of Christ. The Jews however did not understand their own prophecies: they took the

2. The text of his deposition may be found in *Textes inédits de Blaise Pascal,* ed. Jean Mesnard (Paris, 1962), pp. 17–23.

3. My summary owes most to Jean Mesnard's *Blaise Pascal* (Paris: Desclée de Brouwer, series: "Les Ecrivains devant Dieu," 1965), pp. 51–61, and to the still valuable article of M. J. Lagrange, "Pascal et les prophéties messianiques," *Revue Biblique,* N.S. III (1906), 533–60; cf. also J. Mesnard, *Pascal* (Paris, 1962), pp. 148–53, and J. Lhermet, *Pascal et la Bible* (Paris, n.d. [1931]), esp. pp. 377 ff. The late Abbé Jean Steinmann's notorious "Entretien de Pascal et du Père Richard Simon sur le sens de l'Ecriture," *Vie Intellectuelle,* XVII (1949), 239–53, with the replies of Jean Daniélou, Claudel, et al. (*ibid.,* pp. 503–14), tells us more about twentieth-century Catholic attitudes toward Scripture than about Pascal.

promises of victory over their enemies and good things to come literally, and so when Jesus Christ came and preached to them, his message of the spiritual kingdom did not seem to them a fulfillment of the prophecies and they rejected him. But how can we know that the Jews were wrong, and that Christ was indeed the Messiah predicted by the prophets? It is true of course that there are specific prophecies which Christ did fulfill, and also that many of the Old Testament prophets speak of a spiritual kingdom rather than a temporal one; but there are also many prophecies that seem to support the Judaic expectation of a more secular savior.

The Old Testament prophecies, then, are ambiguous: they speak of both temporal goods (this is what Pascal calls the "sens charnel" of the Scriptures), and of spiritual goods (in what he calls the "sens figuré"); it remains to be shown that the figurative meaning is the correct one. There are many "pensées" on this subject and several reasons are given as to why the temporal or earthly meaning cannot be the basic one:

> *Premièrement, que cela serait indigne de Dieu;*
> *Secondement, que leurs discours expriment très clairement la promesse des biens temporels, et qu'ils disent néanmoins que leurs discours sont obscurs, et que leur sens ne sera point entendu. D'où il paraît que ce sens secret n'était pas celui qu'ils exprimaient à découvert. . . .*[4]

In other words the promise of temporal goods had another meaning; but this is still not proof that the other meaning is the only true one. But Pascal points out that if one leaves it at that, not only Scripture, but sometimes even the same prophet, is guilty of gross contradictions; so there must be a larger meaning in which both these meanings are harmonized.[5] Pascal then reasons as follows:

> *Si la loi et les sacrifices sont la vérité, il faut qu'elle plaise*

4. Br. 659; *OC,* p. 1261.
5. Cf. Br. 659, 684; *OC,* pp. 1261–63.

à Dieu, et qu'elle ne lui déplaise point. S'ils sont figures, il faut qu'ils plaisent et déplaisent.

Or dans toute l'Ecriture ils plaisent et déplaisent. Il est dit que la loi sera changée, que le sacrifice sera changé, qu'ils seront sans roi, sans prince et sans sacrifice, qu'il sera fait une nouvelle alliance, que la loi sera renouvelée, que les préceptes qu'ils ont reçus ne sont pas bons, que leurs sacrifices sont abominables, que Dieu n'en a point demandé.

Il est dit, au contraire, que la loi durera éternellement, que cette alliance sera éternelle, que le sacrifice sera éternel, que le sceptre ne sortira jamais d'avec eux, puisqu'il n'en doit point sortir que le Roi éternel n'arrive.

Tous ces passages marquent-ils que ce soit réalité? Non. Marquent-ils aussi que ce soit figure? Non: mais que c'est réalité, ou figure. Mais les premiers, excluant la réalité, marquent que ce n'est que figure.

Tous ces passages ensemble ne peuvent être dits de la réalité, tous peuvent être dits de la figure: donc ils ne sont pas dits de la réalité, mais de la figure.[6]

Now if it is so demonstrable that the true sense of the Old Testament prophecies is the spiritual or figurative one, it is certainly remarkable that the Jews adhered to the literal and temporal view; and Pascal points out that this too serves Christianity, since the prophecies were preserved by a people to whom they were in fact hostile, and so that people's witness is by so much the less suspect.[7] But it is not so surprising that the Jews rejected the spiritual sense of Scripture, for they, like all of us sons of Adam, were under the dominion of concupiscence; they had turned away from the Creator toward his creatures, from the "choses figurées" to the "choses figurantes." Concupiscence cannot understand Scripture, for "l'unique objet de l'Ecriture est la charité." [8]

In this, however, the Jews are no different from anyone

6. Br. 685; *OC*, p. 1263.
7. Cf. Br. 571, 663, etc.; *OC*, pp. 1269–72.
8. Br. 670; *OC*, p. 1274.

else. We today are faced with the same ambiguities in the case of miracles, which are a sort of continuation of the prophecies;[9] that is, they also are signs. Merely to believe that a miraculous event took place is not to believe in the miracle—the Pharisees in Christ's time had ample evidence of his miracles. But one must also see the miraculous event as a sign pointing beyond itself to a higher reality. Miracles, then, have the same ambiguity as prophecies, and those who reject their evidence do so because they are addicted to the temporal, material world, because they are ruled by concupiscence.

A third theme of Pascal's thoughts on religion is one alluded to above: "la perpétuité de la foi."[10] When the Law, rites, and sacrifices of the Jews are seen as figures of the commandment of charity, of the liturgy, and of the self-sacrifice of Christians; when the faith of Christians is seen as a continuation of the faith of the prophets, and the whole of Scripture as witnessing to a continuous history of salvation, with Christ as its center; then one must see this tradition as not only the longest religious tradition we know but indeed as a unique one coextensive with the whole history of man.

Now none of these three arguments—from the prophecies, from miracles, and from perpetuity—would seem to us today to have the validity of proofs. Yet for Pascal they are the only kind of proofs of Christianity that do have validity; rational proofs are ruled out by him as useless or irrelevant. This is partly so because of the primacy of the will and the limitations of human reason. But it also follows from the distinction Pascal borrowed from Jansenius between the rational sciences and the historical sciences: theology and history belong in the same domain, that of memory, not reason. Rational proofs of truths of religion are as much an absurdity as theological proofs of the truths of mathematics or physics. The only proof of Christianity is the history of Christianity: a history with sufficient signs for us to understand it if we will, even though the signs are necessarily ambiguous.

The theory of the prophecies and miracles as ambiguous

9. Cf. Br. 829, 838; *OC,* pp. 1286–88.
10. See Br. 613, 614, 616, 617, 646, 851, 852; *OC,* pp. 1325–28.

signs depends in turn on Pascal's notion of the "Dieu caché." This notion, which recurs several times in the *Pensées*, is best developed in the letter to Mlle de Roannez which was discussed in the preceding chapter (see above, pp. 114–16); it was shown there that the whole concept depends for Pascal on the Augustinian doctrine of predestination. It was only those chosen to be Christ's disciples who saw him as fulfilling the prophecies and believed in his miracles. So today it is only the elect who see Christian history not just as a series of events but as the discourse of God. That discourse cannot be understood by reason, but only by the heart, a heart which in fallen man is ruled by concupiscence; it is only when God's grace intervenes so that the heart throws off the bonds of concupiscence and awakens to love that it can then understand the discourse of history, for the meaning of that discourse is charity. But this whole process, the process of conversion, will be better understood if we understand properly the terms of Pascal's psychology.

What ought to be the most important term to relate to the theology of grace and free will is "will" itself. What does Pascal mean by "will," especially when he says that it is free and also determined by grace? We have seen that in this he only follows St. Augustine, maintaining that it is the nature of the will to follow necessarily the greater "délectation," and yet that all acts of the will are free by definition. But doesn't this last notion involve some sort of logical sleight of hand?

Fortunately, on this very question of definition we have explicit and quite interesting texts by Pascal: the *De l'Esprit géométrique*,[11] which we may supplement by passages from the Port-Royal *Logic*, which incorporates some of Pascal's ideas. In the *Esprit géométrique*, Pascal attempts to show the foundation of geometry in definition and axiom before going on

11. See Mesnard, "Pascal et Port-Royal," p. 17; Mesnard wants to date these notes from the year 1655 rather than 1658 as is often supposed; I cannot see any justification for the later date, seeing that the long passages on the two infinities certainly come out of his preoccupation with similar problems at the end of 1654, and there is also a direct use of the idea of substitution of the definition for the word defined in the fourth *Provinciale*, written in February, 1656; see *OC*, p. 693.

to outline the methods of proof. Geometry allows only nominal definitions, which means that we simply give a name arbitrarily to a concept in order to facilitate discourse. Such definitions, being arbitrary, are also free and cannot be contradicted: they amount to saying, for example, "By 'triangle' I mean a closed figure bounded by three straight lines," or something of the sort; these definitions imply nothing about the existence or nonexistence of what they define. But Pascal goes on to show that with such a rigorous and unexceptionable method, geometry would be impossible, for it is impossible to define all one's terms in this way: one keeps using words to define words and so we should go in a perpetual circle if we didn't stop somewhere. In fact, he points out, there are certain basic words ("mots primitifs") that are left undefined, such as space, time, movement, number, equality, etc. These words are already sufficiently clear to anyone who knows the language, and in any case no definition we could invent would make it any clearer what we mean by them. One of the examples used is close to our own subject:

Quelle nécessité y a-t-il, par exemple, d'expliquer ce qu'on entend par le mot homme? Ne-sait-on pas assez quelle est la chose qu'on veut désigner par ce terme? Et quel avantage pensait nous procurer Platon, en disant que c'était un animal à deux jambes sans plumes? Comme si l'idée que j'en ai naturellement, et que je ne puis exprimer, n'était pas plus nette et plus sûre que celle qu'il me donne par son explication inutile et même ridicule; puisqu'un homme ne perd pas l'humanité en perdant les deux jambes, et qu'un chapon ne l'acquiert pas en perdant ses plumes.[12]

But when we use these basic, undefined terms, we should not be under the illusion that we understand their essences, but only that we may proceed to say something about them with the assurance that those who understand the language will know what we are designating by them. Thus if we say something like "time is the movement of created things" we

12. OC, p. 579.

cannot take this as a definition of time from which we can then deduce certain things, but as either a nominal definition (i.e., "I mean by the word 'time' the movement of created things"), or else as a proposition which must itself be proven before anything can be deduced from it.

Now this radical nominalism seems to exclude any real definitions, and even though the Port-Royal *Logic* allows them, it is easy to see that the examples there ("L'homme est un animal raisonnable," "Le temps est la mesure du mouvement")[13] are specifically rejected by Pascal; and Arnauld, in the *Logic* adds, with Pascal, that real definitions are in fact propositions and need to be proven if they are contested. The *Logic* also points out that usage supplies us with the ordinary or dictionary meaning of words, and if we are to make ourselves understood, we must conform to these ordinary meanings; but this usage is always a little vague and subject to dispute and that is why it is important to have recourse to nominal definitions—substituting a definition for the thing defined—whenever there is equivocation.

This, very summarily, is Pascal's view, and it is easy to see from such a position why any notion of "human nature" might seem a very shaky concept on which to base a morality. It is much less easy to see how a theology of the will could be made to follow from a definition of the will. When Pascal says that the will is both free and determined by its delectations, is he not stating a real definition, i.e., a proposition which must be proven rather than a definition from which he can then draw inferences? Ah, but we have seen that for Pascal the freedom of the will (not, of course, particularly emphasized by him) is merely another way of saying its voluntariness.[14] That is, he has only insisted that what is not involuntary in the sense of compelled by something outside the will, is voluntary; or in other words it is inconsistent with usage and common sense to call acts of the will involuntary (or unfree) in certain cases simply because they do not also conform to other criteria

13. *La Logique,* ed. P. Clair and F. Girbal (Paris, 1965), I, xii, p. 86.
14. Cf. the fourth *Provinciale, OC,* p. 693, and the passage from Aristotle discussed above.

such as that of including a full knowledge of the good and evil involved, etc. So it is rather the Jesuits who, by seeking to read such additional criteria into a definition of the will, have abused the principle of definition.

The same is true in the case of the will's being determined by the stronger delectation, as is seen in the passage quoted earlier from the *Ecrits sur la grâce*: "Car qu'y a-t-il de plus clair que cette proposition, qu l'on fait toujours ce qui délecte le plus? Puisque ce n'est autre chose que de dire que l'on fait toujours ce qui plaît le mieux, c'est-à-dire que l'on veut toujours ce qui plaît, c'est-à-dire qu'on veut toujours ce que l'on veut. . . ." [15] By a series of substitutions, it is shown that to say we are determined by our delectations is the same thing as to say that we will what we will, and this is clear to our common sense. Further, Pascal does not then proceed to deduce anything from these definitions, but is trying only to show that this is the meaning of the term "will" in St. Augustine. The confusions in the interpretations of Augustinian doctrine—they are sometimes willful confusions—come from the attempt to make the will something other than a will: to make it into reason, judgment, or conscience. But when we will something in accordance with our reasons, it is because we have willed to follow our reason, not because reason has willed anything. The will is, in Pascal's sense, a basic term (a "mot primitif"), incapable of clear definition and yet clear enough as long as we don't try to explain it in other terms. It is the same as with "man": though we may not understand human nature, we all know what a man is, and it is only when we try to define him in other terms that we run into trouble.

Let us assume, at least for the moment, that Pascal's use of his terms is consistent with his own discourse on method, the *De l'Esprit géométrique,* and that terms are used as unequivocally as possible. We shall have, of course, to allow for the important exception of passages specifically aimed at the reader's emotions; for, as the second half of that treatise points out, men are less easily convinced by reasons than by passions: "L'art de persuader consiste autant en celui d'agréer qu'en

15. *IIIᵉ Ecrit, OC,* p. 1003.

celui de convaincre." [16] But even if we accept this method as basic to Pascal's thought and make allowances for rhetoric, rigor in our use of undefined terms may still seem to present us with more problems than it eliminates. If we follow Pascal in saying that the will is the will and therefore neither the reason, nor on the other hand some involuntary part of ourselves, we may begin to wonder whether such a thing exists as a will which includes neither deliberation nor involuntary motivation, or if it does, just what it is and how it is related to these latter elements. We must look at the other terms involved, then, in order to see the whole structure of Pascal's anthropology if we are to understand the scope and import of any one term.

The most central word for our subject, the most discussed and the most misunderstood, is the word "coeur" as Pascal uses it. The contradictions in interpretation often seem to correspond to contradictions in Pascal's own use of the term. Many have taken it to imply "sentiment" and think Pascal is a champion of sentiment as against reason; they have only to look at the *Esprit géométrique,* however, to see that the way of the heart is "contre la nature," "basse, indigne et étrangère." [17] Those who find the word "instinct" the best synonym for "coeur" and see him as a precursor of Rousseau and his "instinct divin," have to be reminded that "le coeur de l'homme est creux et plein d'ordure!" [18] And in fact it is obvious that the Jesuit idea of a continual natural inspiration toward the good, which Pascal attacked so vigorously in the fourth *Provinciale,* is much closer to Rousseau's "conscience" than is the Pascalian "coeur."

It is perfectly true that "volonté," "instinct," and "sentiment" are all used as synonyms for "coeur" in Pascal's writings, and

16. *OC,* p. 594; this aspect of Pascal's writings has been studied in detail in a recent book by Patricia Topliss, *The Rhetoric of Pascal: A Study of His Art of Persuasion in the "Provinciales" and the "Pensées"* (Leicester, 1966).

17. *OC,* p. 592.

18. Br. 143; *OC,* p. 1145.

further that the "coeur" is also an organ of knowledge: "Nous connaissons la vérité, non seulement par la raison, mais encore par le coeur." [19] Yet his use of the word is neither inconsistent nor difficult to define. We can safely say, I think, that he uses the word, not as it was used in sentimental novels, and not even altogether as it was used at Port-Royal with overtones of a systematic, rational-theological status: [20] he uses the word "heart" as it is used in the Bible, where it occurs perhaps a thousand times and designates the seat of all the faculties of the soul, whether volitional, affective, or intellectual. [21] Now this may seem a very unsatisfactory definition, since Pascal seems often to contrast "coeur" and "raison," and since the word "soul" seems today so very vague. But the point is that it was not vague for Pascal: the soul is what is saved, the part of us which is directly related to God, and so the heart is the place in us in which God acts, makes himself perceived, as well as felt or loved, and in short operates our salvation. As a result,

19. Br. 282; *OC,* p. 1221. This fragment contains the longest and most complete discussion of the "coeur."

20. Contrary to Jean Laporte, *Le Coeur et la raison selon Pascal* (Paris, 1950; originally published in the *Revue philosophique,* 1927), whose discussion is however one of the best on the subject. The same point of view is carried even further in the remarkable analyses of Mlle Jeanne Russier in her *La Foi selon Pascal,* 2 vols. (Paris, 1949). I do not wish to deny the "accord total" which Mlle Russier finds between Pascal's doctrine and that of Port-Royal (see II, 379), nor that it is possible to "éclairer par la théologie de Port-Royal" texts which are obscure or apparently contradictory (Laporte, p. 11). But, as has often been pointed out, the theology of Port-Royal was by no means monolithic and there were, besides great divergences in emphasis, efforts to systematize the basic Augustinian doctrine leaning variously toward Thomism, Cartesianism, etc., and which if applied to the interpretation of Pascal could both distort his meaning and also destroy our appreciation of his originality, which depends so largely on his "Ockham's razor" approach to philosophical systems. More helpful, perhaps, for a study of the "coeur pascalien" are the remarks of Dom Michel Jungo, *Le Vocabulaire de Pascal* (Paris, n.d.), pp. 113 ff., 169.

21. See H. Lesêtre, art. "Coeur," in the *Dictionnaire de la Bible,* II (Paris, 1899), cols. 822–26. Mlle Russier, *La Foi selon Pascal,* I, 156 ff., also emphasizes this dependence of Pascal on the biblical notion.

the knowledge of God that leads to salvation comes to the heart even though it is genuinely knowledge and not merely "sentiment"; and the knowledge of God that comes by reason alone—rational proofs and the like—"n'est qu'humaine et inutile pour le salut." [22] The heart, then, is not in any sense contrary to reason, any more than it is to instinct or unconscious habit ("la machine"): in Pascal's terms, it is of a different order, of the order of salvation. So the reason, even when employed in proving the existence of God, does not necessarily lead to salvation, for the heart must be touched by grace. In the same way, the mere external practices of religion, when they are mere habits of the "machine," do not lead to salvation unless grace intervenes: "C'est être superstitieux, de mettre son espérance dans les formalités," or again, "Attendre de cet extérieur le secours est être superstitieux." [23] Faith, which is "Dieu sensible au coeur," [24] comes only from God; however, this does not deny all value to proofs, as "la preuve est souvent l'instrument" of faith, and this proof can be either a proof of reason, or be a "preuve par la machine," [25] that is, through submission to the forms and habits of belief.

Yet there is still that other side of the heart, represented in such statements as: "Le coeur de l'homme est creux et plein d'ordure!" [26] For the heart is not only a faculty that enables man to know or love, nor a faculty at all in the usual sense; it is rather a capacity, an empty space capable of charity when filled with grace, but without grace, it has a horror of its own emptiness and fills itself with garbage; it is also then the organ of concupiscence. So, man's "déguisement . . . mensonge et hypocrisie . . . ont une racine naturelle dans son coeur." [27] The heart of fallen man is in a state of alienation, in which it retains its essential structure but has lost its true object; this is true of all our faculties: "L'esprit croit naturellement, et la

22. Br. 282; *OC*, p. 1222.
23. Br. 249, 250; *OC*, p. 1219.
24. Br. 278; *OC*, p. 1222.
25. Br. 248; *OC*, p. 1220.
26. Br. 143; *OC*, p. 1145.
27. Br. 100; *OC*, p. 1125–26.

volonté aime naturellement; de sorte que faute de vrais objects, il faut qu'ils s'attachent aux faux." [28] It is these structured capacities which are all that we can truly call man's nature: a body inclined to habit, a mind that forms judgments, and a heart or will that must love; none of them by itself contains any principle of truth or justice or piety. Nor is any of these faculties adequate to define man. Pascal, inventor of the calculating machine, also saw the implications of his invention for our notions of human reason: "La machine d'arithmétique fait des effets qui approchent plus de la pensée que tout ce que font les animaux; mais elle ne fait rien qui puisse faire dire qu'elle a de la volonté, comme les animaux." [29] The mind without a will is only a reasoning machine, and yet this will is only what we have in common with the animals. What defines man is his condition, which is for Pascal that of being fallen from grace. As most commentators have emphasized, it is the Fall and consequent corruption of man that governs the vision of man we think of as typical of Pascal, and which is expressed in those fragments usually grouped together under the title of "misère de l'homme." However, just what of human nature remains after the Fall and how it operates has occasionally been misunderstood in an attempt to interpret man's faculties in terms of a secular psychology. The reason for such attempts is clear enough; Pascal was an acute observer, first as an empirical scientist, and then in his remarks on human nature; and these remarks carry, often enough, a ring of truth even for naturalistic thinkers. Since the first publication of the *Pensées,* commentators have tried to save what seems true in Pascal and bend it to suit various non-Augustinian and secular philosophies. The result has been either to falsify Pascal's thought or to find it contradictory. But if we keep in mind the central facts of man's historical and collective Fall and its consequences, Pascal's vision of man remains coherent, and the

28. Br. 81; *OC,* pp. 1115–16. Cf. also Br. 423; *OC,* p. 1170, where it is said that man has a "nature capable du bien" but that "cette capacité est vide."

29. Br. 340; *OC,* p. 1156.

truth of his psychological insight can be seen to rest solidly on the truths of his theology.

All this will become even clearer if we look now at that most celebrated Pascalian text, the so-called "pari," or wager.[30] Hastily written and never reworked, the fragment nevertheless gives us useful insight into that movement of the will toward faith which is crucial to our understanding of Pascal's notions of freedom and grace. Without entering into the question of the validity of the mathematical argument from probability,

30. Commentaries on this fragment (Br. 233; *OC,* pp. 1212–16) are too numerous to mention. An excellent reading is that of Mesnard, *Pascal* (1965), pp. 36–44. Also interesting is the little book of George Brunet, *Le Pari de Pascal* (Paris, 1956). Cf. also the article of Jean Orcibal, "Le fragment 'infini-rien' et ses sources" with discussion in *Blaise Pascal* (Cahiers de Royaumont), pp. 159–95. M. Lucien Goldmann's article, with discussion, in the same volume ("Le pari est-il écrit 'pour le libertin'?," pp. 111–58), as well as the section of his *Le Dieu caché* on the "pari" (pp. 315–37) argues that the "pari" is really Pascal talking to himself (not to a "libertin") and so for Pascal, "croire" equals "parier." As M. Bénichou pointed out in the discussion at Royaumont (pp. 150–51), the text makes it abundantly clear that the interlocutor in the fragment is someone very different from Pascal, and to maintain that he represents a position with which Pascal had a secret sympathy is merely psychological speculation. In the long discussion of whether "croire" equals "parier," no one seems to have remarked that Goldmann's view is once again based on a misreading. There are two different meanings of the word "parier" as it is used in the text. In the sentence "Apprenez de ceux qui ont été liés comme vous et qui parient maintenant tout leur bien" (which Goldmann mistakenly supposes to apply to Pascal himself), the verb "parier," used transitively, means "engager son bien." But in the text "on me force à parier . . . [et] je ne puis croire" the verb "parier," in an absolute construction, means only "jouer." The gist of this part of the argument then is: one must bet either for or against God, since not to bet for him is to bet against him; but which way to bet? Pascal shows by the rules of probability that to bet against God is unreasonable. So to bet on God is to do the reasonable thing, but as the text shows, that is not to acquire faith, which (a) comes from God, and (b) is unreasonable and is reached not by reason but by the diminution of the passions. Thus "parier" equals "croire" only in the very limited sense of believing it is reasonable to believe in God; and to suppose that this describes Pascal's own faith is a manifest absurdity.

we can see the importance of the form of the argument, for the point of departure of the "pari" is the nearest equivalent for Pascal to the Cartesian *cogito*. Pascal's famous criticism of Descartes ("Il aurait bien voulu . . . pouvoir se passer de Dieu; mais il n'a pu s'empêcher de lui faire donner une chiquenaude, pour mettre le monde en mouvement; après cela, il n'a plus que faire de Dieu"[31]) has its roots in this fundamental difference in their point of departure. Descartes' pure thought indubitably thinking itself seemed to Pascal dubious, artificial, and superfluous: "Descartes inutile et incertain."[32] The most radical reduction we can make finds man not as reasoning, but simply as faced with the necessity of making a choice: "Il faut parier. Cela n'est pas volontaire, vous êtes embarqué."[33] The one thing man is obliged (willy-nilly) to do is to use his will, to make a choice, and there is no escape from that situation into pure reason or pure doubt. But one may decide to use one's reason to make the choice, and at this point Pascal tries to show that the "règle des partis," or what would come under the general heading "probability theory," is man's best guide because it takes into account man as an interested party, as a *volonté embarquée*. With probability theory we even have an advantage over the ancients: "Saint Augustin a vu qu'on travaille pour l'incertain, sur mer, en bataille, etc.: mais il n'a pas vu la règle des partis, qui démontre qu'on le doit."[34] So the reason no longer has any excuse for refusing this choice, nor for refusing in fact to choose to wager this finite life against "une infinité de vie infiniment heureuse." "Cela est démonstratif et si les hommes sont capable de quelque vérité, celle-là l'est."[35]

Now at this point, Pascal's interlocutor is supposed to be totally convinced by this rational proof but to feel himself nonetheless incapable of faith. Pascal reminds him that since his reason tells him to believe, it can only be his passions which

31. Br. 77; *OC*, p. 1137.
32. Br. 78; *OC*, p. 1137.
33. Br. 233; *OC*, p. 1213.
34. Br. 234; *OC*, p. 1217.
35. Br. 233; *OC*, pp. 1214–15.

hold him back, and recommends he take up the practices of faith as if he did believe. Then comes the line that has caused so much controversy: "Naturellement même cela vous fera croire et vous abêtira." [36] The word which could have furnished a key to this passage for those who were put off by "abêtir" is the "naturellement." For what does it mean to believe "naturally"? It means simply to have the habit of belief, because "la coutume est notre nature. Qui s'accoutume à la foi la croit." [37] Once again, in the *Pensées* as in the *Provinciales,* we see the whole concept of a human "nature" radically undermined. "Qu'est-ce que nos principes naturels, sinon nos principes accoutumés, et, dans les enfants, ceux qu'ils ont reçus de la coutume de leurs pères, comme la chasse dans les animaux?" [38] And so, "la coutume est une seconde nature, qui détruit la première. Mais qu'est-ce que nature? Pourquoi la coutume n'est-elle pas naturelle? J'ai grand peur que cette nature ne soit elle-même qu'une première coutume, comme la coutume est une seconde nature." [39] Belief, then, must become second nature, and the way that it does this is by submitting to custom, which is our human equivalent of the instincts of animals, and it is in this way that we become like animals. And there is no offense to reason as long as we see that this submission to custom

36. Br. 233; *OC*, p. 1216. The article of Etienne Gilson, "Le Sens du terme 'abêtir' chez Pascal," in his *Les Idées et les lettres* (Paris, 1932) is probably still the best on this subject, and I differ from his interpretation only in refusing the primacy of reason, which Gilson attributes to the Cartesian milieux of Port-Royal and by extension to Pascal. A recent article by Brian Foster, "Pascal's Use of *Abêtir*," *French Studies,* XVII (1963), 1–13, tries to do away with the difficulties by an alternative reading that rests on the absurd hypothesis that Pascal, an Auvergnat, and one acutely conscious of language and style, has nevertheless unconsciously used a Norman dialect word. Foster is adequately refuted by Stirling Haig, "A Further Note on Pascal's *abêtir*," *ibid.,* XVIII (1964), 29–32, citing very appropriately a recently discovered text: "L'Ecriture renvoie l'homme aux fourmis: grande marque de la corruption de sa nature. Qu'il est beau de voir le maître du monde renvoyé aux bêtes comme aux maîtres de la sagesse." See Mesnard (ed.), *Textes inédits,* p. 32.

37. Br. 89; *OC*, p. 1212.
38. Br. 92; *OC*, p. 1121.
39. Br. 93; *OC*, p. 1121.

is reasonable: "Il est donc juste que [la raison] se soumette quand elle juge qu'elle doit se soumettre." [40]

So our reason can be made to see that it is to our advantage to believe, and by acquiring the external habits of piety we can diminish the passions, which corrupt the reason and prevent belief. But let us be very clear on two points. First, reason has no primacy here over the voluntary, but only over that area of our lives we generally think of as involuntary, over the passions, fantasies, instincts, which distract or corrupt us but which can to some extent be tamed or integrated into the voluntary life by the discipline of faith; Pascal is not far here from the familiar Christian theme of the war between flesh and spirit. But the reason too has its difficulties, being both impotent to produce real belief, and also subject to the grave (and again traditional) spiritual sins of pride and presumption. So it in turn must submit to the flesh with its needs and habits; "l'homme n'est ni ange ni bête, et le malheur veut que qui veut faire l'ange fait la bête." [41] Beneath this dialectic remains always the necessity of choice, and the essential soul is neither rational nor natural but voluntary, a will or heart that must ultimately move toward God or be eternally separated from him. And so the second point to keep clearly in mind is that the argument of the "pari" is intended primarily to lead man back to himself, and to "ôter les obstacles," [42] but not of course to induce faith, which comes only from the grace of God. This is not a very subtle point and may seem hardly worth repeating, but to forget it would make a nonsense of the end of the text—the external appearance of faith would seem to be faith itself—and would also be in contradiction with Pascal's theology.

Much of the confusion, therefore, which has arisen in the exegesis of the texts dealing with the "coeur" comes from the failure to distinguish the heart and its reasons from the dialectic of reason and "coutume" or "abêtissement" that we have in the "pari" and elsewhere. It is true that the word "instinct"

40. Br. 270; *OC*, p. 1218.
41. Br. 358; *OC,* p. 1170.
42. Br. 246; *OC*, p. 1210.

is used as a synonym for "coeur" but not in the sense of animal instinct: this latter sense is reflected in the term "abêtir" and belongs to what is called "la machine," which is by no means the heart. The heart, as the seat of the faculties of the soul, is behind and above both these other faculties, and "Dieu sensible au coeur" is no closer to the machine and the empty habits of piety than to the reason; the famous distinction of the three orders of "corps," "esprits," and "charité" makes this perfectly clear.[43]

There are, however, a few texts that seem to contradict my interpretation, and have caused some commentators to see Pascal's thought as itself contradictory.[44] For he says, "Nous connaissons la verité, non seulement par la raison, mais encore par le coeur; c'est de cette dernière sorte que nous connaissons les premiers principes," and then he goes on to explain that "la connaissance des premiers principes, comme qu'il y a espace, temps, mouvement, nombres, [est] aussi ferme qu'aucune de celles que nos raisonnements nous donnent. Et c'est sur ces connaissances du coeur et de l'instinct qu'il faut que la raison s'appuie, et qu'elle y fonde tout son discours." [45] Now the idea of primitive notions which cannot be proved or defined but are basic to all our reasoning is already familiar to us from its development in the *Esprit géométrique* and is no doubt what Pascal has in mind here.[46] But the seat of these notions is, in this fragment, "coeur," "instinct," "sentiment," and the end of the text makes it clear that it is the real "coeur pascalien"

43. Br. 793; *OC*, pp. 1341–42. Perhaps the rather frequent failure to see that Pascal's thinking in these matters is essentially trinary rather than binary is due to nothing more than the habit of putting the fragments on the "esprit de géométrie" and the "esprit de finesse" at the beginning of the *Pensées*, thereby inducing us to take this as a fundamental distinction which determines what follows; in fact this distinction seems to have very little to do with the rest of the *Pensées* and is really nothing more than a reflection on a cliché of the mundane thought of the period. It was probably related, in Pascal's mind, only to questions of rhetoric, to the *Art de persuader*.

44. See, for example, Bénichou, *Morales*, p. 93, note.

45. Br. 282; *OC*, pp. 1221–22.

46. A note in the margin of the MS would seem to indicate this reference; see *OC*, p. 1222, n. 1.

that is involved, for it is there he says that without the "sentiment du coeur" given by God, "la foi n'est qu'humaine et inutile pour le salut." It would be easy then to read for "coeur" here, a natural instinct quite distinct from reason and closer to God. Yet it is equally certain that the heart or instinct described here is also in fact the soul. The "pari" itself begins: "Notre âme est jetée dans le corps, où elle trouve nombre, temps, dimensions." [47] So this knowledge of the heart is attributed also to the incarnate soul, and my definition seems to hold. What it comes to is this: our soul has an instinctive knowledge of what it experiences, namely space, time, movement, etc., and the seat of that knowledge is the heart. This knowledge is "natural" in the sense that it is a direct experience of nature. Now with this knowledge we project to other knowledge both by reason and also by habit or custom. So by reason we try to discover natural laws, but our attempts to systematize nature are doomed ultimately to failure: "Il y a sans doute des lois naturelles; mais cette belle raison corrompue a tout corrompu"—after "raison" here, Pascal first wrote "dogmatisante." [48] "La nature . . . est toute familière et commune," but our logic is only able to "guinder l'esprit" and turn us away from it.[49] However, habit is no more reliable than reason: "qui a démontré qu'il sera demain jour, et que nous mourrons? Et qu'y a-t-il de plus cru? C'est donc la coutume qui nous en persuade." [50] But on the other hand, of atheists who doubt the resurrection, we read: "Quelle raison ont-ils de dire qu'on ne peut ressusciter? quel est plus difficile, de naître ou de ressusciter? . . . La coutume nous rend l'un facile, le manque de coutume rend l'autre impossible: populaire façon de juger!" [51] In short, the only true knowledge of nature we have is our immediate experience, which is hardly knowledge at all, and must be aided both by reason and habit, both of which are fallible. So neither of these principles can lead us to salvation,

47. Br. 233; *OC*, p. 1212.
48. Br. 294; *OC*, p. 1150.
49. *De l'Esprit géométrique*, *OC*, p. 602.
50. Br. 252; *OC*, pp. 1219–20.
51. Br. 222; *OC*, p. 1182.

though Pascal seems to give habit a certain advantage over reason in this domain. But even sentiment has its dangers ("La fantaisie est semblable et contraire au sentiment, de sorte qu'on ne peut distinguer entre ces contraires" [52]), and as we have shown it is only when God Himself touches the heart that any knowledge useful for salvation ensues.

But the fact that the heart is the seat, even without an additional grace, of the immediate experience of space and time, though not of any further knowledge about them, shows us that the knowledge which is useful for salvation must be of the same sort: an immediate presence of God to the soul, not a rational proof or an habitual devotion. If we recall certain passages evoked in the preceding chapter, we may remember that Pascal insists that "le présent est le seul temps qui est véritablement à nous, et dont nous devons user selon Dieu," and again, "ce n'est que faute de savoir bien connaître et étudier le présent qu'on fait l'entendu pour étudier l'avenir." [53] And this is certainly the meaning also of this aphorism from the *Mystère de Jésus*: "Si Dieu nous donnait des maîtres de sa main, oh! qu'il leur faudrait obéir de bon coeur! La nécessité et les événements en sont infailliblement." [54] Even when touched by grace, the heart does not become an enlightened reason or an habitual knowledge, but a continual renewal of a present immediate knowledge of God's will operating in events, of our being in the hands of God, in a way analogous to the ungraced heart's knowledge of its spatio-temporal condition, which it has directly without reason or habit.

There is one other way in which the Jansenist theology can be related to the argument of the "pari," and that is in the question of its appeal. One of the commonest arguments against Pascal's wager is that it appeals only to self-interest, it asks us to believe without regard for the truth of the content of that belief or even for the morality of such a belief; a rapprochement is often made between Pascal and William James. That there is some truth to this criticism is undeniable, and a

52. Br. 274; *OC*, p. 1221.
53. Letter no. 8 to Mlle de Roannez, *OC*, p. 517.
54. Br. 553; *OC*, p. 1313.

confrontation with his theology seems to confirm this. In making his argument by analogy with a game of chance, Pascal clearly appeals to the desire for gain, and this desire, purely selfish as it is, would certainly come under the theological heading of concupiscence. Does Pascal imagine that, by a simple wager, concupiscence can be converted into charity? Let us recall how Pascal and the Augustinians conceived of concupiscence: it is seeking one's happiness in created things when the only true happiness is to be found in God—it is loving the world rather than God. The role of the wager then is simply to eliminate reason as an ally to concupiscence; it is not reasonable, Pascal argues, to seek infinite happiness in finite things, one must look for an infinite being to satisfy such a desire. One may then argue: yes, but who needs infinite happiness? Why can't we be satisfied with finite pleasures? At this point we must recall the place the wager was to occupy in the context of the Apology; for all that was to precede the wager was to be exactly a demonstration of the transitoriness, futility, vanity, the nothingness, in short, of our worldly pleasures and diversions. By the power of his rhetoric, Pascal would first make man feel the desire to transcend such "plaisirs empestés." No one knew better than Pascal that all proofs rest on unproved assumptions. His assumptions are those of his theology: that man is a fallen creature with an eternal destiny for which he retains an obscure but powerful nostalgia, and which he is totally powerless to realize by his own efforts. He is in need of liberation and healing (both words occur frequently in Pascal's writings), and the wager is an answer to those needs. It is for this reason that the argument has a therapeutic goal rather than aiming at philosophical irrefutability—this last being rejected by Pascal as useless. If one cannot accept Pascal's assumption that man is in need of therapy, then his argument will of course remain without validity. Pascal does not attempt to prove this assumption, only to make one feel it is true with all his "art of persuasion."

So far we have attempted to show that Pascal's psychology of the faculties of mind, heart, and will has consistency and is also consistent with his theology. Such a psychology has of course many traditional elements, has even a rather Scholastic ring to it. However, there is another dimension to the Pascalian psychology which is less traditional, and includes some of his more radical positions. He also sketches for us a relational psychology, a series of observations of man in relation to others, and to himself, and ultimately to God.

Man's life in society has furnished the material for many of Pascal's most famous observations, although in these "pensées" he is perhaps least original, owes most to Montaigne. Virtually all our human activities, our social relations, are shown to be something other than they appear to be, to be governed by other laws. They may be governed by pure fantasy, or what Pascal calls "imagination"; so, for example, judges and doctors are all charlatans practicing "sciences imaginaires," but who make us believe they possess true justice or real power of healing by their imposing costumes or impressive apparatus.[55] Or our actions may be governed by a more general principle—in which, however, imagination plays a part; this is the principle of "divertissement," which Pascal defines as follows: "Divertissement.—Les hommes n'ayant pu guérir la mort, la misère, l'ignorance, ils se sont avisés, pour se rendre heureux, de n'y point penser."[56] And this desire not to have to think about ourselves and our situation motivates not only what we usually think of as our diversions or distractions (gaming, hunting, the theater, etc.), but indeed most of our activities: "Sans examiner toutes les occupations particulières, il suffit de les comprendre sous le divertissement."[57] Even the concern over one's business, one's reputation, one's family, the desire for learning, for good health or good looks, all these things that occupy us day by day are sought not for their own sake but because concern with them keeps us distracted from our true selves and our true destiny, helps us to forget that "le dernier acte est sanglant, quelque belle que soit la comédie en tout le reste: on jette enfin de la terre sur la tête, et en voilà

55. Br. 82; *OC*, p. 1118.
56. Br. 168; *OC*, p. 1147.
57. Br. 137; *OC*, p. 1138.

pour jamais." [58] Under this view virtually all human activity then represents an alienation of man from himself; man seeks his happiness by trying to forget what the conditions of his existence (and therefore of his happiness) are. How is this possible? Only by a ruse which would hide our true self, cover it with another self. This ruse is called "amour-propre."

A long fragment develops this notion of "amour-propre" and its mechanism:[59] "La nature de l'amour-propre et de ce *moi* humain," he begins, "est de n'aimer que soi et de ne considérer que soi. Mais que fera-t-il? Il ne saurait empêcher que cet objet qu'il aime ne soit plein de défauts et de misères." This state of affairs produces what Pascal calls "la plus injuste et la plus criminelle passion qu'il soit possible de s'imaginer," which is the desire to hide this disparity both from himself and from others. Now this passion has for Pascal a precise theological genesis and explanation, which is best summed up in the letter on the death of his father, discussed earlier, and which in turn recapitulates material in the *Écrits sur la grâce*.[60] Man was created with two loves: a love for God, which was to be infinite, and a love for himself, which was to be finite; both loves were just and blameless in the state of innocence. But with Adam's sin, the first love was lost, and a soul capable of loving infinitely was left with only itself to love. "Cet amour-propre s'est étendu et débordé dans le vide que l'amour de Dieu a quitté; et ainsi il s'est aimé seul, et toutes choses pour soi, c'est-à-dire infiniment." [61]

It is this infinite (and therefore criminal) love of oneself that characterizes all human activity since the Fall, and that poisons all human relations, for as he shows, it leads to deceit, lies, flattery, hypocrisy.[62] It is because of this "amour-propre" that "le *moi* est haïssable"; because "chaque moi est l'ennemi et voudrait être le tyran de tous les autres," and it is so because "il se fait centre de tout." [63] This famous "pensée" is not an

58. Br. 210; *OC*, p. 1148. Cf. Br. 143; *OC*, p. 1145.
59. Br. 100; *OC*, pp. 1123–26.
60. See above, pp. 66–68.
61. *OC*, p. 496.
62. Br. 100; *OC*, pp. 1123–26.
63. Br. 455; *OC*, pp. 1126–27.

example of what Voltaire thought was sublime misanthropy; it is addressed to Miton, a "libertin" and "honnête homme," whose manners were self-effacing and obliging toward others. But Pascal insists that such manners may eliminate the disagreeable social consequences of the "moi" but not its fundamental injustice; so he is simply trying to show that, in accordance with his Augustinian theology, man's basic disease cannot be cured by the superficial remedies proposed by the philosophy of the "honnête homme." The cure must necessarily be more radical; we must both learn to hate ourselves and also seek "un être véritablement aimable pour l'aimer. Mais comme nous ne pouvons aimer ce qui est hors de nous, il faut aimer un être qui soit en nous et qui ne soit pas nous. . . . Or il n'y a que l'Etre universel qui soit tel. Le royaume de Dieu est en nous; le bien universel est en nous, est nous-même et n'est pas nous." [64]

Now this last passage may seem to smack of the metaphysical; but Pascal was not only uninterested in metaphysics, he believed ontology to be strictly impossible. Of all the "mots primitifs" discussed above, "being" is the most primitive, the least capable of definition.[65] He instead tends to use the word "être" in a sense akin to the "existence" or "Dasein" of the existentialists and to turn his reflections to the psychology of the Ego. The most precise and important fragment for understanding Pascal's thought on this subject is the following:

Nous ne nous contentons pas de la vie que nous avons en nous et en notre propre être: nous voulons vivre dans l'idée des autres d'une vie imaginaire, et nous nous efforçons pour cela de paraître. Nous travaillons incessament à embellir et conserver notre être imaginaire, et négligeons le véritable. Et si

64. Br. 485; *OC*, p. 1306.
65. In the *Esprit géométrique*, Pascal lays down as a rule of definition that the word defined must not appear in the definition or otherwise there is tautology—he makes great fun of a Jesuit who had said, "La lumière est un mouvement luminaire des corps lumineux." He also points out that one cannot define "Being" without saying "Being is. . . ." "Being" is thus incapable of even a nominal definition and so all metaphysical systems are based on an absurdity. See *OC*, pp. 579–80.

nous avons la tranquillité, ou la générosité, ou la fidélité, nous nous empressons de le faire savoir, afin d'attacher ces vertus-là à notre autre être, et les détacherions plutôt de nous pour les joindre à l'autre; nous serions de bon coeur poltrons pour en acquérir la réputation d'être vaillants. Grande marque du néant de notre propre être, de n'être pas satisfait de l'un sans l'autre, et d'échanger souvent l'un pour l'autre! Car qui ne mourrait pour conserver son honneur, celui-là serait infâme.[66]

This passage, which underlies Pascal's observations on "gloire" and "honneur" and "vanité," and relates to the whole seventeenth-century complex of "être-paraître," [67] demands that we give some attention to its terms. We have first "notre propre être" (or "être véritable"), which, however, we neglect in favor of our "être imaginaire." Now this second term is described as our existence "dans l'idée des autres," an existence which is imaginary in the sense that it is strictly illusory. In another fragment, where Pascal begins by asking, "Qu'est-ce que le *moi*?" he goes on to show how our existence for others is purely that of the attributes they see in us, that we never really exist for them as ourselves. He shows that if I am seen from the window by someone standing there to watch the passersby, I exist for him only as a passerby, not as myself; and this is equally true of those with whom we are most intimate: "On n'aime donc jamais personne, mais seulement des qualités." [68] Our existence in the "regard d'autrui" is strictly fragmentary, as well as ephemeral; yet out of the qualities which others occasionally attribute to us (or which we hope they do) and for which we are (or hope to be) admired, we construct an imaginary being, another self, a "moi idéal," to the great detriment of our true being. Well, we may now want to ask, just what is this true being we so readily neglect? If we equate it simply with consciousness, we shall not be far from the thought of a psychoanalyst like Daniel Lagache, who sees the consciousness

66. Br. 147; *OC*, pp. 1127–28.
67. See, for example, the analyses of Jean Rousset, *La Littérature de l'âge baroque en France: Circé et le paon* (Paris, 1953).
68. See Br. 100; *OC*, p. 1165.

as always in danger of being ensnared by its fascination with the "moi," but capable of real knowledge when directed toward real objects.[69] But for Pascal something else is involved. As we saw in the theology of "amour-propre," it is not just consciousness, but love which is involved; to stay with the psychoanalysts, we should say that man has undergone a displacement of his cathexis from the Father to his ideal Ego. In the Pascalian vocabulary, it is the heart which now finds itself trapped by this narcissistic illusion and incapable of escaping from it.[70]

Now if we keep this psychology in mind, we can also see one of the deep reasons why Pascal rejected so vehemently the Molinist view on grace and free will. The great danger (psychologically speaking) inherent in the Pelagian or Molinist doctrine of merit is that it leaves the "moi" trapped in this same futile attempt to create an image of itself which God

69. Cf. D. Lagache, "Fascination de la conscience par le moi," *La Psychanalyse,* III (1957), 33–45.

70. I see no difficulty in reading Jacques Lacan's celebrated schema (see his *Ecrits* [Paris, 1966], p. 548), the simplest form of which is:

in which S = the Subject, a = his objects (l'autre), a' = his "moi" (in Pascal's sense), and A = l'Autre, as a diagram of Pascal's notion of the results of Original Sin. However, Lacan, "grand lecteur de Pascal" though he may be, clearly does not rejoin him on all counts. Even though, for Lacan, the "Autre" is found in the same position in the schema as the "Nom-du-Père" (p. 553), and this position is described as "le lieu d'où peut se poser [au sujet] la question de son existence," Lacan does not seem to accept that the alienation thus represented is the result of a real historical event—though Freud, incidentally, apparently did. For Pascal, then, the aim is for the "discourse of the Other" (Lacan's definition of the Unconscious) to be precisely the discourse of God in history, discussed earlier, or, for the Christian, the discourse of the Church; it is for this reason that mechanical acceptance of the practices of the Church is exactly appropriate, for they are the representations of a discourse that not only calls our existence into question, but actually reestablishes it in the symbolic (rather than the imaginary) order.

will find admirable for its good works and virtues, and will be forced to love and save. Such a doctrine was, in Pascal's own observation, psychologically false, as well as theologically mistaken. But if, with Pascal, we renounce the "moi" with its narcissistic illusion, we at least open ourselves to the possibility of salvation, though that salvation must always come from God: "Consolez-vous: ce n'est pas de vous que vous devez l'attendre, mais au contraire, en n'attendant rien de vous, que vous devez l'attendre." [71] We must recognize our radical dependency on God and recognize the falsity of that most far-reaching of Renaissance errors, the notion of the autonomy of the Ego. And we must do so not to prove our humility (and attribute even that virtue to our Ego) but simply because it is the truth.

It would seem then that Pascal, who developed a theology of freedom in the *Ecrits sur la grâce,* offers us in the *Pensées* the basis, not for a philosophy of freedom, but for the psychology of freedom. And the first tenet of this psychology is, not the autonomy of the Ego, but its ambiguity. We may recall how in the first *Ecrit* he emphasized the saying of Christ, "Ce n'est pas moi qui fais les oeuvres, mais le Pére qui est en moi," to which Pascal adds: "Jésus-Christ ne veut pas être principe, et vous le voulez être." [72] And again the saying of St. Paul, "Je vis, non pas moi, mais Jésus-Christ en moi." [73] So both the ambiguity and the arrogance of the "moi" have a theological, even a scriptural basis. Pascal seems further to have been aware of the linguistic ambiguity of the first personal pronoun, that is, that the "je" of a linguistic utterance is not identical with the speaker, does not even signify the speaker in the usual way; as he understood it, the "je" of any linguistic utterance normally designates the "moi" of the speaker, that is the speaker as he presents himself to the other (the listener, or reader of the utterance), in other words, the "moi imaginaire." And it is this very "moi" which a Christian wishes to suppress.

71. Br. 517; *OC,* p. 1296.
72. *OC,* p. 950.
73. *OC,* p. 949.

According to one witness, Pascal went so far as to try to avoid the use of the first personal pronoun altogether in his own speech.[74]

A very large portion of our discourse, then, or indeed of our conscious lives, is really in the service of this "moi," is the slave of its needs. Even reason, the creator of systems which are either tautological (as geometry) or misrepresent nature (e.g., Cartesian physics), is for Pascal at the service of our "amour-propre": it is what we should call nowadays "rationalization." Our most rational statements are still always at least partially determined by what Pascal would call the passions or concupiscence, what we would call unconscious motivation. Yet our concupiscence is not, as we have just seen, a simple selfish desire, a mere hedonistic craving. It is complicated by its attachment to the "moi"; so in the wager text, and more explicitly in many of the "misère de l'homme" fragments of the *Pensées,* it is not only the "plaisirs empestés" that lead us astray, but even more it is "gloire" and "honneur," that is, the desire to "build up our egos" in the ways we discussed earlier. If we look at the "wager" in psychological terms, we see that Pascal's therapeutic has two fundamental goals: first, to convince us that our reason is really only rationalization, for once this is recognized we can proceed to deal with the forces that really govern our lives—our unconscious motivations based in concupiscence. The second step is to show that our real self-interest (as opposed to a concupiscence complicated and confused by its preoccupation with the "moi") leads us to opt for God. However, we are not really ready to make this choice, which so far could only be made on the rational level, without any deeper motivation; the sources of a true decision remain inaccessible to us. What is accessible, however, is a purely physical level (what Pascal calls the "machine"), so we can go to Mass, etc., as Pascal admonishes. In this way he apparently believes that the unconscious may be conditioned to the point where its resistance is dissolved, and we not only give rational and physical assent but the assent of the heart as well.

74. Nicole in the *Logique,* III, xx, 6, p. 267.

These levels may be seen schematized in a diagram borrowed (slightly modified) from another psychoanalyst:[75]

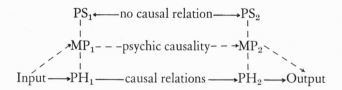

$$PS_1 \longleftarrow \text{no causal relation} \longrightarrow PS_2$$

$$MP_1 - - \text{psychic causality} - - \rightarrow MP_2$$

$$\text{Input} \longrightarrow PH_1 \longrightarrow \text{causal relations} \longrightarrow PH_2 \longrightarrow \text{Output}$$

This schema shows stimuli which in time produce responses as operating in a way that can be traced causally on the purely physical level (the bottom line), but which also involve mental processes (the middle line) in which psychic causality operates. The top line is the level of our conscious lives and between one conscious moment and the next there is no causal relationship; this is of course strictly true, for we do not say that at the level of our conscious discourse one statement *causes* another, or even that a statement or a conscious intention *causes* the actions we proceed to do. Now, looking at such a schema, we can see without difficulty where freedom fits in: it clearly belongs to the top line. That is, lacking any external constraint, we have the impression or feeling that we are free, for one moment of our conscious lives does not cause another; they simply succeed one another, although they are in fact the results of unconscious physical and psychic causation. So the feeling of being free, as also the feeling of being fated, are both epiphenomena that prove nothing about our actual condition; both feelings are obviously considered by Pascal to be irrelevant if not detrimental to our understanding of ourselves. To say with the libertarian (or Molinist), "I have free will," is to attempt to attribute to our "moi" a quality that belongs only to the conscious subject (and a trivial quality at that) and so further enslave the subject. To say with the predestinarian (or extreme Calvinist), "My actions are predes-

75. E. Hartmann, "The Psychophysiology of Free Will: An Example of Vertical Research" in *Psychoanalysis—A General Psychology: Essays in Honor of Heinz Hartmann,* ed. R. M. Loewenstein et al. (New York, 1966), p. 523.

tined," is (as Augustine also saw) to try to say, "My *moi* is blameless," and so to remain in the same snare. Both positions are psychologically false and detrimental to the spiritual life.

The preceding analysis, which is, I believe, an accurate schematization of the Pascalian psychology, has nevertheless done exactly what I criticize some other writers for doing: it has ignored the properly supernatural or theological dimension. When we say that for Pascal the mechanical acts of faith seem to condition one for the true assent of the heart, we must also bear in mind that that assent will never come without an act of grace which originates in God alone. Yet there is some assurance that this grace will come ("seek and you shall find"); and this being the case, are we not right back with the Molinists, seeing God's grace as a reward for pious acts? No, for as we saw in the *Ecrits sur la grâce,* the pious acts are themselves a result of God's grace. Yet this too is paradoxical, for it is Pascal's wager that is supposed to lead to the performance of these acts. But what Pascal said of metaphysical proofs of the existence of God is just as true of his own argument: proofs are useless for salvation unless they are instruments of grace. There have always been many who have remained unconvinced by, or indifferent to philosophical proofs, and so since the publication of the *Pensées,* many have been unmoved by the argument of the wager; but this does not mean the argument is invalid, only that the reason is too blinded by passions, the heart too grave with concupiscence to accept its implications. Pascal's Apology, with the argument of the wager, was to be at best a discourse which would so undermine the rational discourse of the "free-thinker" that this latter would be ready to accept, and enter into the discourse of the Church instead. Pascal was certainly aware that his argumentation, a human discourse, was no more certain of attaining its end than any other, and in fact was much less so; for opposed to its success was not just reason but also concupiscence, and to overcome the latter God's grace had to come to the aid of Pascal's words. But the role of an apology such as Pascal undertook was not an irrelevant or indifferent one; for it was not only to recommend the discourse of the Church as the only one worthy of adherence, but also to become part of that discourse. For the conversion of the heart, seen by Pascal and the Port-Royalists generally as the very center of the Christian life, was not a conversion to a life of spiritual contemplation: it was a conversion to life of charity, a life Pascal would say was infinitely above the life of the spirit. But this life of charity was to be lived in and through the Church, a Church consisting not merely of religious and ecclesiastics, but of all the Elect: "hommes de tout sexe, âges, conditions, complexions, de tous les pays, de tous les temps, et enfin de toutes sortes."[76] The words and actions of any of its members become part of the history of the Church and are thus relevant to salvation. Pascal did not wish his Apology to have more than this relevance; it could not have the weight of doctrine, and specifically denounced the pseudo-gravity of metaphysical proof. But for him there was no paradox, even in a Jansenist context, in giving it whatever force his own reason, rhetorical ability, and faith could give it, knowing that in the realm of conversion it was strictly impossible to rival or supplant God's grace, but also that it was a diminution of the life of the Church, a sin against charity, to refuse one's efforts.

It is for these reasons that, in this relation of the individual to the action of God in the Church, or of the individual will to God's predestining will, the doctrine of the Mystical Body takes on great importance for Pascal. In the fragments on the "membres pensants," Pascal develops the "figure" that perhaps best expresses the relation of our wills to the Divine will: "Si les pieds et les mains avaient une volonté particulière, jamais ils ne seraient dans leur ordre qu'en soumettant cette volonté particulière à la volonté première qui gouverne le corps entier."[77] And if our hearts are indeed converted by God's grace and we enter into the full life of the Mystical Body, even our "amour-propre" is transformed and the "moi" is no longer "haïssable": "on s'aime parce qu'on est membre de Jésus-Christ. On aime Jésus-Christ parce qu'il est le corps dont

76. II*e* Ecrit sur la grâce, OC, p. 966.
77. Br. 475; OC, p. 1304. Other important passages on the Mystical Body include Br. 473–76, 480, 482–83, 485; OC, pp. 1304–6.

on est membre." [78] But for this submission of the will to be complete, it must recognize that the will of God is absolute and his justice is not to be questioned; so Pascal says of a member which had discovered its participation in the Body, "avec quelle soumission se laisserait-il gouverner à la volonté qui régit le corps, jusqu'à consentir à être retranché s'il le faut! . . . car il faut que tout membre veuille bien périr pour le corps, qui est le seul pour qui tout est." [79]

Again in this context it is interesting to note the peculiar dialogue between the individual will and the Divine will. It is not a relationship of causality: God, moving one of his members, does not cause it to move in the sense of physical causation, any more than we would normally say, "I caused my hand to go up," but rather, simply, "I raised my hand." And likewise we don't say, "I predict my hand will go up," but "I am going to raise my hand"; and the notion that our hand at that moment might be thinking, "Well, I think I'll go up now," would make us either laugh or be angry at its presumption. When the individual will acts as it is predestined to act, by grace, it acts as God intends it to, not as he causes it to. And if the dignity of man consists in his ability to think (as Pascal says), the one true goal of his thought is to recognize his radical dependency on God, his membership in the Mystical Body: the "roseau pensant" becomes the "membre pensant."

The doctrine of the Mystical Body, however, also serves as a bridge between Pascal's theology of grace and his notions concerning the Christian in society. If the Mystical Body is composed essentially of the Elect, the notion of such a body depends ultimately on the fact that we are all descended from Adam; as Pascal notes of the Jewish people, "C'est un peuple tout composé de frères, . . . tout sorti d'un seul homme, et, étant ainsi tous une même chair, et membres les uns des autres, [ils] composent un puissant état d'une seule famille." [80] If all mankind is not a single family, the Augustinian theology is nonsense; but if we are all brothers, the Christian has no ex-

78. Br. 483; *OC,* p. 1306.
79. Br. 476; *OC,* p. 1305.
80. Br. 620; *OC,* pp. 1195–96.

cuse for remaining aloof, separated from the lives of other men. Many commentators seem to have been led astray regarding Pascal's attitude on the Christian's relation to society, perhaps because, as Pascal himself recognized, certain phases of the Jansenist doctrine seemed to induce despair. And in pointing out that even very young children are indoctrinated by society with the desire for glory—that supreme illusion of the Ego—he then notes: "Les enfants de Port-Royal, auxquels on ne donne point cet aiguillon d'envie et de gloire, tombent dans la nonchalance." [81] At least one illustrious reader of Pascal has found in the *Pensées* only a sort of contemplative ideal for man, one which denies all value to human action. [82] And yet such an interpretation cannot be sustained. First, the notion of a "quietist" Pascal who wished only to "demeurer en repos, dans une chambre" [83] is completely contrary to what we know of Pascal's life. He was a person of great energy and enormously varied activity, one who even when almost totally immobilized by illness undertook the quite secular task of organizing a sort of bus line. Another "pensée," less frequently quoted than the above, says that "notre nature est dans le mouvement; le repos entier est la mort." [84] It is no doubt correct to say that Pascal had a very strong nostalgia for Paradise or for the beatific vision, which may have arisen from the longing for his lost mother, and was perhaps encouraged, as I mentioned, by the experience of the *Mémorial*. But if the goal of the Apology is the conversion of the heart, the true goal of the heart is not contemplation but charity: "Tous les corps ensemble, et tous les esprits ensemble, et toutes leurs productions, ne valent pas le moindre mouvement de charité." [85] The result of conversion is not withdrawal from human life or activity but a renewal of it.

Others would point to the so-called political fragments that

81. Br. 151; *OC*, p. 1128; cf. Br. 781; *OC*, p. 1293.
82. Paul Bénichou in *Blaise Pascal* (Cahiers de Royaumont), pp. 216–17.
83. Br. 139; *OC*, p. 1139.
84. Br. 129; *OC*, p. 1137.
85. Br. 793; *OC*, p. 1342.

seem to make Pascal out as an ardent defender of the *status quo;* and in his life Pascal does seem to have been politically conservative—a devoted royalist during the Fronde at least. But let us look at these fragments. One of the main themes is that "les opinions du peuple sont saines." [86] Albert Béguin has shown that these fragments are part of the "renversement du pour au contre" and thus reflect a tactic of the Apology rather than a supposed political theory of Pascal's; in fact, Béguin's main reproach is that Pascal did not seriously trouble himself over such matters.[87] Underlying the dialectic is a contrast of the three orders of body, mind, and heart and their respective ways of knowing. We begin with "la pure ignorance naturelle où se trouvent tous les hommes en naissant";[88] if one remained in this ignorance one would be all right. But the mindless masses, who judge correctly on the basis of habit and appearances, i.e., within the realm of the physical, think their opinions are founded on reason, and so "le peuple est vain quoique ses opinions soient saines: parce qu'il n'en sent pas la vérité où elle est." [89] But even worse are the "demi-habiles" who, using their reason, see that the mass of people are unreasonable and their laws unjust: "Ceux-là troublent le monde, et jugent mal de tout." [90] The true "habiles" judge things by "une pensée de derrière . . . en parlant cependant comme le peuple";[91] we are still within the order of reason, but, as at the end of the "pari" of reason submitting to custom. When the order of the heart is invoked, however, although it resembles this last point of view, the "chrétiens parfaits" honor the opinions of the people "par une autre lumière supérieure," which is, as we have seen, the knowledge that events—the way things are—are the will of

86. See Br. 313, 316, 324, 328, 335, etc.; *OC,* pp. 1163–66. Cf. the analysis of Br. 298 (*OC,* pp. 1160–61) by Erich Auerbach in "On the Political Theory of Pascal" in his *Scenes from the Drama of European Literature* (New York, 1959), pp. 101–29.

87. See "Pascal sans histoire" in his *Pascal par lui-même* (Paris, 1952), pp. 81–92.

88. Br. 327; *OC,* p. 1166.

89. Br. 328; *OC,* p. 1166.

90. Br. 327; *OC,* p. 1166.

91. Br. 335; *OC,* p. 1167.

God. This is the view of the "grandes âmes, qui, ayant par-couru tout ce que les hommes peuvent savoir, trouvent qu'ils ne savent rien, et se rencontrent en cette même ignorance d'où ils étaient partis." [92] Now this last position much resembles that of the clever man who sees the need for reason to respect custom; but while in the clever man such a view might be interpreted in the direction of political conservatism, in the true Christian, it cannot. For the true Christian respects only the order of God, and the events that express this order may include radical changes as well as an established order. We shall see this difference more clearly as we develop an analysis of this condition of the true Christian; what is clear in these texts is that whatever social action a Christian takes must be motivated not by the sort of political reasons which even the clever man might use, but by charity. Without charity, all is concupiscence, and this is the foundation of the political thought of even the cleverest nonbeliever: "on s'est servi comme on a pu de la concupiscence pour la faire servir au bien public; mais ce n'est que feindre, et une fausse image de la charité." [93] It seems then that it is as hard to find a political theory either progressive or conservative, activist or quietist, in the *Pensées* as it is in the New Testament; it is excluded primarily by the demands of the Apology; it remains to be seen whether it is also excluded, as Béguin seems to think, by a timeless other-worldliness characteristic of the Jansenist milieu.

The historicity of man's condition is certainly one of the most difficult of all theological principles to discuss and keep firmly in mind. Rational thought is by its nature opposed to historical truth, aiming as it does at a truth that transcends historical vicissitudes. Yet, as we have seen, every important element of Pascal's analysis of man must be defined historically. There is no human nature separable from the story of a mankind that was created sane, just, and free, and which lost

92. Br. 327; *OC*, p. 1166.

93. Br. 451; *OC*, p. 1126. Cf. also the remarkable article of Marcel Raymond, "Du jansénisme à la morale de l'intérêt," *Mercure de France*, no. 1126 (June 1957), pp. 238–55, on the development of this notion in the seventeenth and eighteenth centuries.

those attributes through Adam's Fall. The attempt to define a nonhistorical human nature is the worm in the apple of Thomism which the Jesuits swallowed whole and brought forth as the viper's tangle of casuistry and the new morality. And the attempt to interpret the *Pensées* as a description of such a permanent human nature leads to the idea of the "sublime misanthrope" or the anguished preromantic, or other mistaken views of their author.

It may seem untoward to insist so on the historical nature of Pascal's thought when one of his most distinguished modern critics has taken him to task exactly for lacking a sense of history.[94] The question raised by M. Béguin is in fact several questions which we must try to keep distinct. There is the first and fundamental question as to whether the unfolding of time plays an essential rôle in his thought, or whether Pascal's vision is classical, timeless, nonhistorical. Here, it seems to me, we must insist most strongly on the essentially historical nature of his vision. In an age of philosophical systems, and a physical mechanism that transcended and destroyed time, Pascal more than anyone in his age and society—even among his Augustinian friends—upheld the Augustinian vision, not only against the Jesuits, but against Thomists and Cartesians, scientists and mathematicians: "Dieu d'Abraham, Dieu d'Isaac, Dieu de Jacob, non des Philosophes et des savants."[95] The revelation of Christianity is essentially a Sacred History, and the events of that history from the Creation and the Fall of Adam to the Incarnation and the awaited Second Coming are, for Pascal, more important and more enlightening than any philosophical system known or possible; philosophical systems are in fact shown to be themselves mere temporal manifestations and are seen in the light of an historical development that transcends them.[96] It is hardly necessary to emphasize the role of this "theology of history" in Pascal's thought: it was to play an enormous part in the Apology, and the ramifications of it fill

94. Béguin, "Pascal sans histoire," pp. 81–92.

95. *Mémorial, OC,* p. 554.

96. See Br. 73, 366, 367, 369, 370, 436, and *passim; OC,* pp. 1114–15, 1135–37.

only slightly less than half of the total pages of the *Pensées*. And one of the main points of the rest of the Apology was to show that man is a "monstre incompréhensible" as long as he tries to understand himself in purely philosophical terms without reference to his historical situation. But this is of course always with reference to Sacred History; Béguin's criticism is rather that Pascal's thought seems to have no place in it for secular history, or rather to describe secular history as pure vanity—an enormous waste motivated by concupiscence and doomed to damnation.

Once again a distinction must be made between two questions: the first would concern the individual's attitude toward secular life, i.e., to what extent the Christian is called to participate in the society of his time and in the better aims of that society; we shall return to this question shortly. The other question is the intellectual question of how we conceive secular history, particularly in its relation to the History of Salvation. Here, as Béguin recognizes, we are outside the scope of the Apology and consequently need not expect to find very many helpful texts, but there are nonetheless indications of Pascal's position. As Béguin says, there is none of the meditation on the density and mystery of historical becoming that characterizes some thinkers since the nineteenth century, and also perhaps certain passages of St. Augustine. But the elements of the Augustinian view are all there: the emphasis on the Mystical Body and the insistence on the invisibility of election, which we saw developed in the *Ecrits sur la grâce* as an essential difference between Jansenists and Calvinists; this doctrine sees God's intentions as hidden and mysterious until the end of time: a doctrine which in fact puts considerable weight on an historical development which cannot exclude secular history, since it cannot really distinguish it from the History of Salvation.[97] And finally there is the generosity and justice of God toward all men (not just the elect) and the desire of Christ for the salvation of all.

This last position, involving the fifth condemned proposition

97. Besides the *Ecrits sur la grâce*, see in the *Pensées*: Br. 515, 518, 521; *OC*, pp. 1297–99.

of Jansenius, has led some commentators to see Pascal as abandoning the Jansenist position on this point.[98] However, this is difficult to maintain: the position in the texts in the *Pensées*[99] is exactly that of the *Ecrits sur la grâce* and of the *Abrégé de la vie de Jésus Christ*,[100] namely, that the statement "Christ died for all men" can be understood in two ways depending on whether you are considering Christ as man or Christ as God. This is merely a matter of common sense; Pascal goes further, however, and finds fault with those who emphasize the fact that his death did not benefit all men, rather than the fact that it was offered for all. It is possible that he has in mind some of his Jansenist friends,[101] but possible also that, as in the *Ecrits sur la grâce*, he means the Calvinists, and wishes to preserve the Augustinian doctrine from the gloomy air they seem to give it. In any case, it is clear that although all humanity will not finally be saved, only God's judgment will discern, at the end of time, the Elect from the damned. So, what Henri Marrou says of the Augustinian doctrine could also express the conception of Pascal: "Nous possédons le sens de l'histoire, mais par la Foi, c'est-à-dire d'une connaissance qui demeure partiellement obscure. C'est le sens global de l'histoire qui nous est révélé; non le détail, les modalités de sa réalisation." [102] Although the unbeliever must be made to see the vanity of the ideals of secular society, the Christian, enlightened as to the ultimate direction of history, will look for the hand of God at work even through the vanity of men, drawing good out of evil. Pascal was more concerned to lead the unbeliever to the point where he could receive this vision than to produce meditations upon it which might please the mind but leave the heart untouched. For a philosophy of history remains always a philosophy and therefore is itself ahis-

98. See, for example, Br. 781; *OC*, p. 1293, and nn. 1 and 2, *OC*, pp. 1513–14.

99. Br. 774, 775, 781; *OC*, pp. 1292–93.

100. *OC*, p. 649.

101. This could explain the only authentic anti-Jansenist statement in the *Pensées*: Br. 865; *OC*, p. 1331.

102. *L'Ambivalence du temps de l'histoire chez saint Augustin* (Montreal and Paris, 1950), p. 79.

torical; but an apology that rejects philosophy and attempts rather to move its readers into a religion that is in its very essence historical hardly deserves the reproach of lacking a sense of history. In the History of Salvation, Pascal is undoubtedly more interested in the salvation than in the history, but the one cannot exist without the other, and Pascal was one of the very few in an age of philosophy and science to see this clearly and to base all his thinking on it.

Finally, concerning the question as to what extent the Christian is called to participate in the society of his time and in general to contribute to the better aims of society, it seems incredible that anyone familiar with Pascal's life could suppose that he somehow rejected society or life in the world. It is true of course that he admired and encouraged those who chose to withdraw for the sake of the religious life—his sister Jacqueline and Charlotte de Roannez are notable examples. But his attitude on the question of the signature also made it clear that he did not consider even the religious as exempt from the cares and obligations of other Christians, and indeed in the seventeenth century they were not. In any case, although Pascal must have considered the religious life for himself, he not only rejected such a withdrawal but seems to have accepted his worldly condition with an equanimity bordering on lightheartedness.

Nor do the *Pensées* anywhere contradict such an attitude. On the contrary, near the end of the wager he reminds his interlocutor of the advantages of choosing God and losing oneself: "Vous serez fidèle, honnête, humble, reconnaissant, bien faisant, ami sincère, véritable." [103] And elsewhere he says, "Nul n'est heureux comme un vrai chrétien, ni raisonnable, ni vertueux, ni aimable." [104] The import of these statements is clearly that the Christian convert does not withdraw from human society, but becomes more truly human. He has of course undergone a change of heart: his activity is no longer mere diversion or distraction, motivated by concupiscence and

103. Br. 233; *OC,* p. 1216.
104. Br. 541; *OC,* p. 1301.

egoism—although these are never in this life entirely absent; his motivation is now primarily charitable, done not for his own gain or glory, but for others, and so for God. Conversion, for Pascal, was never a refusal of society or history, of the world as our scene of operations, our very condition of life. It was rather a reentry into human society with purified motives, an entry into history with a fuller understanding and acceptance of its process. And to return to our old question of freedom, the true Christian's activity in the world will actually be freer. Because, although it is always possible for him to fall from grace, he is yet free from the anxiety of having to merit his salvation. His most characteristic virtue is hope, a virtue that presupposes existence in time and precludes both a fatalistic attitude and also a Pelagian one, for, as Pascal notes, if we could truly earn our salvation, "le juste ne devrait donc plus espérer en Dieu, car il ne doit pas espérer, mais s'efforcer d'obtenir ce qu'il demande!" [105]

The very real contrast between the outlook of Pascal and that of the "humanisme dévot" of the sixteenth and seventeenth centuries has led too many to suppose that Pascal is a sort of antihumanist. The following passage, besides giving us a clear picture of Pascal's goal as apologist, also shows much about his assessment of man.

Contrariétés. Après avoir montré la bassesse et la grandeur de l'homme.—*Que l'homme maintenant s'estime son prix. Qu'il s'aime, car il y a en lui une nature capable de bien; mais qu'il n'aime pas pour cela les bassesses qui y sont. Qu'il se méprise, parce que cette capacité est vide; mais qu'il ne méprise pas pour cela cette capacité naturelle. Qu'il se haïsse, qu'il s'aime: il a en lui la capacité de connaître la vérité et d'être heureux; mais il n'a point de vérité, ou constante, ou satisfaisante.*

Je voudrais donc porter l'homme à désirer d'en trouver, à être prêt, et dégagé des passions, pour la suivre où il la trouvera, sachant combien sa connaissance s'est obscurcie par les passions; je voudrais bien qu'il haït en soi la concupiscence qui

105. Br. 514; *OC*, p. 1297.

le détermine d'elle-même, afin qu'elle ne l'aveuglât point pour faire son choix, et qu'elle ne l'arrêtât point quand il aura choisi.[106]

This passage summarizes much of what I have tried to bring out already: man's true nature as a "capacité vide," the need to both love and hate oneself, and so forth. It also shows the precise limits of Pascal's ambition, not just for his Apology, but for self-knowledge and the efforts of human reason. It has been said that Pascal's vision is essentially discontinuous, there being no communication between the three orders of body, mind, and heart; and that there exists likewise an unbridgeable abyss between man and God. One author says that Pascal wished to "couper les ponts de l'homme à Dieu sans renoncer à les faire exister l'un pour l'autre."[107] Such a notion, however, presupposes that outlook, characteristic of Renaissance Humanism, in which man sets out to reach God and can do so only by deeds of valor or towers of intellect. The ideal of a St. Ignatius, at least in the early stages of his conversion, was totally that of the heroic deeds to be done to reach God, and the ideal of the chivalrous saints does not seem so far from that of the chevalier of metaphysics, Descartes. The bridges built in the name of an all too human rationalism and "gloire" had to be destroyed. Yet Pascal did not accept the total lack of communication that seems to be characteristic of both Calvinism and the fideism of Montaigne; they are accused of fostering despair or a "nonchalance du salut." The true way to God, then, was not through building great edifices, which could only be towers of Babel, nor in despairing of all communication, but, as the above passage says, in being ready and alert and wanting to find the bridge that God built to man. So the "humanisme dévot" of the Renaissance depended on a notion of man as fundamentally independent of God but with the power to reach God through his efforts. Pascal, on the other hand, notes that "l'homme n'est ni ange ni bête, et le malheur

106. Br. 423; *OC*, p. 1170.
107. Bénichou, *Morales*, p. 90.

veut que qui veut faire l'ange fait la bête." [108] Man's efforts to scale the heights are doomed, but once he recognizes his radical dependency on God and accepts God's efforts to reach him through Jesus Christ, he is more truly human in this life and destined for a glory greater than that of the angels. Pascal's humanism thus lies more in his hope for humanity than in his confidence in man's powers; but his descriptions of the spiritual life of the true Christian show far more than a narrow theologism. Hatred for self is counterbalanced by a new self-acceptance, and, as one no longer feels endangered by other Egos, one's relations to others are also transformed in the direction of self-effacement and generosity. And even one's relation to nature is affected; as one learns to abandon the "esprit de système" and live in the present, nature is no longer merely an object to be subjected to laws, but speaks directly to the heart in a relation that approaches intersubjectivity. There is no doubt a dimension that is properly mystical involved here, though this is a debated point;[109] the relation to a recognized Christian mystical tradition is not so clear. But there are points in Pascal that suggest closer parallels may be found in oriental mystical doctrines, in particular that of Zen Buddhism with its emphasis on an immediate and mindless relation to the world, however different may be the paths that lead to this new awareness.

Theology, as I have tried to show throughout this book, played a far more important role in the development of Pascal's thought than is usually supposed. His interest in theology and his efforts to acquire a serious understanding of its implications date from the time of his first conversion (1646), and his interest, his study and meditation of the Bible, and even the presumption that he understood some aspects of theology better than the professionals: all can be traced to this early period. Further, there is no reason to suppose that this interest was lost

108. Br. 358; *OC*, p. 1170.
109. See the interesting analysis by H. Gouhier in his *Commentaires,* chap. I, and in the Royaumont volume, with discussion, pp. 296–341.

even in the so-called mundane period; and there is no justification at all for supposing that when he came to the writing of the *Lettres provinciales* he was still theologically naïve and had to have his theology dictated to him by Arnauld and Nicole.[110]

As to what his theology was, there is not the slightest doubt that it was the Augustinian theology as interpreted by Jansenius and Saint-Cyran and their followers. Difficulties over Pascal's Jansenism invariably arise out of the habit of regarding Jansenism as some sort of bugbear, a pernicious and monolithic heresy that taints all associated with it. A sensible historical perspective reveals that it is merely a label given to a group of defenders of the Augustinian doctrine of grace as that doctrine was undermined and threatened with extinction in the Renaissance. Nor is this to say that the Jansenists were right and the Molinists wrong: both groups can claim their ancient authorities—the Molinists echoed not only Pelagius but also the almost unanimous sentiment of the pre-Augustinian Fathers. And if the Jansenists can claim the weight of Conciliar support, Molinists nevertheless represented something like a new mind of the Church struggling against Augustinian conservatism.

Pascal claims to have looked at both sides of these questions and opted most decisively for the Augustinian view, for reasons that may originally have had more to do with the question of reason and revelation than with questions concerning grace and free will; our knowledge of Pascal's early thought is too sparse to allow of any definite conclusions on that point. In any

110. The question of Pascal's debt to Port-Royal is a thorny one, already discussed in part earlier. In a recent debate on the subject, J. Dedieu has taken issue with the thesis of Mlle Russier (in her *La Foi selon Pascal*); see *XVIIᵉ Siècle*, nos. 9–10 (1951), pp. 35–49; the replies of Mlle Russier and others are in the same periodical, nos. 17–18 (1953), pp. 59–77. In my view Mlle Russier is entirely right to emphasize Pascal's fundamental agreement with Port-Royal doctrine, as well as the latter's orthodoxy; Dedieu's attempts to oppose Pascal to Port-Royal seem misguided. However I agree with Dedieu that in many cases of congruence of ideas it is at least reasonable to suppose that the influence went from Pascal to Port-Royal rather than the reverse.

case he clearly never abandoned the basic Augustinian doctrines but rather proceeded to elaborate on them in his own way with a view, perhaps again dating from soon after the first conversion,[111] to the writing of an Apology for Christianity. In both the projected Apology and in the *Lettres provinciales* the Augustinian (or Jansenist) theology is not only very much present, but supplies the real intellectual basis for both works, being at the source of all the apparently diverse discussions and attacks in the *Provinciales,* and supplying the framework for understanding the whole anthropology of the *Pensées.* Even the tactics of the Apology presuppose a Jansenist view of man, and not only as regards the role of reason. For example, Pascal offers us no vision of damnation such as we find in a Dante or a Bernanos, and the reason is that fear was not considered, in the Jansenist theory of "delectatio," to be an adequate motive force to turn the heart toward God.

But in looking at Pascal's own attempts to write real theology —the so-called *Ecrits sur la grâce*—we discover that although the doctrine is Jansenist, the style is not. Here Pascal shows not just a clarity and conciseness which contrast strongly with the style of an Arnauld, but as always an originality of approach. His emphasis on linguistic analysis is virtually unique in theological writing before the twentieth century. It is not at all the same sort of thing that occupied the Scholastics, who were concerned with precision of concepts; Pascal was keenly aware that theological statements, even those of a Pope or a Council, were made by men who meant something by them in a particular historical, intellectual context; so, although their truth is *not* therefore relative, their meaning is.

And this characteristic of his theological writing carries over into all his writing, especially into the *Pensées.* It is an almost unparalleled ability to rethink man's problems entirely from within the limitations of our condition. So when writing against the vanity even of philosophers, who are after all only seeking their own glory, Pascal adds, "Et ceux qui écrivent

111. This notion, which I suggested in a thesis some years ago, has been recently put forward in considerable detail by Henri Gouhier, *Commentaires,* esp. chap. II.

contre veulent avoir la gloire d'avoir bien écrit; et ceux qui les lisent veulent avoir la gloire de les avoir lus; et moi, qui écris ceci, ai peut-être cette envie; et peut-être que ceux qui le liront. . . ." [112] Denouncing "amour-propre" does not make one exempt from it; quite the contrary. Of course, as a thinker who saw that a fly could disrupt a metaphysical proof, that a pretty face or a kidney stone could change the course of history, and who considered a sneeze to be as worthy of philosophical reflection as deeds of valor, Pascal was not so original; the example of Montaigne was always before him. But Pascal refused the Montaignian shrug of the shoulders ("que sais-je?") and sought always to get as near to the truth as the condition of our language and our reason allow. Questions such as that of the existence of God and of the immortality of the soul are real questions of vital importance to every man; but philosophical answers are not real answers, because philosophers assume they can be answered in the abstract, out of time, free from the passions which animate us, ignoring the role of the questioner. This, then, is the primary characteristic of that strange argument, the wager, which has enticed but often repelled philosophers: that it tries to give the best answer possible to these questions without attempting to rise above the conditions of human existence to do it. So much of what seems to be paradoxical in the *Pensées* arises out of the same point of view. It is not, as M. Goldmann would have it, a refusal of the world from within the world: it is rather a total acceptance of the world in the knowledge that all our aspirations are other-worldly; it is the application to our intellectual life of the mystery of the Incarnation.

Yet this also echoes, and for Pascal probably arises out of meditation on the Augustinian doctrine of grace. For man's will is free, but he cannot freely will his salvation unless predestined to do so, and God's predestination is entirely beyond our grasp. In fact it was the aspiration toward freedom as independence that lost us our freedom in the Garden of Eden, and which still distorts our notions of freedom so that we cannot abide grace. For even grace does not restore the absolute

112. Br. 150; *OC*, p. 1129.

freedom Adam enjoyed, but only a present sense of radical dependency on God's will which enables one to reason in good faith, to live in hope, and to act in charity. We become, at best, free as the birds are free, that is, in harmony with a nature that is the always actual expression of God's will.

The Augustinian theology would seem to me then the only basis for a consistent interpretation of Pascal's thought, for that thought is largely theological in its origins and in its continued inspiration. It is a theology which, in Pascal's version, leaves a large place to observation, because events are direct expressions of the will of God and because "les choses corporelles ne sont qu'une image des spirituelles." Behind the observations of human nature and society in the *Pensées,* however, there is almost always a theological understanding which alone supplies their coherence. And it is because of this underlying unity of his thought that Pascal never feared to stretch his ideas to their limits, for in so doing he felt neither contradiction nor anguish but only the omnipresence of a central and substantial Truth.

The dating of the *Ecrits sur la grâce* will, of course, involve some notions concerning their nature and purpose. The date most often given for them is 1657–58; the reason given is that they show us a Pascal "mieux informé sur les dogmes de la grâce qu'il ne l'était au début des *Provinciales*." [1] Or as Jean Mesnard has put it: "La rédaction des *Provinciales* aura fourni à Pascal l'occasion d'acquérir une culture théologique qui sera ultérieurement mise en oeuvre dans les *Ecrits sur la grâce*." [2]

This reasoning seems to me to involve two assumptions not justified by the evidence. The first is that of Pascal's theological naïveté at the time he undertook to write the *Provinciales*. According to this tradition, based largely on the account of Marguerite Périer, when Arnauld turned to Pascal in January 1656 and asked him to do something about their plight, Pascal undertook to write the first *Provinciale* and in doing so discovered his talent as a popularizer of theology, a subject with which he had only a superficial acquaintance. Again according to Marguerite Périer, Pascal admitted that he was aided in writing the *Provinciales*; as Steinmann would have it, "Il écrivait à la hâte et sous la dictée de ses maîtres," [3] and it has become common to say that the wit, style, and presentation of the *Provinciales* are Pascal's, while the theology is entirely due to Arnauld and Nicole. However, the remarks attributed to Pascal by Marguerite Périer give rather a different account

1. Lafuma (ed.), "L'Intégrale," p. 311.
2. "Pascal et Port-Royal," *Revue de théologie et de philosophie*, 1963, no. 1, pp. 12–23.
3. *Pascal*, p. 164.

of the aid received; what Pascal says is that he had his friends read the books of the Jesuits, for otherwise, "il aurait fallu que j'eusse passé ma vie à lire de très mauvais livres."[4] There is no suggestion that his friends also did his reading for him in St. Augustine or Prosper or Fulgentius, or even in Jansenius. And the Jansenist pamphlets, discovered by Mlle Jansen,[5] annotated in Pascal's own hand, certainly show that for an amateur he knew the specialized literature rather well, and made direct use of it in the writing of the *Provinciales*. Scholars have perhaps tended to identify too readily the "naïf" whom Pascal created as his narrator in the early *Provinciales* with Pascal himself. It is true that such scholars as Cognet and Orcibal, well informed in theological matters, consider that Pascal's theological writings are unprofessional and naïve, as they undoubtedly are compared to those of Arnauld and Nicole; yet they admit that in the case of Pascal such naïveté can be a virtue. In any event, they apply these views to both the *Provinciales* and the *Ecrits sur la grâce,* in which case nothing is implied regarding the anteriority of one to the other.[6] What is clearly inconsistent is to hold, as did Steinmann, that Pascal's theological writings are both amateurish and also dictated by Arnauld and Nicole.

There is, moreover, much evidence opposed to the tradition of Pascal's theological ignorance before 1656. Shortly after his first conversion in 1646, he was reading Saint-Cyran, Jansenius' *Réformation de l'homme intérieur,* probably Arnauld; and the *Préface pour le traité du vide* (written at the latest in 1651, more probably in 1647) seems to indicate he had read at least part of the *Augustinus*. Again in 1647 he seems to have felt sure enough of himself in theology to go before the local bishop to challenge the orthodoxy of a well-known lecturer on theology, Jacques Forton, sieur de Saint-Ange.[7] In the letter of

4. *OC*, p. 1458.

5. Paule Jansen, "La Bibliothèque de Pascal: les sources des *Provinciales* d'après les notes autographes inédites de Pascal," *Revue historique*, October–December 1952, pp. 228–35.

6. See *Blaise Pascal* (Cahiers de Royaumont), I, 20–21, 39, 45.

7. See Mesnard, *Pascal* (1962), pp. 31–33; also E. Jovy, *Etudes pascaliennes,* Vol. I: "Pascal et Saint-Ange" (Paris, 1927).

January 26, 1648, to Gilberte, Pascal tells of his visit to the Jansenist, M. de Rebours, to whom Pascal says that

nous avions vu leurs livres et ceux de leurs adversaires; que c'était assez pour lui faire entendre que nous étions de leurs sentiments. . . . Je lui dis ensuite que je pensais que l'on pouvait, suivant les principes mêmes du sens commun, démontrer beaucoup de choses que les adversaires disent lui être contraires, et que le raisonnement bien conduit portait à les croire, quoiqu'il les faille croire sans l'aide du raisonnement.[8]

M. Henri Gouhier has analyzed this episode in detail,[9] but, his interest being the origins of Pascal's apologetic, he seems to me to miss the unmistakable implication that what Pascal thought he could show[10] by reason or common sense had to do with the position of the Jansenists and the attacks of their enemies, in other words, with specifically Jansenist positions and not simply with general Christian truths. It seems quite undeniable, then, that within a couple of years after the first conversion Pascal had not only acquired a considerable knowledge of the theology of the Augustinians but he even thought himself capable of making original contributions to their defense; this may represent only the enthusiasm of an amateur, but Pascal was never at any period more than a well-informed amateur in this domain, and I would argue that he was so already by the end of 1647. In the years leading up to the second conversion of 1654, Pascal's interest in these questions no doubt slackened, but not so much that he couldn't write the eloquent letter on the death of his father (very much à la Saint-Cyran) in 1651. And if Professor Goldmann is correct, in spite of his quarrel over Jacqueline's dowry, Pascal took enough interest in the Port-Royal position to side with Barcos against submission to the Bull *Cum Occasione* in 1653.[11] It seems inconceivable,

8. *OC*, pp. 481–82.
9. *Commentaires*, pp. 105–25.
10. "Montrer" is apparently the correct reading; see GE, XI, 349.
11. See L. Goldmann, *Correspondance de Martin de Barcos* (Paris, 1956), Introduction, p. 25. J. Orcibal challenges Goldmann's evidence

then, that Pascal, who had given the Augustinian theology serious study since 1647, and continued even through his "mundane" period to identify himself with that theology and its Jansenist interpreters, should need—or be able, given his extraordinary intellectual verve—to place himself at the feet of Arnauld in order to learn enough theology for either the *Ecrits sur la grâce* or the *Provinciales,* which are, after all, by all accounts, still only the work of a clever amateur. Isn't it clear rather that for all we know Pascal could perfectly well have written the *Ecrits sur la grâce* entirely unaided as early as 1648?

The second error found in most speculation about the *Ecrits sur la grâce* is to take them *en bloc* and assume they were written at roughly the same time. There is no evidence for this, and the many differences of form, style, and vocabulary seem rather to argue for their separation in time.

As to any positive evidence for an earlier date for the *Ecrits sur la grâce,* the most striking fact is that of the sources so far identified for these writings none was published later than 1649. "Fait curieux," says M. Mesnard, that these sources are "des théologiens de Louvain, Conrius, Sinnich, les plus proches de Jansénius; en revanche Arnauld n'est pas utilisé." [12] The fact is not only curious but completely incomprehensible if Pascal is supposed to have waited until 1656–57 to learn his theology from Arnauld himself in order to be able to write the *Ecrits.* If, *before* writing the *Ecrits sur la grâce,* Pascal had already written the *Provinciales* and had used in their preparation Jansenist books and pamphlets published between 1649 and 1656, why then didn't he use them for the *Ecrits sur la grâce?*

In order to attempt to assign plausible dates to the *Ecrits sur la grâce* then, we must first distinguish the five or more different works represented: the two doctrinal expositions (Cheva-

---

on this matter; see his review of Goldmann in the *Revue d'histoire écclésiastique,* Vol. 52 (1957), pp. 877–99. However, one of Orcibal's arguments is that Pascal would not have taken an interest in the matter before the *Provinciales,* which is just the view I am challenging.

12. "Pascal et Port-Royal," p. 17.

lier's *Ier* and *IIe Ecrit*); the one or more letters on the possibility of the commandments, etc. (Chevalier's *IIIe Ecrit* and a fragment of the *IVe*); and two treatises, one unfinished (in Chevalier's *IVe Ecrit*).

Of these, the *IIe Ecrit* would seem to be the earliest, being a simple exposé of the Augustinian doctrine in which the Molinists are referred to only as "les restes des Pélagiens" as they often are in the *Augustinus*. There is nothing here arguing for an advanced theological culture, only for a clear and intelligent assimilation of basic Jansenist doctrine. It certainly could have been written in 1647, and the simple matter-of-fact tone indicates it is an attempt to put forth these doctrines as clearly as possible for someone concerned but not well acquainted with the theological disputes. It could well have been written for Jacqueline or Gilberte.

The *Ier Ecrit* is more complex; of the two fragments, the second seems to begin as a continuation of the first but breaks off and goes back over some of the same material—an apparent reworking—and ends with the ambitious project of tracing the doctrine of grace back from the seventeenth century to the Church Fathers, though it breaks off with Peter Lombard. The method of the first fragment could suggest a rapprochement with either the "raisonnement bien conduit" which Pascal mentioned to M. Rebours as applying to these questions in 1648, or to a similar attitude as expressed to Nicole, presumably around 1656–58.[13] The extensive and ambitious use of citations of other theologians suggests a later date, as do also the similarities with the *Ve Ecrit des Curés des Paris* that have been noted.[14] It is perhaps the likelihood of a later date for this *Ier Ecrit* that has led scholars to assume a later date for all the fragments.

The fragments of a letter (or letters) on the possibility of the commandments, the "délaissement des justes," and related matters (Chevalier's *IIIe Ecrit* and one fragment in the *IVe*) are perhaps the richest in suggestions for dating. Why does Pascal say, "Je n'ai ni loisir, ni livres, ni suffisance pour vous

13. See GE, XI, 100–102.
14. E.g., in the GE, XI, 102.

répondre . . ."? Where is he, and when, that he has no books and has to rely on his old favorites Conrius and Sinnich—books he probably owned—rather than the resources of Port-Royal? To whom is he replying? To someone concerned first about the reconciliation of Jansenist doctrines with the Council of Trent, and a familiar of Pascal (he says he is going to put in writing things he has already discussed with him), who is now separated from him. M. Mesnard has suggested that this letter (or letters) was written for the Duc de Roannez;[15] M. Mesnard promises to discuss this hypothesis in the Introduction to Volume II of his edition of the *Oeuvres complètes* (not yet published at the time of this writing). It is an interesting suggestion, which fits all the known facts, and which, if true, would help us to date the fragments more precisely. We should feel sure then that it was written: (1) after Pascal's second conversion when he was concerned with the conversion of the Duc; (2) when the Duc was absent from Paris; and (3) before the *Provinciales*—as I would argue contrary to Mesnard. For Mesnard sees a rapprochement of these fragments with the letters to Mlle de Roannez (written in the fall and winter of 1656–57) on the grounds that the theology of the *Ecrits sur la grâce* underlies the spiritual doctrines of the letters to Mlle de Roannez; but the *Ecrits* could then just as well have preceded the letters. Also, the lack of polemical tone in the *IIIᵉ Ecrit* argues against these fragments being written at the same time as the *Provinciales*, for they would surely have been affected as indeed the letters to Mlle de Roannez are affected by the preoccupation with the *Provinciales*: as Mesnard says, "Pascal n'aurait-il pas été obsédé par la lutte qu'il menait alors?"[16] On the other hand, the Duc was absent from Paris from August 17, 1655, to May 8, 1656; the fall of 1655 seems to me a far more likely date for such a letter (or letters) to have been addressed to the Duc. A further advantage to this earlier date is that putting the *IIIᵉ Ecrit* just before the writing of the *Provinciales* offers an explanation for another riddle: when Arnauld asked Pascal to do something for their cause, he

15. *Pascal et les Roannez*, I, 515, n. 1.
16. *Ibid.*, I, 509.

presumably did not suggest what form Pascal's effort should take; but if Pascal had just been writing a theological letter (or letters) to his friend the Duc in Poitou, what would suggest itself to him more readily than a *Lettre écrite à un provincial par un de ses amis?*

The fragments of treatises in the *IVᵉ Ecrit* treat the same subject matter more systematically. The method used (which I discussed in Chapter II) suggests a rapprochement with the work on definitions that is found in the *De l'Esprit géométrique* and again in the Port-Royal *Logic*.[17] The period at which Pascal was engaged on such work is again usually taken to be 1657–58, but Mesnard suggests that most of this activity took place in 1655,[18] an hypothesis that is supported by Jacqueline's letter of October 1655[19] concerning Pascal's method for teaching children to read, a method which found its way into the Port-Royal *Grammar*.[20] As I have tried to show, there is no valid reason for not placing the *IVᵉ Ecrit* in this same period, before the *Provinciales*.

I am well aware that I offer no conclusive evidence for any of these suggested dates; perhaps M. Mesnard, with his extraordinary genius for this sort of research, will come up with something positive in his edition of the *Ecrits*. I have, however, tried to show that there is no better evidence for putting the *Ecrits* in 1657–58 than there is for the earlier dates I have suggested for some of them.

17. *La Logique*, pp. 86–93.
18. "Pascal et Port-Royal."
19. *OC*, p. 1455.
20. *Grammaire générale et raisonnée* (Paris, 1660), Iᵉʳᵉ partie, chap. VI; for further discussion of Pascal's contribution to the *Grammar*, see J. Miel, "Pascal, Port-Royal, and Cartesian Linguistics," *Journal of the History of Ideas*, Vol. 30 (1969), no. 2 (April–June), pp. 261–71.

Translations from
the *Ecrits*

From the *Ier Ecrit; OC*, pp. 948–49.

If, then, one asks why men are saved or damned, one can
say in a sense that it is because God wills it, and in a sense that
it is because men will it.

But it is a question of ascertaining which of these two wills,
namely, the will of God or the will of man, is master, is dominant, is the source, principle, and cause of the other.

It is a question of knowing whether the will of man is the
cause of the will of God, or the will of God the cause of the
will of man. And the one which will be dominant and master
of the other will be considered as in some sort unique; not that
it is so, but because it includes the cooperation of the subordinate will. And the action will be attributed to this first will and
not to the other. This is not to say that the action cannot also
be attributed in a sense to the subordinate will: but it is
properly attributed only to the master will, as its principle. For
the subordinate will is such that one can say in a sense that
the action proceeds from it, since it cooperates in it, and in a
sense that the action does not proceed from it, since it does not
originate the action; but the primary will is such that one can
well say of it that the action proceeds from it, but one cannot
at all say that the action does not proceed from it.

———

From the *Ier Ecrit; OC*, p. 954.

That all men are obliged to believe, on pain of eternal damnation and of sinning against the Holy Spirit, a sin irremissible

in this world and the next, that they are of that small number of the Elect for whose salvation Jesus Christ died; and they are obliged to think the same of any men on earth, however wicked or impious they may be, as long as they have still an instant of life remaining, leaving the discernment of the Elect from among the reproved as God's impenetrable secret.

From the *Ier Ecrit; OC,* p. 955.

[The Church] is consoled in that these contradictory errors establish her truth; that it suffices to leave them to themselves in order to destroy them, and that the weapons that these diverse enemies use against her can do her no harm and can only ruin them.

It is not only in this instance that she experiences contradictory enemies. She has virtually never been without this double combat. And as she has experienced this contradiction in the person of Jesus Christ, her head, whom some have called man only, and others God only, she has felt this contradictoriness in almost all other facets of her belief. But, in imitation of her Head, she stretches out her arms to both sides to call them all and embraces them all together to form a happy union.

From the *IIe Ecrit; OC,* pp. 964–67.

THE DOCTRINE OF ST. AUGUSTINE

St. Augustine distinguishes two states of men, before and after sin, and has two opinions appropriate to these two states.

Before the Sin of Adam

God created the first man, and in him all human nature.
He created him just, sound, strong.
Without any concupiscence.
With a free will equally flexible toward good and evil.

Desiring his beatitude, unable not to desire it.

God could not create any man with the absolute purpose of damning him.

God did not create men with the absolute purpose of saving them.

God created men with a conditional intention of saving them all generally if they observed His injunctions.

If not, of treating them as would a master, that is, of damning them or granting them mercy according to His own pleasure.

Innocent man, issuing from the hands of God, although strong and sound and just, could not observe the commandments without God's grace.

God could not with justice impose injunctions on Adam and innocent men without giving them the grace necessary to carry them out.

If men at their creation had not had a grace sufficient and necessary to observe the injunctions, they would not have sinned in transgressing them.

God gave to Adam a sufficient grace, that is, one beyond which no other was needed in order to carry out the injunctions and remain in a just state. By means of which he could persevere or not persevere according to his own pleasure.

So that his free will, as master of this sufficient grace, could render it efficacious or useless, according to his pleasure.

God left and allowed to Adam's free will the good or bad use of this grace.

If Adam by means of this grace had persevered, he would have merited glory, that is, being eternally established in grace without danger of ever sinning: as the Angels merited it by the merit of a similar grace.

And each of his descendants would have been born in justice with a sufficient grace similar to his, by which he in turn would have been able to persevere or not, according to his pleasure, and to merit, or not, eternal glory like Adam.

Adam, tempted by the Devil, succumbed to temptation, rebelled against God, broke His commands, wished to be independent of God and equal to Him.

Since Adam had sinned and rendered himself worthy of
eternal death,

to punish his rebellion

God left him in the love of creatures.

And his will, which before was not in any way drawn toward creatures by any concupiscence, was now filled with concupiscence, sown there by the Devil, not by God.

Concupiscence thus arose in his bodily parts and stimulated
and delighted his will in evil, and darkness filled his mind so
that his will, previously indifferent toward good and evil, not
delighted or stimulated one way or the other, but without any
anticipatory appetite of its own, following what it knew to be
best suited to its happiness, this will now fell under the spell of
the concupiscence that arose in his bodily parts. And Adam's
mind, so strong, so just, so enlightened, was darkened and in
ignorance.

Since this sin passed from Adam to all his posterity, which
partook of his corruption like the fruit that issues from a bad
seed, all men sprung from Adam are born into ignorance and
concupiscence, guilty of the sin of Adam and worthy of
eternal death.

The free will remained flexible toward good and toward
evil but with this difference: while in Adam it had no attraction toward evil, and it was enough for it to know what was
good in order to be able to proceed to it, now it has through
concupiscence a sweetness and a delight in evil so powerful
that it proceeds to it infallibly as to its good, and it chooses
evil voluntarily and quite freely and joyfully as the object in
which it senses its beatitude.

All men in this corrupt mass being equally worthy of eternal
death and the wrath of God, God could with justice abandon
them all without mercy to damnation.

And yet it pleases God to choose, elect, and discern from
this equally corrupt mass, in which he sees only demerit, a
number of men of each sex, age, condition, complexion, from
every country and time, in short, of all sorts.

God has distinguished His Elect from the others, for reasons unknown to men and to Angels, by pure mercy, without any merit involved.

The Elect of God form a sum total which is sometimes called "world" because they are scattered throughout the world, sometimes called "all" because they form a totality, sometimes called "many" because they are many to each other, sometimes called "few" because they are few in proportion to the totality of the abandoned.

The abandoned form a totality which is called "world," "all," "many," and never "few."

God, through an absolute and irrevocable will, willed to save His Elect with a purely gratuitous goodness; He abandoned the others to their evil desires, to which He could with perfect justice abandon all men.

In order to save His Elect, God sent Jesus Christ to satisfy His justice and merit from His mercy the grace of Redemption, the medicinal grace, the grace of Jesus Christ, which is nothing other than a sweetness and a delight in the Law of God sown in the heart by the Holy Spirit; this grace, which not merely equals but even surpasses the strength of concupiscence of the flesh, fills the will with a greater delight in good than concupiscence offers it in evil, and so the free will, charmed more by the sweetness and the pleasures which the Holy Spirit inspires in it than by the attractions of sin, chooses infallibly and of itself the Law of God, by this sole reason that it finds greater satisfaction in it and feels that in it lies its beatitude and felicity.

So that those to whom it pleases God to grant this grace bring themselves by their own free will infallibly to prefer God to creatures. And that is why one may equally well say either that the free will moves of itself by means of this grace because it does in effect move itself, or that this grace moves the free will because whenever it is given the free will does so move infallibly.

And those to whom it pleases God to give this grace to the end of their lives persevere infallibly in this preference and so, choosing by their own will right up to their death to fulfill the Law rather than to violate it, because they feel greater satisfaction in so doing, they do merit glory both by the help of this grace, which overcame concupiscence, and by their own choice and the movement of their free will, which moved of itself voluntarily and freely.

And all those to whom this grace is not given, or is not given up to the end, remain so stimulated and charmed by their concupiscence that they infallibly prefer sinning to not sinning, for the reason that they find greater satisfaction in it.

And thus, dying in sin, they merit eternal death, since they chose evil with their own free will.

So that men are saved or damned according as to whether it has pleased God to choose them as recipients of this grace from out of the corrupt mass of men, in which He could with justice abandon them all.

All men being for their part equally guilty before God's discernment of them.

From the *II*^e *Ecrit; OC,* p. 983.

The commandments are possible to the just. And yet who does not see that the word "power" [implied in "possible"] is so vague that it includes all sorts of ideas. For indeed, if one says a thing is "within our power" when we do it when we wish to, which is a very natural and familiar way of speaking, does it not follow that it is within our power, in this sense, to keep the commandments and to change our will, since as soon as we will something not only does it happen but there is contradiction if it does not happen? But if one says a thing is "within our power" only when it is within a power we call "proximate," in this sense we no longer have this power except when it is given by God. Thus this proposition of St. Augustine's is Catholic in the first sense and Pelagian in the second.

From the *III*^e *Ecrit; OC,* p. 985.

It seems, then, that God abandons only because He has been abandoned, and that man abandons only because he has been abandoned; thus it is absurd to conclude that according to St. Augustine God is never first to abandon simply because he has said that God is not the first to abandon; both are true together, that He is the first and is not the first to abandon [man], given the different ways of abandoning.

From the *IIIe Ecrit; OC,* p. 1003.

He is now the slave of delight; that which most delights him attracts him infallibly: which is so clear a principle, both to common sense and in St. Augustine, that one cannot deny it without renouncing one as well as the other.

For what is more clear than this proposition, that one does always what delights one the most? Since this is no different than saying that one does always what pleases one most, that is, one wants always what pleases one, that is, one wants always what one wants; and in the state to which our soul is now reduced, it is inconceivable that it want anything other than what it pleases it to want, that is, than what delights it most. And let us not think we can be subtle and say that the will, to show its power, will sometimes choose what pleases it least; for then it will simply please it more to show its power than to want the good it gives up, so that when it attempts to flee what pleases it, it is only in order to do what pleases it, since it is impossible that it should want anything but what it pleases it to want.

From the *IIIe Ecrit; OC,* pp. 1005–6.

And so you see to what extent this proximate power is contrary both to common sense and to the dictums of St. Augustine, besides being ridiculous in itself and not to be seriously propounded; for since man changes all the time and can never remain in the same state, therefore in the measure that he attached himself to, or detached himself from, the things of this world (which it is always in his power to do more or less, though not entirely), it would be necessary for this delectation of grace, which establishes him in the proximate power, to change all the time in accordance with man's inconstancy, and (what it would be monstrous to say of grace) it would have to increase in proportion to his attachment to the world, and diminish its force in proportion to his detachment from the world.

From the *IIIe Ecrit; OC*, p. 1007.

Is it not obvious that it is the opinion not only of St. Augustine but of the entire Church without exception, even of the one who seems to be urging the contrary view on you, that one never has the assurance that he will persevere, and even the most just are not exempt from the fear [of not persevering], and nothing would so destroy justice as the destruction of that fear; and yet how is that fear supposed to subsist in the just when they are assured they have always the proximate power of prayer, and that the Gospels, moreover, assure them that they will always obtain what they ask with justice?

Can there be anything so contrary to common sense and to truth? Not only their fear would be destroyed, but also their hope, for since one doesn't hope for things of which one is certain, they will not hope for the continuation of this help since it is certain; nor will they have hope of obtaining what they ask as that also is certain. So what will be the object of their hope, except perhaps themselves, of whom they will hope for the good use of a power of which they are assured?

From the *IIIe Ecrit; OC*, pp. 1010–11.

It is true that God has put himself in the obligation to give [his aid] to those who ask it; and that is why it is never refused. But no one should think he can twist the meaning of this by saying that he can ask for perseverance in prayer and thus obtain it; and thus that by asking in the present moment for the grace of prayer in some future moment, one will obtain it, and thus one can be assured of perseverance: that is simply to play with words. For God gives to those who ask, not to those who have asked, and that is why one must persevere in asking in order to obtain; for it is not enough to ask with a pure mind today for continence for tomorrow, for if subsequently one descends into impurity, who should not see that this change of heart destroys the effect of the earlier prayer, and that to have continence tomorrow, one must not cease to ask for it. And thus, if in the present moment one asks for the gift of prayer for the following moment, isn't it obvious that one will not obtain it unless one continues to ask it? Now to say that one will have the spirit of prayer in the following moment if one prays in the following moment, isn't this the same as to say that one will have it if one has it, and so simply to play with words?

From the *IVe Ecrit; OC,* pp. 1012–13.

1. The first step will be to examine the terms of the proposition to see what meaning we naturally take to be the one they express.

2. The second, to examine which of two meanings the Fathers and the Council meant, by examining the purpose they had in making the decision.

3. And the third will be to examine the rest of their discourse and the other passages from the Fathers and the Council which clarify it, in order to determine the true meaning.

From the *IVe Ecrit; OC,* p. 1014.

And if there is any need to clarify by examples a thing already so clear, is it not true that it is not impossible for men to make war? And yet it is not always in the power of all men to do so.

And it is not impossible for a royal prince to become king,

and yet it is not always fully within the power of royal princes to do so.

It is not impossible for men to live to the age of sixty, and yet it is not fully within the power of all men to reach that age, or even to assure themselves of a single moment of life.

Index of Names

Dates are given for writers from the seventeenth century and earlier used primarily as sources in order to distinguish them from more recent scholars or commentators. Omitted from the list are Biblical names and that of Pascal himself.

 THE JOHNS HOPKINS PRESS

Designed by James C. Wageman

Composed in Granjon, text and display,
printed on Warren's "1854," and
bound in Holliston Roxite and Kivar 6
by The Colonial Press, Inc.